ADVERTISING MEDIA

GRID SERIES IN ADVERTISING AND JOURNALISM

Consulting Editors
ARNOLD M. BARBAN, University of Illinois
DONALD W. JUGENHEIMER, University of Kansas

Bailen, *Student Workbook to Accompany Basic Advertising*
Barban, Jugenheimer & Young, *Advertising Media Sourcebook and Workbook*
Burton, *Advertising Copywriting,* Fourth Edition
Burton & Ryan, *Advertising Fundamentals,* Third Edition
Dunn & Lorimor, *International Advertising and Marketing*
Ernst, *The Creative Package, A Working Text for Advertising Copy and Layout*
Fletcher & Bowers, *Fundamentals of Advertising Research*
Francois, *Beginning News Writing: A Programmed Text*
Francois, *Introduction to Mass Communications and Mass Media*
Jugenheimer & Turk, *Advertising Media*
Jugenheimer & White, *Basic Advertising*
Michman & Jugenheimer, *Strategic Advertising Decisions*
Patti & Murphy, *Advertising Management: Cases and Concepts*
Pickett, *Voices of the Past: Key Documents in the History of American Journalism*
Porchey & Carlson, *Style: A Guide to Journalism Expression*
Quera, *Advertising Campaigns: Formulations and Tactics,* Second Edition
Rotzoll, Haefner & Sandage, *Advertising in Contemporary Society: Perspectives Toward Understanding*
Simon, *Public Relations: Concepts and Practices,* Second Edition
Simon, *Public Relations Management: Cases and Simulations,* Second
Simon, *Publicity and Public Relations Worktext,* Fourth Edition
Smeyak, *Broadcast News Writing*
Zeigler & Howard, *Broadcast Advertising: A Comprehensive Working Textbook*

OTHER BOOKS IN THE GRID SERIES IN ADVERTISING AND JOURNALISM

Francois, *Mass Media Law and Regulation,* Second Edition

ADVERTISING MEDIA

Donald W. Jugenheimer
University of Kansas

Peter B. Turk
Syracuse University

Grid Publishing Inc., Columbus, Ohio

4666 Indianola Avenue
Columbus, Ohio 43214

Printed in the United States

1 2 3 4 5 6 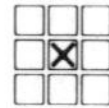 5 4 3 2 1 0

Library of Congress Cataloging in Publication Data

Jugenheimer, Donald W
Advertising media.

(The Grid series in advertising-journalism)
Includes index.
1. Advertising. I. Turk, Peter B., joint author. II. Title.
HF5821.J8 659.1 79-23007
ISBN 0-88244-210-4

TABLE OF CONTENTS

SECTION I: DEVELOPMENT 1

1 INTRODUCTION AND OVERVIEW 3

2 MEDIA PLANNING PROCESS 11

SECTION II: MARKETING PREPARATION 31

3 MARKET PROFILES 33

4 CONSUMER PROFILES 45

5 GEOGRAPHIC AND TIMING CONSIDERATIONS IN MEDIA PLANNING 59

SECTION III: MEDIA PLAN ANALYSES 73

6 MEDIA CHARACTERISTICS 75

7 COST ESTIMATING IN MEDIA PLANNING 93

8 AUDIENCE FACTORS IN MEDIA SELECTION 105

9 COST FACTORS IN MEDIA SELECTION 127

10 QUALITATIVE FACTORS IN MEDIA SELECTION 137

SECTION IV: REPORT PREPARATION 145

11 REPORT FORMAT AND ORGANIZATION 147

SECTION V: PURCHASING TECHNIQUES 157

12 MEDIA BUYING TACTICS AND PROCESSES 159

APPENDIX A 177

APPENDIX B 187

APPENDIX C 203

INDEX 219

SECTION I
DEVELOPMENT

INTRODUCTION TO SECTION I

This book is organized in the same way that the advertising media planning and buying process is organized: start with evaluation, then plans, then selection, and then complete the media buying. This type of logical organization should help the reader follow and understand the media process.

One warning, ... however: do not attempt to read only the first section or two of the book, and then complete that much of the media planning process, and later go on to other sections of the book. You should read the entire book, understand the entire process thoroughly, and only then attempt to apply the information and the process to the actual media situation. Better still, try to work with the problems and illustrations and examples that you will find throughout the book, and then put them together in an integrated approach to the advertising media process.

Before you can understand the details of the media process as it is used in advertising, you will need some sort of overview to help you comprehend the "bigger picture" of how the process functions and how the various parts fit together. That is what this first section of the book does: it provides a look at the development of advertising media planning with an introduction, an overview, and an understanding of how the parts of the process work and fit together.

1

INTRODUCTION AND OVERVIEW

Advertising media planning, as an significant part of the advertising process, has only within the last ten years come into its own. For a long time, the media function in advertising received less than its share of attention. The creative function, as copywriting and artwork and layout are termed, received most of the emphasis. The advertisement itself is what sells a product or service or idea (and also may likely sell an advertising campaign idea to a potential advertiser), so the processes involved in creating that advertisement were given most of the attention and emphasis. When making presentations of prospective campaigns, advertising agency executives would devote most of their time to the copy and art and layout of the advertisements, with relatively little time for research, media, budgeting, or postcampaign effectiveness.

IMPORTANCE OF THE MEDIA FUNCTION

There may be more natural inherent interest in the advertisements themselves than there is in the evaluation and selection of the media in which those advertisements are to appear. Research and media and budgeting and follow-up evaluations involve, by necessity, great amounts of hard work with data and facts and figures and numbers, and there is less evidence of creative genius than in copywriting or in art.

In recent years, however, advertising media operations have earned more attention. In times of economic difficulties, saving money became important. Rising inflationary spirals created even more pressures on advertisers, their agencies, and the advertising media, to avoid squandering resources, especially financial resources, and to become more frugal. Stretching advertising budgets suddenly became an important goal, and deriving every possible benefit from a set amount of money evolved into an important objective of advertising practice.

The problem was, however, that there was little saving possible in most areas of advertising. Creative work is essential, and to scrimp on copywriting is a selfdefeating solution. Research must also be done, although perhaps advertisers could save by relying on facts that are already available rather than performing their own primary research surveys and experiments. In the media function, too, it was impossible to do without media planning or buying or checking, for all are important contributions to the total success of an advertising campaign.

The media function is the one area, however, where many persons reasoned that advertising could become more efficient. Attempting to reach more people in larger audiences with less waste has provided real opportunities to economize in advertising without sacrificing any important communication effectiveness. In fact, making advertising media operations more efficient not only saves money, but focuses on the best prospects and thereby makes the advertising *more* effective and productive.

Because of this return on the investment in advertising media analysis, it has been possible for marketing-media managers to contribute even more to the overall success of advertising. It also has been possible for advertising to save time for members of the media audiences because increased advertising media efficiency has meant that people who are not bonafide prospective customers for a product or service are now less likely to see advertising for goods and services that do not interest them. More people are being communicated to for each dollar of advertising investment; greater selectivity on the part of the media themselves has replaced the once-popular consideration of audience size as the only critical factor; fewer messages need be directed to people who are not interested or who are not prospective customers.

The emergence of the media function has brought a new realization that the media function not only controls and spends most of the monies that flow through advertising, but it also commands most of the campaign expenditure. Take a typical advertiser of a packaged good, using advertising to promote the product and induce sales. The actual advertising effort is coordinated by an advertising agency. The agency takes care of most of the strategic and tactical problems that are associated with advertising; the advertiser (the agency's client) is involved principally in the planning and budgeting stages, with approval powers over all aspects of the advertising effort. The advertising agency receives a commission from the media in which the advertisements are placed, and the standard industry practice is for the media to grant a 15 percent commission to the agency. The remainder, 85 percent of the advertising budget, goes directly to the media. Of the commission, part of that 15 percent is again devoted to the media function within the advertising agency. Commonly, about 90 percent of all the money spent on advertising, then, is devoted to the media or to the media function, and the remaining amount is left for all the other advertising functions: research, copywriting, art, layout, evaluation, planning, budgeting, and the like.

With the realization that most of the advertising budget is, in one way or another, expended on media, the media function has risen higher in the hierarchy of advertising functions.

MARKETING MIX

One way to look at the media function is as part of the overall advertising effort, but then one must also consider that advertising is but a part of the overall marketing effort. It is vital that advertising's contributions to marketing be thoroughly understood before we examine the media contribution to advertising.

Within marketing there are four basic variables, which the well-known marketing educator Jerome McCarthy describes as "Product, Place, Price, and Promotion."[1] The *product* can be an actual good that is to be marketed, or it can be a service or an idea. In the study of marketing and advertising, it is convenient to think of a *product* that is being sold and advertised, but the principles that apply to goods apply equally well to ideas and to services that are to be sold and advertised, too. The *place* portion of the marketing mix is involved with distributing the product, service, or idea to the proper target. *Price* is the agreed-upon value that is set on the item to be sold. And *promotion* is telling the customer about the product for sale, to communicate and help the sale take place. There may, of course, be other incidental variables that arise within the marketing mix, such as packaging (which may be part of the product, or of promotion, or a combination of both), product planning (which is usually involved with the product itself), brand policy, service, and other similar considerations. Most marketing functions however can be found in one of the four basic variables that are mentioned above.

Next, it is important for us to examine what is involved in promotion. It may involve a variety of functions, such as sales promotion (premium offers, contests, cents-off deals, and the like), personal selling (sales clerks in stores or sales representatives calling on business), public relations, publicity, and advertising.

Then advertising can itself be broken into a kind of "advertising mix" that includes research, creative, and evaluative efforts, and, of course, media. A diagram of the marketing mix, promotion mix, and advertising mix may look something like this.

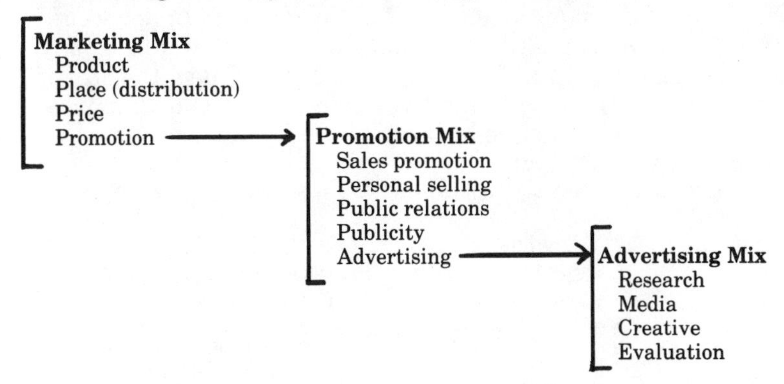

Later, there will also be a discussion of the "media mix" which is a way of looking at the variety of media to be used for a particular advertising campaign and how those media overlap and reinforce one another.

The word "media," incidentally, is plural; the singular form is "medium." The word comes from the Latin for "middle," and that is exactly what an advertising medium is: something in the middle that acts as a go-between or intermediary, which serves to join together a writer or performer with an audience, or a marketer with potential customers. Some modern American usage allows for the plural form to be *mediums,* but *media* is the word most often used by educated people in advertising. A single *medium* might be television, and the broadcast channels together would constitute the broadcast *media* of radio and television.

THE MEDIA PLANNING AND BUYING PROCESS

Before we can understand the specifics of how advertising media are evaluated, selected, and utilized, it is necessary to examine the process that is used within the advertising media function.

The normal process involves starting with setting objectives, then developing strategies, and finally using tactics to achieve the objectives. The words "strategies" and "tactics" have evolved from their formal military usage into business because of the competitive nature of the advertising business. *Strategies* are plans, and *tactics* are the implementations of those plans. For example, once the formal goals for the marketing program have been established, and these goals then have been detailed into advertising and finally into media objectives, the planning or strategy phase begins. This might involve planning to reach certain kinds of people, called our *target group,* who are likely prospects for buying the product, as well as defining the *target markets,* where the product will be sold and advertised to the target group.

Further planning will involve comparing all the types of media; each medium, such as newspapers, magazines, network television, business publications, local (or "spot") radio, and the like are called *types* of media. The specific media *vehicles* are the actual outlets of the media; the medium of television may have a program on the network as the actual vehicle, or an individual television station as the vehicle. In magazines, an individual magazine such as *Reader's Digest* would be a vehicle. In newspapers (the medium), the vehicle would be any individual newspaper, such as the *New York Times.* Then, the size of the advertisement or the length of a television commercial announcement is the *unit* of advertising to be used.

It may be useful to envision the relationship between a medium, a media vehicle, and an advertising unit with these kinds of examples.

Media	Vehicle	Unit
Radio	WBBM-AM	60-second announcement
Magazine	*Family Circle*	full-page black-and-white
Newspaper	Cincinnati *Enquirer*	4 columns x 8 inches
Television	Three's Company	30-second participation (sponsorship)

Other strategic plans would include the relative importance of each of the types of media to be used in an advertising effort; assigning certain "weights" or numerical values to represent the importance or the specific functional contribution of each of the media is often done at this stage.

Because the potential customers for a product or service must be reached through the mass media, these people must be grouped according to their attributes and then matched up with the audience characteristics of the people who are exposed to each medium or vehicle. These attributes and characteristics are called the *audience quality,* and the number of people within each of these groupings would constitute the audience *dimension.* Any surrounding influences that might affect and even limit the effectiveness of the advertising also must be considered in the plan, because the editorial content of a magazine or the emotional involvement of a television audience may affect the type of advertisement to be run, and may also affect the ability of an advertisement to communicate efficiently and effectively. Likewise, the need for regular advertising in certain patterns, called *continuity,* must be part of the plan.

All these attributes and considerations lead to media selection, the ultimate outcome of the strategy phase that will be discussed in detail in subsequent chapters.

In the tactical phase of the media process, implementation of the strategic plans is the important business. Someone must *estimate* how much the planned media program will cost, and then contact the vehicles involved and negotiate for the specified units and for the best prices. The final negotiated price for the time and space ordered will then be tallied in the *costing* process to keep a complete record of how much of the budget has been spent and to compare back to the media plan. The actual *ordering* of the time and space in the media vehicles and the *scheduling* of the advertisements to be run are other tactics, as is the postpurchase evaluation of the vehicles to learn if they performed as planned.

With the use of terms such as strategies and tactics in advertising media, it may be useful to use the term *logistics* to describe the supporting activities that are necessary. These logistics do not contribute to the actual media plan nor to advertising effectiveness, yet they are vital to the businesslike operation of advertising departments and agencies. Sending bills or invoices from the medium to the advertising agency is part of this logistical activity, as is *recording* every agreement, reserving and buying and paying for advertising time and space in the media vehicles.

Checking on the media to see that the advertisements ran as ordered with no mechanical problems is another vital job, which may be done by advertisers or by their agencies or by special firms that hire out to perform this checking function.

Now that you have an overview of how the media function operates, the next chapter will show you how these functions are put to work in preparing a media plan.

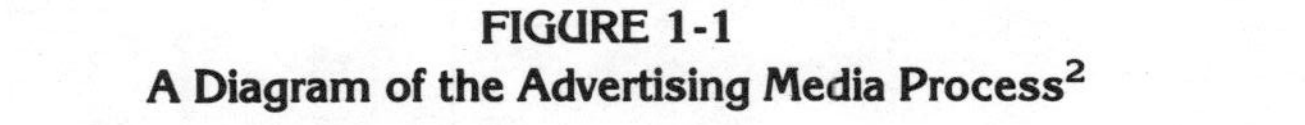

FIGURE 1-1
A Diagram of the Advertising Media Process[2]

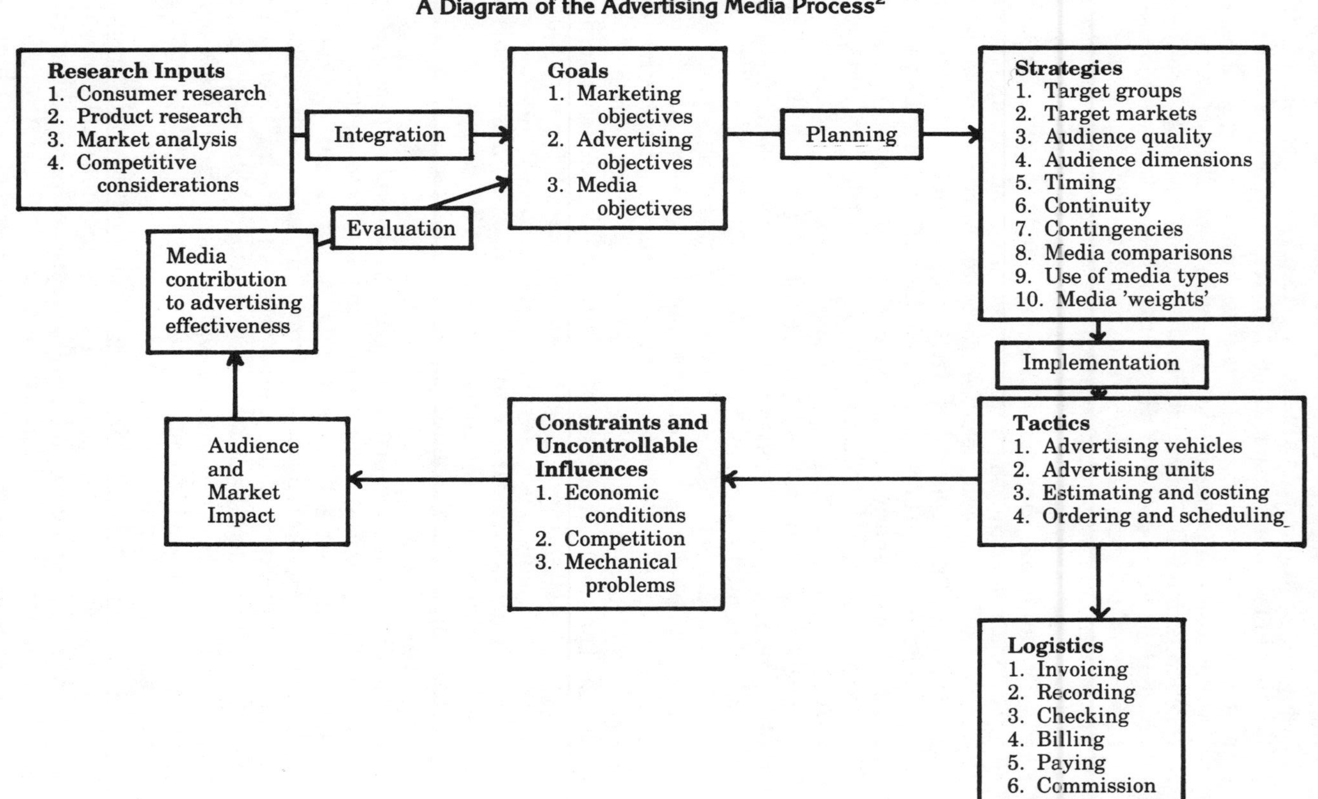

QUESTIONS

1. Why is the topic of advertising media considered more important by advertisers than it was a few years ago?

2. How are the marketing mix and the advertising mix related? How do both terms relate to the use of mass media for promotional purposes?

3. What are the differences between strategies and tactics? What is the purpose of each?

4. Which must come first in the advertising decision process: the selection of the medium to be used, or the selection of the vehicle to be used? Then, which is first: the vehicle or the unit?

ENDNOTES

1. E. Jerome McCarthy, *Basic Marketing* (4th edition), page 44.
2. The conceptual basis for this diagram was suggested by Arnold M. Barban.

2

MEDIA PLANNING PROCESS

Before you attempt to understand the details of preparing an advertising media plan, you must know how the entire media planning process fits together. The remaining chapters of this book explain how each major step in the media planning process is undertaken and carried out. This chapter will help you understand the flow of these steps from one to another.

To help in your understanding, you may wish to refer back to the diagram of the media process in Chapter 1. We will also be using parts of that diagram to explain in more detail just what is involved at each stage of the process.

MARKETING INTERFACE

All advertising campaign plans, including media plans, should start with the overall marketing effort and must be coordinated with the more general marketing operation. The media planning process is a flow from one stage to another, each phase coordinated and blended with another. But all elements must first be in conjunction with the marketing goals and objectives. This interaction or interface with the marketing effort is essential if the advertising and media plans are to support the general marketing programs.

In addition, the media planning process cannot be viewed simply as a series of individual steps, with various persons working on various phases of the overall plan. There is a sequential flow to the media planning process, from marketing to setting objectives for the advertising and media effort, on through the strategy of the plans, to such details as estimating costs and allocating the media budget, to the actual media allocations. Finally, there is the plan implementation, such as ordering and buying the advertising time or space on the media, scheduling the specific times for broadcast commercials, confirming orders, and the like.

Before we go on, it will be useful to explain a few terms that will be used throughout the book. Plans are usually known as *strategies,* whereas the implementation of those plans are the *tactics,* as you learned in the first chapter. *Marketing* involves product development, packaging, distribution, and promotion, and part of the promotional effort involves *advertising.* Advertising, in turn, has component parts, one of them the *media* function. And there are several stages in the flow of media planning — setting objectives, strategic planning, tactical implementation, logistical support, and evaluating the effects of the campaign. The diagram in Chapter 1 shows how these processes flow together.

It is also easiest to understand the media planning process if we use the advertising campaign for a product as an example. Of course, the same process could apply to the advertising plans for a service or even for an idea, just as it can fit a product advertising campaign.

THE STEPS IN A MEDIA PLAN

MARKETING ORIENTATION

The media planning process begins with a client briefing, a meeting in which the advertiser's staff and the agency's media department get together. Together they go through the most recent available information on this particular product or service account, along with any special instructions that apply or have been learned from past advertising efforts. After this briefing, the agency media planner meets with other associates, known as a Media Planning Unit. The various media experts give their viewpoints, ideas, suggestions, and provide direction and counsel. Then the group reviews the basic marketing and advertising strategy for this account that will affect the media functions, and also determines what, if any, additional information is needed. These needs are forwarded to the research department of the agency, in most cases; however, if a great deal of research is needed, or if other departments also need complicated questions answered through research, the task may be assigned to an independent marketing research firm.

Then the Media Planning Unit begins to set the direction of the media plan. It is necessary to analyze the product and become more aware of its intended uses and functions, and to consider the marketing and advertising plans that may already have been approved by this time. Any additional consumer research or market analysis may also be performed at this stage. Such things as determining the market potential for the product will be done now, if it has not already been completed. For a product or service that is already firmly established in the market place, a media spending history will be gathered, containing information about all the media plans that have been used in the past, how well they worked, what problems with them were incurred, and similar information. The group may review media plans for as many as the preceding five years, both for this particular product as well as for competing products. Comparisons between the product and those of competitors as to sales trends and profits during these preceding years will be examined. Any previous media tests, such as test markets, also will be analyzed, including the kinds of tests, the products involved, the places used, the monies invested (both in absolute dollars and in investment per thousand prospects reached or per unit of sales), the media used, and the results of the tests.

Background information on the activities of the competition is also reviewed, even though this information may not actually be used until later in the plan. In fact, the initial stage of the planning process is often used to gather *all* the information that eventually will be needed, both from primary research and from secondary sources of data. Information about consumers, products or services to be marketed, markets where the product or service may be sold — all will be important, as will be the competitive information.

Media planners need this kind of information to provide the marketing insights that are essential to the formulation of an effective and efficient plan. Sales trends of the product and of competing products will indicate strengths and weaknesses, as well as provide an idea of the scope of the marketing task at hand. Certain types of advertising media may be considered more suitable for certain kinds of products or services; a product intended for a high socioeconomic group might not be suitable being advertised in a movie fan magazine — but this kind of media sensitivity may not show up in a simple quantitative evaluation of the media situation.

Figure 2-1, which is a detail from the flow of the media planning process shown in Chapter 1, portrays how the information is gathered and combined and integrated, then sent along to be used in the rest of the media planning process.

FIGURE 2-1
Marketing Orientation

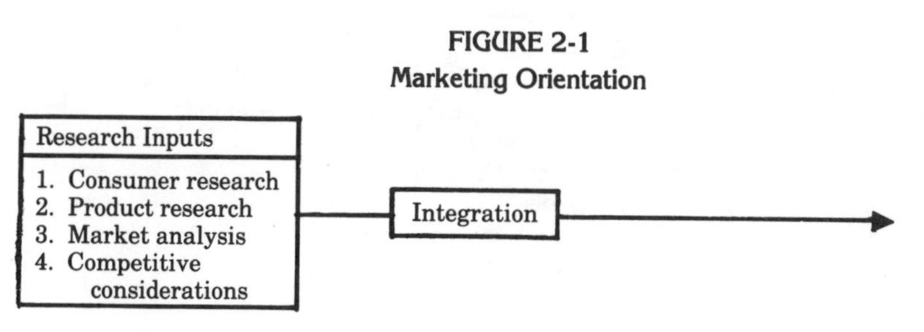

Another important consideration at this early stage is the advertising budget. If the advertiser is using a budget that is goal-related, there then may be enough money made available to provide the kind of media effort that the planner desires. This approach to budgeting is often called "open end" or "objective and task" or the "task" approach because the advertising effort that is necessary to accomplish the marketing and advertising goals is the primary consideration. Once the advertising plans are made, the budget will be determined by how much that advertising effort will cost. Certainly, this kind of budgeting approach provides much more flexibility to the media planner than a set amount of money from a "fixed sum" budget, where the advertising campaign is subject to the constraints of some predetermined amount of money.

Once all information and data are gathered and sorted and the general budget picture is understood, the specifics of the media plan can begin.

DEVELOPING OBJECTIVES

Clear and precise objectives are essential if a good plan is to result. Planning must be oriented toward the goals and must support the goals. If the goals are not specifically stated in advance, it is impossible for the plan to work toward the direction and accomplish the same ends as the rest of the marketing effort. Media, creative work, research, and the rest of the advertising campaign must work in conjunction with one another, and all the advertising elements must work together with the rest of the marketing effort.

Objectives are a critical task in any planning process (Figure 2-2). But there is an irony in dealing with objectives for the media plan: the media themselves are not objectives. The selected media are part of the strategies, or plans, that will be used to help meet the objectives. Media objectives are the final results that you propose to accomplish, and your use of advertising media assists you in achieving the proposed results.

FIGURE 2-2
Determining Objectives

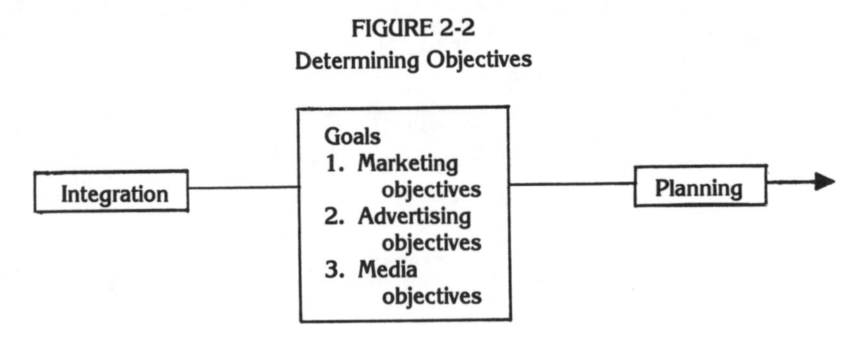

When you design objectives, it is desirable to establish specific levels of accomplishments that are to be measured. In marketing, some measurable levels of sales, either in units sold or in a percentage share of market, are a logical goal. In advertising, the percentage of certain kinds of people who will be aware of the new product can be specified as goals. In media, the proportion of the audience exposed is an objective. There is, unfortunately, a tendency for advertising agencies to attempt to design objectives in rather loose terms, because aiming for specific percentages or amounts of sales, awareness, reach and similar measures means that the agency is locked into a mandatory goal, and the goal may not be entirely within the control of the agency. On the other hand, in recent years there has been considerable pressure from advertisers to establish specific objectives. Only by setting specific objectives and then measuring the advertising's results against those objectives can it be determined whether the campaign is successful. In practice, some leeway is often given by both sides, and ranges may be set as the goals at which the advertising campaign is aimed.

MARKETING OBJECTIVES

Usually, the marketing objectives are determined by the advertiser or someone else outside the media operation. A marketing objective involves the sales levels for the product, most often in terms of the number of items to be sold during the upcoming period. Another common way is to set sales objectives in market shares, that is, a percentage of the sales for the entire industry.

Marketing objectives can often deal with the geographic territories in which the product or service is to be sold. In many cases, the sales may be nationwide, but a newly introduced product may be expanding into new territories as it attempts to "roll out" from a limited area into national distribution. Similarly, a new product may be in test marketing and limited to certain areas. Some companies only operate in a certain region of the country, so this kind of geographic distribution might also be a marketing objective.

Basic promotional intentions, such as special times of the year that are earmarked for intensive selling or a special promotional program that will need to be supported by the advertising effort, or maybe a change in the packaging that requires special promotional support, may also be included as marketing objectives.

Other examples of marketing objectives might include special consideration of the competing firms, special pricing policies, distributive goals such as increasing the number of stores or other retail sellers who might handle the product or service, and the positioning of the product against the competition.

ADVERTISING OBJECTIVES

After the marketing objectives are established, it is time to consider the role advertising is to play. Advertising objectives must support and be consistent with the marketing objectives, and they must identify the specific contributions that advertising will make toward the success of the campaign.

Advertising objectives might be concerned with the lifestyle or way of life in which the product is portrayed in the advertising, or which is anticipated among the prospective buyers. In fact, target prospects might be segmented according to their various lifestyles, or according to other factors: demographic characteristics such as their age, educational level, family income, and the like; or perhaps the prospective buyers may even be segmented according to their personalities or other psychographic characteristics.

Advertising objectives might also concern creative demands or the need for a particular creative environment in the advertisements. The need for color (a common requirement for food product advertising), sound, and motion places limits on the kinds of advertising media that can be recommended. Similarly, a special frame of reference or editorial environment will be needed, such as placing advertising on sports pages of newspapers or in food-oriented broadcast programs or print magazines.

If certain geographic or timing goals were included in the marketing objectives, then certainly these must be followed up in the advertising objectives insofar as the advertising campaign is affected. The advertising may need to be run at a certain time in advance of the popular selling season, or it may be limited to certain areas of the country.

The advertising objectives may even indicate whether the advertisements should mention the competition or should show what the package looks like (a good idea for a new product or if the package has been changed). If such detailed information is to be included, it may affect the media plan because the selected media must lend themselves to such requirements.

While these objectives must be weighed against what units of time and space actually are available and affordable, the media planner must also balance the impact gained through the use of expensive units of space or time, against the values of repeat exposure gained by buying less expensive advertising units.

At the same time, general characteristics of advertising media may be stated. For example, an above-average degree of flexibility in media to provide for unforeseen changes in the advertising campaign or the ability to distribute coupons through the advertising media may be desired, especially for a new product. These general media guidelines are not intended to be the final decision on which advertising media will be used and which will not be used; instead, only general characteristics that might apply to several media, or that might eliminate only one or two types of media, are common at this point.

Not all advertising objectives influence media choice, but the planner must be aware of possible directions resulting from any objective.

MEDIA OBJECTIVES

Media objectives must fit in with and support the marketing and advertising objectives that have already been determined. Some of these may be refinements of the other objectives.

For example, some basic audience characteristics may have been established to give a general idea of the kinds of people to whom the advertising is to be directed. The media planner determines the relative importance of men, or women, or children as likely prospects for the advertised product. Most often this is accomplished by outlining the demographic characteristics, or demographic profiles, of the potential customers.

Similarly, the areas or territories where the advertising is to be directed may be refined into a media objective. This may be a two-level process: first, special considerations for local advertising as opposed to regional or national advertising, and then, if localized, which portions of the country or which metropolitan areas. For example, if the advertising is regional in nature, should it cover the entire region, such as the East North Central states, or only a part of that region? And if the advertising is national, does that mean that an equal number of advertisements must appear in all markets and regions, or should there be heavier weights of advertising in portions of the country? These audience and geographic decisions are often reidentified in media objectives. But media objectives are not limited to refinements of marketing and advertising objectives. Some objectives for media are unique.

Media Mix

It is often helpful if the media planner has some idea in mind as to what kind of media mix is desirable. A combination of various types of media will often aid the media plan by providing additional reach to different kinds of people and different regions or markets. In addition, because many persons are exposed to a variety of different media, the media mix may also add frequency of exposure.

Some media planners prefer to think of this kind of concept as "media mix versus media concentration." The use of only one or two types of media is a concentration, while the use of several different media types is a mix. Still, the term "media mix" usually refers to a blending of media, and that kind of "mix" may occur when only two or three types of media are used. "Media mix" refers to the composite use of media types or vehicles, and is often recommended as a communication objective.

Reach and Frequency

The media planner must also decide which message exposure property is most important — reach, frequency, impact, or continuity. *Reach* is the size of the audience or the number of different people to which the advertising will communicate; it may be set in absolute numbers, such as 42,000,000 people, or as a percentage of a group such as 30 percent of all the female heads of households in the western United States. *Frequency* is the number of times, on the average, that each person in the audience will be exposed to an advertisement in this advertising campaign. *Impact* is the intrusive force of impression that the message makes in the minds of the audience; does a full-page newspaper advertisement have more impact than only a half-page; does a full-color magazine advertisement have more impact than the same advertisement in black-and-white; does a full minute on radio offer more impact than thirty seconds? *Continuity* is the need for a pattern within the advertising campaign, so that the advertisements reinforce one another and are timed properly to increase awareness without creating irritation in the audience.

The media plan does not need to have absolute levels of reach, frequency, impact, and continuity as objectives, but some advertisers require some sort of specification as a goal. In any event, these values are stated in a range or are "plugged in" later on, when the affordable level of advertising is more clear.

The importance of reach, frequency, impact, or continuity is priority. The planner must decide which of these four factors is most important to this advertising campaign, which is next in importance, and so on. If reach is considered twice as important as frequency early in the campaign, and three or four times as important as either impact or continuity, it should be stated. After the initial phase of the campaign, the decision may be to reduce reach in favor of additional frequency or some other factor. Again, this should be specified. In fact, this pattern of reach shifting later to frequency is often used for new product advertising campaigns.

The relationship between reach and frequency is that for any given amount of money you can get only so much reach and frequency. Increase the amount of reach, and some repeat exposure is usually sacrificed. As a formula:

$$\$ = R \times F$$

where the budget is constant ($), reach (R) is the number of people in the audience while frequency (F) is the number of times the average audience member sees the advertising. If you want to reach more people and you cannot afford more money for advertising, then you will need to reduce the number of times that each person can see the advertising. The relationship between reach and frequency and the amount of money that is in the advertising budget must be kept in mind, because each one affects the other. The same relationship exists with impact and continuity — each has a value and a price. Accurate objectives try to balance needs with cost limitations. It is a demanding process.

Other media objectives include supporting the advertising creative effort, or avoiding or facing up to the media usage of a competitor; if the competitor is well known for quality magazine advertising, you may want to avoid magazines in your media plan. Merchandising intentions, such as the use of coupons, may become a media objective.

Remember, however, that the media themselves are *not* objectives. You do not want to select media at this time: you want only to establish the objectives that the media will eventually be expected to accomplish.

Certain desired accomplishments of a media plan may not be presented because the planner lacks sufficient control to bring them about. You may know your prospective customers demographically but you cannot "create" an advertising medium that reaches all those kinds of people and only them. Likewise, you cannot tell newspaper publishers to measure newspaper audiences in ways that will identify lifestyle or buying habits. In fact, most planners do not know much about a newspaper's *audience* (that is, the people who receive the newspaper). The information planners deal with the *circulation* of the newspaper, which is the number of copies that are sold. Thus, there may be an objective that deals with reaching the audience, yet newspaper selection must be satisfied only with circulation.

The objectives guide and direct the strategic planning that follows. Each strategy then should attempt to achieve at least one or more of the marketing, advertising, or media objectives, and all the strategies should complement the objectives. The objectives are not necessarily what you plan to do; they are what you expect to accomplish through the marketing and advertising efforts.

STRATEGIC TECHNIQUES

Strategies are the plans for the advertising campaign while the tactics are the implementations of those plans. Objectives, or "goal planning," concentrate on the final achievements that are intended, whereas the strategies are the plans that will be followed to assure those goals and objectives. Figure 2-3 lists some of the major advertising media strategies.

To start on strategies, the media planner must evaluate the proposed budget that has already been provided. An attempt will be made to relate the budget investment in advertising to the expected sales levels that have been set in the marketing objectives, to find out if the goals actually can be achieved with the amount of advertising that the budget will afford. Seldom will there be more than enough money to do the job; more often, the campaign goals can be achieved only by making every dollar count.

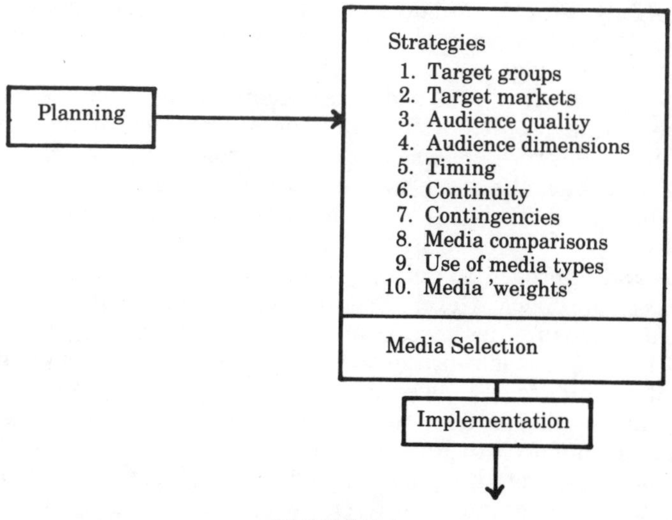

FIGURE 2-3
Planning Strategies

TARGETS

Determining the audience or "target group" to be reached by the media is the next job. Generally, there are two methods that can be used to determine these target groups.[1] In the *demographic matching* method, the demographic categories that describe the best potential customers of the product are matched with demographic information about the audiences of certain media types and vehicles.

The target groups are outlined, based on the demographic information that is available about prospective customers. The target group descriptions might look like this:

Primary Target Group (1st priority):
Women, ages 18-24, not employed outside the home, with school age or younger children living at home, some college education, and a family income of $15,000 or higher.

Secondary Target Group (next best):
Women, 18-50, employed or not employed outside the home, with children living at home, high school education or better, and a family income of $10,000 or higher.

Tertiary Target Group (Also identified for some special value):
Men and women, 19-50, with children or other dependents, completed high school, and a family income of $8,500 or higher.

Notice how the descriptions of the target groups become progressively less restrictive as they go from primary to secondary to tertiary targets. This allows the media effort to be aimed specifically at the primary target group, but it also identifies other media audiences who are also valued targets to receive the advertising. Because it is usually difficult to find media that exclusively reach the primary target, media selections may be evaluated on ability to expose the secondary or tertiary groups. Besides, it would be an unusual advertiser who would want to restrict his message only to the "best" prospects.

Once the target groups are outlined, media planners seek media that have similar profiles in their audiences. There are many sources of information about the demographic characteristics of potential customers and about the audience characteristics of the mass media, and these will be discussed in detail in a later chapter dealing with media strategies.

A second approach to defining audience targets is known as the *product user approach*. Here, instead of examining target groups, the media planner examines media audiences and determines how much usage of the product is represented by the members of each audience. The media audience is viewed as representing a certain quantity of consumption of the product to be advertised. The various media or vehicles are compared to find out which ones offer the greatest numbers of consumers of the product, and the greatest amount of total consumption of the product, for the most economical advertising media investment.

At the end of this targeting step, the media planner has in hand either a description of the demographic characteristics of the intended target group, or a list of the media and vehicles that offer audiences who consume significant quantities of the product.

Whether the target group is identified in terms of its demographic characteristics or any other measure, the numerical size of the target group must now be determined. It is naive to attempt to plan to reach a given audience without first knowing the total audience size and the size of each product-user segment.

While the term "target group" refers to the kinds of people to whom the advertising will be directed, "target market" is used to talk about the geographic locations where those people will be communicated to or sold. As with the target group, the selection of the target market involves outlining the specific characteristics of the kinds of markets that are desired, and then matching these definitions with the actual characteristics. Eventually, the media planner may be able to specify the kinds of markets wanted, such as "top 25 metro (metropolitan) areas," or "A- and B-sized counties" (those counties with populations of more than 120,000), or "the Middle Atlantic, North Central, and Southeastern Sections" of the United States. And the planner must again attempt to delineate the numerical sizes of the target markets and of the target groups within them.

AUDIENCE CONSIDERATIONS

Although it is useful to know how many persons there are in the audiences of various advertising media, absolute numbers are not the most useful way to report that information. A percentage may be more valuable than the actual number of persons might be.

The most popular of these percentages is the *gross rating point* (GRP). This term evolved from television, where a *rating* or program rating is the percentage out of the total number of homes that have television receivers (called TV households) that are tuned in to a particular program or station or network. If there are a million television households in a certain market, and one-fifth (200,000) of them are tuned to a program on one of the local stations, then there is a rating of 20 percent, or simply 20.

$$\frac{200{,}000}{1{,}000{,}000} = 20\%$$

The sum of the ratings for a series of commercial placements is the gross rating points. Assume that you have purchased advertising on four programs in a single week in this market.

Advertisement	Time	Rating
1	9:30 p.m. Tuesday	13
2	7:15 p.m. Thursday	22
3	6:45 p.m. Friday	12
4	2:00 p.m. Saturday	13
		60GRP

The sum of your exposure is 60 or 60 gross rating points.

The gross rating concept spread from television to radio and then to outdoor advertising. Currently, some practitioners express print (magazine and newspaper) audience values in GRP. This is done primarily to standardize the way media opportunities are evaluated.

The term *gross* is a designation meaning a measure of *individual* audiences for each vehicle. However, an important dimension of selection strategy is to find the unduplicated audience (the audience members receive no repeat exposures). Thus, it is important when dealing with rating points to know if they are "gross" (that is, duplicated) or "net" (unduplicated). Later chapters will demonstrate how media planners determine "gross" and "net" and how the evaluations are used.

The media planner may also find it useful to calculate the number of *total* audience impressions, which counts every time the advertising campaign is seen or heard or read by someone. Obviously, it is impossible to count each of these exposures, but if you estimate the number of people who see any of the campaign and multiply by the average number of times that each person sees the advertisement, you will arrive at total audience impressions.

TIMING AND SCHEDULING

The eventual media selection and the total media plan must also consider when the advertising will be run. Some products or services depend on seasonality and are best advertised at certain seasons of the year. Other products fit in with advertising on certain days of the week, usually because they are most often sold on certain days of the week; grocery stores do most of their sales on Saturdays and the few days preceding the weekend, and so grocery advertising may run on a Tuesday or Wednesday each week, what is known as the "best food day" for advertising in that particular locality.

Some products are even advertised at certain times during the day. Some advertisements may be on television late at night because they are not appropriate for children to see, while toys may be advertised during morning television programs when many children are watching.

Certain timing patterns may also be used. Some media planners use what they call a "wave" pattern, which is so-named because there are peaks of high frequency of advertising that are separated by periods of reduced advertising or even no advertising. The peaks are called the "flights" and the periods of reduced or no advertising is called the "hiatus." Advertising for a new product often starts out with a heavy barrage of advertisements in a flight, followed by a hiatus, followed by more flights. The "flighting" may look something like this. Eventually the advertising may level off with less frequency than during the flighting periods; this level of maintaining some advertising is called a "sustaining period."

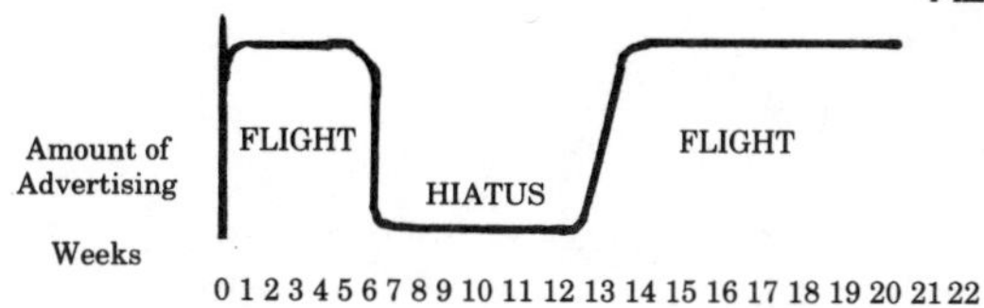

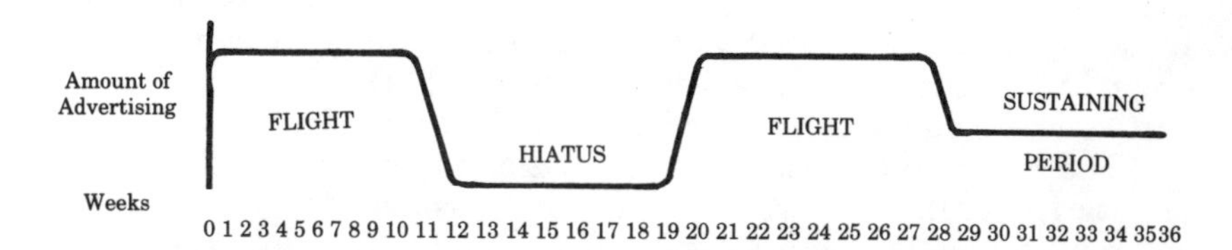

The actual scheduling of each advertisement will be done in the tactical stages of buying the actual advertising vehicle time and space. But the media planner can outline the needs for certain timing patterns when establishing the objectives, and it is also possible to draw up a flow chart that reflects how the media can be utilized to meet those scheduling objectives.

CONTINGENCY PLANNING

Finally comes what is known as the contingency plan. This establishes a program to be used if unforeseen events occur that upset the already-established plan. Generally, the contingency plan should concern adjustments that must be made in the media plan if the advertising campaign is more successful than was anticipated, or if the campaign is not as successful as anticipated, or if a competitor does something unexpected such as developing a new competing product or making an improvement in an old competing product.

Too many media plans are concerned with a "reserve fund," but that concept may be mistaken. If part of the advertising budget is put aside as a "reserve," the advertising agency is demonstrating that it does not need the entire budget to operate an effective campaign, so the client may not permit all the budget to be spent. It is more sensible to make the original plan flexible enough so that some of the budgeted funds can be shifted, if needed, into other uses. The contingency plan implies that there is a planned program if and when it is needed.

Some advertisers also ask for "back-up" campaigns to be prepared by the agencies. These are not exactly the same as contingency plans. Instead, they are complete new programs, including creative as well as media plans, that can be put into operation should they be needed. Some advertisers may ask for such "back ups" because they are uncertain about how well a proposed campaign may work, or because the campaign is a total departure from the past marketing direction for this product line, or because of the volatile nature of some product categories that does not allow for much planning time if a new campaign should suddenly be needed.

MEDIA SELECTION PROCESSES

Now the media planner can begin on the general media selection. Here an attempt is made to determine the types of media (but not the specific vehicles at this time) that may be used in the upcoming advertising, as well as the types of media that will not be used. For a while, some media may be considered as alternative choices if the budget will permit their use, and the media types are often placed in descending order of importance so that those listed last (the least vital to the success of the advertising), can be dropped from the list.

The selection process can make use of quantitative factors and of qualitative factors about the media under consideration. Here are some of the more popular factors used in media and vehicle selection.

Quantitative Factors

You already have learned that audience size is one of the quantitative factors to be considered. The gross audience is the number of persons in the marketplace who may read a certain publication or see a certain telecast. The net audience is that part of the gross audience who are exposed *once* to the program or advertisement. Net audience measures are most important in consideration of multiple message units (that is, using more than one program, more than one magazine, more than one issue of a magazine, and so on).

Another factor is cost and comparing the cost efficiencies of various media or vehicles. Most often, the cost of reaching a thousand members of the audience is the comparison that is used, because it allows comparisons of costs on a dollar-and-cents basis. This figure is known as *cost per thousand* (CPM). This measure relates the size of the audience to the cost of exposing the audience. Consumer advertising in the mass media ranges at about $5 to $15, but the CPM can vary according to the audience segment desired. It is also possible to use the gross rating point that was discussed earlier and calculate the *cost per rating point,* which is another useful quantitative media comparison.

Timing flexibility is important, too. If there is a need for making changes on short notice, some media may be much more suitable than others. Magazines have long preparation times and advertising space must be ordered far in advance, for example, while radio messages can be changed right up until broadcast time.

Audience selectivity is another factor. Some media are quite selective in that they permit the advertiser to reach prospective customers without a lot of waste circulation. Certainly, if there is a specific kind of person who is the best prospect for some certain item, then a medium that reaches those persons and few other persons would be desirable.

Qualitative Factors

The quality of the audience is an intangible factor in selecting media, but important nonetheless. Some popular magazines attract a rather low socioeconomic class of people in their audiences, as do some daytime television programs. On the other hand, some sophisticated magazines and special event television programs attract a very select audience of above-average income, education, and social status.

Then, too, the environment in which the advertisement will appear may be important to some advertisers. Some media are simply not deemed appropriate in their editorial and entertainment content, even though the audience make-up may be quite suitable.

MEDIA SELECTION

With multiple selection criteria, it is important to organize how each factor will contribute to the selection decision. One way to help select the media types is to rank them in their order of importance, but that is difficult when many factors must be considered. Beginning media planners often find it useful to list all the important criteria that have been determined for the media objectives of the campaign, and then evaluate each type of medium against the individual criteria. Because some of the criteria will be more important than others, depending upon the product, it may be desirable to "weight" them accordingly, giving heavier emphasis to those criteria that are deemed most important, as in Figure 2-4. The media have been evaluated on a five-point scale, with "5" indicating that the medium is very good in this category, and "3" being an average rating. The characteristic of showing the color of the package has been rated very important for this product, so it has been given a weight of "3x," meaning that each medium's score on this characteristic will be multiplied by 3 to indicate that factor's importance. Similarly, the need for demonstrating the product to consumers has been judged important enough to multiply each medium's rating by 2, along with the selectivity and efficiency factors. By using this kind of quick chart, a media planner can have a quantitative estimate of the relative importance of each of the media, in order of importance based on the total "score" each medium receives. Of course, the success of this kind of approach is based on having correct weights and complete lists of characteristics in advance. As a result, the setting of objectives becomes a critical stage in the subsequent success of selecting media types.

As a kind of double check on the rankings, the planner will now go back to the original objectives and make sure that the media now being considered for use meet all the objectives. The planner wants to know that all the objectives can be accomplished with these media and will detail which of the objectives can be met with each type of medium, as a kind of justification for their selection. The planner also wants to give reasons why other media were not selected for use in the plan.

The media planner will be certain to determine how each medium is a logical choice for the media plan by listing its advantages for the product and for the plan along with its possible disadvantages. The planner will also indicate how each medium contributes to the attainment of the objectives and where each one has shortcomings. The planner must also determine how well the composite mix of all the media meet the objectives. A chart, similar to the one in Figure 2-4, may help in this task, because of the quantified and weighted characteristics and decisions based on those numerical values.

FIGURE 2-4
An Example of a Quantitative Evaluation of Media

CRITERIA (from marketing, advertising, and media objectives)	WEIGHT	MEDIA BEING CONSIDERED Daily newspapers	Network television	Spot television	Network radio	Spot radio	Consumer magazines	Farm publications	Outdoor	Transit
GENERAL										
Reach	1	3	5	5	3	3	3	2	4	3
Frequency	1	3	5	5	4	4	2	2	3	3
Repetition	1	3	5	5	5	5	2	3	3	4
Selectivity	2	1 (n = 2)	1 (x2 = 2)	2 (x2 = 4)	3 (x2 = 6)	3 (x2 = 6)	5 (x2 = 10)	5 (x2 = 10)	2 (x2 = 4)	1 (x2 = 2)
Efficiency	2	3 (x2 = 6)	3 (x2 = 6)	3 (x2 = 6)	5 (x2 = 10)	5 (x2 = 10)	3 (x2 = 6)	3 (x2 = 6)	3 (x2 = 6)	3 (x2 = 6)
SPECIFIC										
Allows for coupons	1	5	1	1	1	1	4	4	1	2
Demonstration	2	2 (x2 = 4)	5 (x2 = 10)	5 (x2 = 10)	1 (x2 = 2)	1 (x2 = 2)	2 (x2 = 4)	2 (x2 = 4)	2 (x2 = 4)	2 (x2 = 4
Show package in color	3	2 (x3 = 6)	5 (x3 = 15)	5 (x3 = 15)	1 (x3 = 3)	1 (x3 = 3)	5 (x3 = 15)	5 (x3 = 15)	5 (x3 = 15)	5 (x3 = 15)
Merchandising support	1	5	2	2	1	1	4	4	2	2
TOTALS		37	51	32	55	35	50	50	42	41

Each of these decisions must be justified, of course. It may be obvious that the media planner must provide specific reasons for using each medium selected; one way to do this is to demonstrate how each chosen medium fulfills some of the marketing, advertising, and media objectives. What may not be quite so obvious is that there must also be specific reasons for *not* selecting the other media. A complete justification will cover all the media that were considered, telling why some were selected for use and why the others were not selected.

OTHER STEPS

There are other steps in the media process that remain, although they are not properly part of the "strategy" process because they follow these planning decisions. Instead, these other steps involve implementing the planned strategies.

As Figure 2-5 shows, the tactics involve some detailed selection of the advertising vehicles to be used: which magazines and newspapers, which television and radio stations and programs, and other specific vehicle selections. Actually, these choices may be included in the strategic plan, but in the process of the tactical negotiations the media planner may discover that certain vehicles are not available or cannot be scheduled when they are needed, so the plans may be changed to meet the actual conditions that exist.

FIGURE 2-5
Implementing Tactics and Logistics

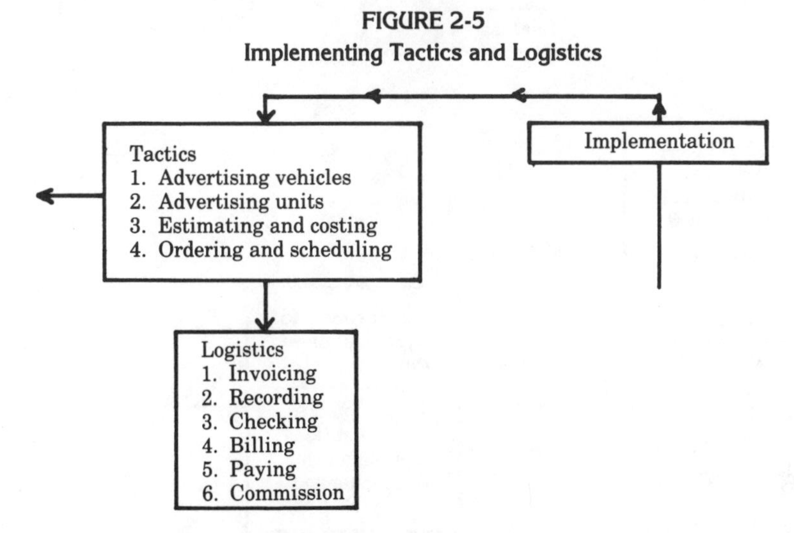

Then the costs of the media effort must be estimated, and eventually the actual costs must be matched up with these estimates. Further, the advertising times and space must be ordered and confirmed and placed on the media schedule.

There are logistics, too, of processing the space/time contracts, as also seen in Figure 2-5. The media will send an invoice for each insertion, which must be matched up with what was ordered and with some evidence that the advertisement actually was run as it was supposed to. If everything is all right, when the bill comes from the media it must be paid, using the advertiser's funds and keeping a commission for the advertising agency.

When the advertising runs, there may be influences on the plan that cannot be controlled for, as indicated in Figure 2-6. Certainly the economy will determine how many people can afford to buy the advertised item and what they are willing to pay for it. Competitive products may alter or increase advertising, either of which may affect the current advertising campaign. Sometimes the schedule changes because advertisements do not always appear in the media as they should — maybe the film breaks in the middle of the commercial, or maybe the printing press throws ink all over the newspaper pages.

FIGURE 2-6
The Results of the Media Process

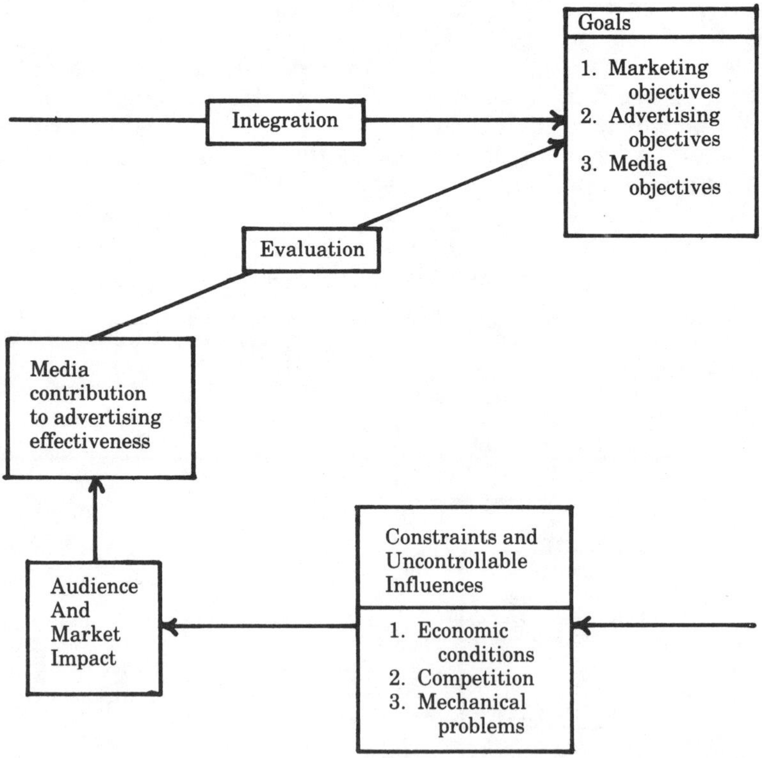

Goals
1. Marketing objectives
2. Advertising objectives
3. Media objectives

Integration

Evaluation

Media contribution to advertising effectiveness

Audience And Market Impact

Constraints and Uncontrollable Influences
1. Economic conditions
2. Competition
3. Mechanical problems

Eventually, however, the advertising runs, exposes an audience, and if the advertising is successful there will be some reaction in the marketplace as well. If one can measure the part that the advertising played and specifically what part the advertising media plan has played, an evaluation will be made of how well the plan satisfied the objectives. In part, this process is establishing the groundwork for the next advertising campaign. Figure 2-6 also shows how this information must be worked in with other research findings that were discussed at the beginning of the media planning process.

This, then, is an overview of the media planning process in advertising. The following chapters will provide details on how each step may be accomplished.

QUESTIONS

1. What is the marketing interface?
2. Why are objectives considered such an important part of the media planning process?
3. What is the relationship between marketing objectives and advertising objectives? Between advertising objectives and media objectives?
4. What is a media mix? How does it compare to media concentration?
5. What is a contingency plan, and how is it used in advertising media planning?
6. How are gross rating points different from total audience impressions? How are they alike?

ENDNOTES

1. Additional examples may be found in Roger Barton's excellent book, *Media in Advertising* (New York: McGraw-Hill, 1964).

SECTION II

MARKETING PREPARATION

INTRODUCTION TO SECTION II

Most consumer product companies insist that advertising planning be firmly anchored in the marketing situation of each brand. Modern advertising media planning begins with a full immersion into marketing. The intent of this section of the book is to acquaint the reader with those aspects of marketing that are of greatest significance in the media planning process.

Chapter 3 gives a basic orientation to market definition, area identifications, sources used, and the tactics of market analysis. It is this identification of sales potentials that characterizes current media strategies. The consumer is key to any plan, so Chapter 4 focuses upon how a sales prospect is identified and found in media audiences. The courses and techniques of this identification are essential to the media planner. The marketing foundation concludes with Chapter 5, which demonstrates the interface between marketing data and media planning. This chapter illustrates how marketing data are used to develop media plan objectives.

3

MARKET PROFILES

To understand the specifics of how media plans are put together, it is necessary to examine in some detail the various steps that are involved. What you have read in the preceding chapter provided an overview so that you could see how the various stages fit together, but you still must study how to perform each one of the steps.

There are two steps that fit together very closely — defining the *target market,* and defining the *target group.* Remember, the target market is the geographic territories, regions, metropolitan areas, cities, or other geographic divisions in which you wish to sell your product, service, or idea and to which you wish to direct your advertising. The target group is the kinds of people who are likely prospects for your selling effort and to whom you want to direct the advertising messages. In this chapter, we shall examine the profiles of the target market, which we can call the "market profile," and in the next chapter we'll take a look at the target group, or "consumer profile."

There are three elements of market data that will be discussed in this chapter: standard statistical information, product performance by market, and competitive analyses.

Standard Market Statistics

First, in dealing with the market profile, you may need some basic information about the markets that are available to you. In some cases you may be talking about certain cities; in other cases you may be talking about a city and the socially and economically integrated area around a major city, which is called a *metropolitan area.* A metropolitan area is defined by the U.S. Department of Commerce and is called Standard Metropolitan Statistical Area (SMSA). Such a long title is cumbersome in the everyday advertising business, so it is commonly referred to as "metro area."

There are some readily available sources of information about these markets that make it unnecessary to do primary research. In fact, because there is so much information available from the government, syndicated research firms, and the media and the markets themselves, most of the research is secondary research from information sources that are already available.

For the markets themselves, four standard reference sources that are widely available in advertising businesses and in some large libraries are most often used. The *City and County Data Book* provides information on, as its title implies, cities and counties around the country. Local population statistics, income information, ages, and similar kinds of demographic information can be found here, and comparisons can be made between various cities and counties to determine which ones would seem to be the best prospective markets in which to advertise.

The *Editor and Publisher Market Guide* does much the same thing for markets that have daily newspapers in them. It also tells about the kinds of stores and banks that can be found in a city. Some of the information is quite detailed and can be quite useful. The climate information can tell a marketer of anti-freeze or of swim suits when to start selling the product in that market. The number of automobiles can help a manufacturer of tires. The number of electric and gas meters may be useful to appliance manufacturers who are trying to determine the potential sales from that market. Even the condition of the tap water in the local water system may be important; by looking in the *Market Guide,* a toothpaste maker can find out if the water is fluoridated, and a detergent manufacturer can locate those towns that have soft water or acidic water. Because the *Market Guide* is compiled and published by *Editor and Publisher* magazine, which serves the newspaper industry, information on the local newspapers and how to contact the newspapers is also included in each listing.

Another business publication, *Sales and Marketing Management*, also publishes information about markets. Here, the information is specifically about the incomes, population, ages, and amount of retail sales in each market. This source is called the *Survey of Buying Power*, and it also includes indices of how much money is available and how much money is spent by the populace on various kinds of products and services. If you look in this source and find that a market has only 0.144 percent of the population of the country, but that it has 0.208 percent of the "buying power," then you know that the people who live there make good incomes and spend much of their incomes on products and services — an important factor for marketers. You can also use this Buying Power Index to compare one market with another on their sales potentials, and you can use the indices to allocate an advertising budget to individual markets, giving each market its prorated share of the budget based on its proportion of the total buying power in the markets you are considering.

Although most people who work with advertising media use *Standard Rate and Data Service* to locate advertising prices, the volumes of

SRDS that cover spot television and radio and newspapers are organized geographically and offer market data by states. At the beginning of each state's listing there is some useful information about that state and each county in it, as well as the major metropolitan areas within that state. Population, income, and retail sales data, along with the number of passenger cars and farm population and income, can be found for each county and for the state as a whole. If the media planner is not certain exactly where a certain market is located, or how close together two newspapers or two broadcasting stations are, there is also a map of each state with the major cities and their major media outlets clearly shown. This information in certain editions of SRDS is usually right at hand, and the media planner need not go to a library or to another office to look up this desired market information.

So far, we have reviewed several sources of information about markets and about product movement. The value of these data has prompted a combination of some of these kinds of information to furnish a source that would tell about the kinds of people who purchase various products *and* about what advertising media these people may see and hear.

The advantages are so obvious that there have been several attempts in the advertising and marketing research business to produce this kind of media and marketing information source. At this time, the best-known and probably widest used source of this type is *Target Group Index,* known best by its initials, TGI. Target Group Index provides basic background information about magazine and television audiences, as well as basic demographic information about the population of the United States and subgroups within that population. Then TGI goes further, providing data about the kinds of people who purchase various consumer products and services, including the amount of this kind of item that they purchase, their demographic make-ups, and even a summary of their psychographics, i.e., their psychological types. Most important for us, TGI then tells how much television these people watch, how much radio they listen to, how much they read magazines and newspapers, and even how much outdoor advertising they see — even the specific programs they watch and the kinds of radio stations they listen to and the newspaper and magazine sections they read. This kind of information may be provided for a generic product category, such as riding lawn mowers. Or the information may be provided for the amount of margarine that people buy or whether they buy stick margarine or soft margarine. Or the information may be provided for specific brands of headache remedies.

Target Group Index is not the first syndicated advertising research service to provide this kind of detailed information on marketing, advertising, and media, and that may be an advantage. Some of the earlier services were difficult to decipher; the information is very detailed and therefore can also be complicated and complex. Thousands of pages of printed numbers must be read and understood and applied properly. To the credit of TGI, the millions of individual data are still relatively easy to scan and comprehend, even for beginners in the advertising field.

Let's take a look at the kind of information TGI provides and see how these data are interpreted. We shall use the example in Figure 3-1.

FIGURE 3-1

Example of Target Group Index Information

	TOTAL	CURRENTLY CARRY				DON'T CARRY			
	US	A	B	C	D	A	B	C	D
			%	%			%	%	
	'000	'000	down	across	index	'000	down	across	index
ALL ADULTS	145434	97864	100.0	67.3	100	47569	100.0	32.7	100
MEN	68836	51645	52.8	75.0	111	17192	36.1	25.0	76
WOMEN	76597	46220	47.2	60.3	90	30377	63.9	39.7	121
ADULTS 18-24	26930	13285	13.6	49.3	73	13645	28.7	50.7	155
25-34	31606	22344	22.8	70.7	105	9262	19.5	29.3	90
35-44	23027	16850	17.2	73.2	109	6177	13.0	26.8	82
45-54	23429	17878	18.3	76.3	113	5551	11.7	23.7	72
55-64	19696	14744	15.1	74.9	111	4952	10.4	25.1	77
65 OR OVER	20744	12764	13.0	61.5	91	7981	16.8	38.5	118
18-34	58537	35629	36.4	60.9	90	22908	48.2	39.1	120
18-49	93202	61332	62.7	65.8	98	31870	67.0	34.2	105
25-54	78063	57072	58.3	73.1	109	20991	44.1	26.9	82
35-49	34665	25703	26.3	74.1	110	8963	18.8	25.9	79
NORTH EAST	34166	23751	24.3	69.5	103	10415	21.9	30.5	93
NORTH CENTRAL	39414	27807	28.4	70.6	105	11607	24.4	29.4	90
SOUTH	46748	30858	31.5	66.0	98	15890	33.4	34.0	104
WEST	25106	15449	15.8	61.5	91	9657	20.3	38.5	118
NEW ENGLAND	7033	5012	5.1	71.3	106	2021	4.2	28.7	88
MID ATLANTIC	30953	21315	21.8	68.9	102	9638	20.3	31.1	95
EAST CENTRAL	19293	13927	14.2	72.2	107	5366	11.3	27.8	85
WEST CENTRAL	23326	15986	16.3	68.5	102	7340	15.4	31.5	96
SOUTH EAST	26184	18015	18.4	68.8	102	8169	17.2	31.2	95
SOUTH WEST	14389	8715	8.9	60.6	90	5674	11.9	39.4	121
PACIFIC	24256	14895	15.2	61.4	91	9362	19.7	38.6	118
COUNTY SIZE A	57782	39222	40.1	67.9	101	18560	39.0	32.1	98
B	38589	27338	27.9	70.8	105	11251	23.7	29.2	89
C	25177	17155	17.5	68.1	101	8022	16.9	31.9	97
D	23885	14149	14.5	59.2	88	9736	20.5	40.8	125
SMSA CENTRAL CITY	50970	34187	34.9	67.1	100	16783	35.3	32.9	101
SMSA SUBURBAN	52276	36598	37.4	70.0	104	15678	33.0	30.0	92
NON-SMSA	42187	27079	27.7	64.2	95	15109	31.8	35.8	109

Source: Courtesy Target Group Index.

The figures in TGI are projections onto the entire population of the United States, and most of the figures are rounded off to the nearest thousand (always look for the rounding, indicated in TGI by the '000 at the top of a column). So the 145434 figure at the top of the first column of the TGI data means that there are an estimated 145,434,000 adults in the country. The next four columns deal with those adults who carry life insurance (indicated by the term *currently carry* at the top of the columns). There are 97,864,000 adults, then, who have life insurance, as indicated in the column headed with an *A* and with the "'000" rounding to the nearest thousands.

To understand an entire TGI listing, let's read across the next line in the example — *Men*. In the first column, the number 68,836 means that there are an estimate 68,836,000 adult men in the United States. Then, under the *currently carry* heading in column *A*, it is estimated that 51,645,000 of those adult men carry life insurance. The *B* column is the percentage of all the people in the top line going across (all adults who carry life insurance) who are in the category at the left of this row (in this case, men). You could figure this out yourself by dividing the number of men who carry life insurance (51,645,000) by the total number of adults who carry life insurance (97,864,000).

$$\frac{51{,}645{,}000}{97{,}864{,}000} = 0.528 = 52.8\%$$

If you did, then you would know that 52.8 percent of all the adults in the United States who carry life insurance are men; TGI has already completed that calculation for you with the 52.8 figure under the (%) percent sign in column *B*.

You might also want to know what percentage of the adult men in the United States already carry life insurance. To do so, you would take the number of men who carry life insurance (51,645,000) and divide it by the total number of men (68,836,000).

$$\frac{51{,}645{,}000}{68{,}836{,}000} = 0.750 = 75.0\%$$

You would again find that TGI has already done this calculation for you, this time in column *C* where the figure 75.0 is under a percent sign to indicate that 75 percent of the men in the United States carry life insurance. So in TGI, column *C* indicates what percentage the column *A* number is of all the people in the first column heading.

For you to know whether these numbers are important to you, however, you would need to compare the estimate (that 52.8 percent of all adults who carry life insurance are men) with the percentage of the entire population who are men, and you would need to compare the fact that 75.0 percent of adult men carry life insurance with the percentage for all adults. You could then combine these statistics into a complicated formula to tell you how much these figures vary from the average. Once again, however, TGI has already done that calculation for you. In column *D*, under the heading *index*, is the number 111. In this case, the average index number is 100, and anything above 100 is above average while anything below 100 is below average. You can take the difference between the index number and 100 to find out how far above or below average your category might be. In this case, the difference between the index 111 and the average of 100 is 11, so men are about eleven percent above average in their ownership of life insurance. Right below, for women, the index is 90, and the difference from 100 is 10, so women are about ten percent below average in their ownership of life insurance.

You can see, then, that Target Group Index provides very specific information on the ownership of various products and services. And as you read through the rest of the TGI example, you will also see that detailed information is given on how old these people are; in fact, there are two age "breakdowns" so that you can match up the TGI data with various other sources of information that may use a variety of different age classifications, and also so you can do some simple calculations to determine other age categories.

Target Group Index also provides two different categories of geographic territories or regions within the United States, because there are two different widely used classifications. The U.S. Bureau of the Census uses only four geographic regions, while the American Association of Advertising Agencies suggests at least seven separate regional classifications. There is also information on the size of the counties in which people live; these are divided into four county-size categories: A, B, C, and D. For a detailed listing of the Bureau of the Census geographic regions and the AAAA geographic regions, as well as the four county-size classifications, see Figure 3-2.

Looking through the rest of the typical TGI listing, you will see indications of whether the product and service purchasers live in the central city area of a Standard Metropolitan Statistical Area (SMSA) or in the suburban portion of a metropolitan area, or if they live outside a metropolitan area.

The entire Target Group Index listing is not shown in the Figure 3-1 example because it requires eight pages of information to present it all. The rest of the listing provides information on the respondents' educational levels, types of employment, racial characteristics, marital status, household incomes, and numbers of children.

PRODUCT PERFORMANCE

Besides simply collecting data about markets, it would also be useful to determine to some extent how well this advertising seems to be working. In fact, the entire marketing effort can be traced to some degree by finding out how well competitors' products and services are selling. There are syndicated research services that are available to tell us this kind of information.

Selling Areas-Marketing, Inc. is known in the advertising business by its initials, SAMI. This service traces warehouse withdrawals of products. You can find out how much of the competitors' products were shipped out of major wholesale warehouses around the country, and how these shipments compare with those during the past year and with those of other competing products in the same generic category. The advantage of the SAMI information is that major cities throughout the country are included in the survey, so most of the product sales can be traced. A possible disadvantage is that warehouse shipments may not be made at the same time the product is selling; the product may have been sold a week or so before, and the warehouse shipment is a follow-up replacement, or a store may anticipate future sales and order an

FIGURE 3-2
Definitions of County Sizes and Geographic Regions

Geographic Regions (according to Bureau of the Census)

North East includes Maine, Vermont, New Hampshire, Massachusetts, Connecticut, Rhode Island, New York, Pennsylvania, New Jersey.

South includes Delaware, Maryland, District of Columbia, Virginia, West Virginia, North Carolina, South Carolina, Georgia, Florida, Kentucky, Tennessee, Mississippi, Alabama, Louisiana, Arkansas, Oklahoma, Texas.

North Central (or Central) includes Ohio, Indiana, Illinois, Wisconsin, Michigan, Minnesota, Iowa, Missouri, Kansas, Nebraska, South Dakota, North Dakota.

West includes Montana, Idaho, Wyoming, Colorado, New Mexico, Arizona, Utah, Nevada, Washington, Oregon, California.

Geographic Regions (according to American Association of Advertising Agencies' recommended standard breakdowns for consumer media data)

New England includes Maine, Vermont, New Hampshire, Massachusetts, Connecticut, and Rhode Island.

Metro New York includes New York, Kings, Queens, Richmond, Bronx, Westchester, Rockland, Nassau, and Suffolk counties in New York State, and Bergen, Essex, Hudson, Middlesex, Passaic, Union, Somerset, and Morris counties in New Jersey.

Metro Chicago includes Cook, DuPage, Lake, Kane, McHenry, and Will counties in Illinois and Lake and Porter counties in Indiana.

East Central includes Michigan, Ohio, Kentucky, West Virginia, and balance of Indiana, and Alleghany, Armstrong, Beaver, Butler, Clarion, Crawford, Erie, Fayette, Forest, Greene, Indiana, Jefferson, Lawrence, Mercer, Venango, Warren, Washington, and Westmoreland counties in Pennsylvania.

Middle Atlantic includes the balance of New York, New Jersey, and Pennsylvania counties, all of Delaware, Maryland, the District of Columbia, and Fairfax County (including Fall Church) and Arlington County (including Alexandria City) in Virginia.

West Central includes the balance of Illinois, and Wisconsin, Minnesota, Iowa, Missouri, North Dakota, South Dakota, Nebraska, Kansas, Montan, Wyoming, and Colorado.

Southeast includes the balance of Virginia, and North Carolina, South Carolina, Georgia, Florida, Tennessee, Mississippi, and Alabama.

Southwest includes Arkansas, Louisiana, Oklahoma, Texas, and New Mexico.

Pacific includes Washington, Idaho, Utah, Arizona, Nevada, Oregon, and California.

County Sizes

County Size A: All counties belonging to the 26 largest metropolitan areas.

County Size B: Counties over 120,000 population that are not in Class A plus counties that are a part of the metropolitan area of cities in such B counties.

County Size C: Counties not included in Class A or Class B having over 32,000 population plus counties that are a part of the metropolitan area of cities in such C counties.

County Size D: All counties not included in Class A, Class B, or Class C.

early shipment from the warehouse. Still, this is very useful and very complete information that can be purchased for specific products and for specific competitors.

The *A. C. Nielsen Company* is perhaps best known for its broadcast program ratings surveys, but it also provides a product movement service. For example, Nielsen surveys a sample of drugstores and grocery stores to find out what products are selling and in what amounts. Because the survey is made in retail stores instead of in warehouses, the data may be more current than those of other similar services. On the other hand, because there are so many more retail stores than there are wholesale warehouses, the survey is only of a sample of stores and there may be sampling errors involved.

COMPETITIVE INFORMATION

In addition to market information, it may also be useful to learn about the competition. If you are trying to sell a product, the advertising done by other firms that make similar products may be important to the success of your own advertising effort. You may want to avoid certain media where the competition is particularly strong, or you may decide to concentrate your advertising in the same media as your major competitor and demonstrate "head to head" how your product is superior or less expensive or more versatile. Knowing about your competition's advertising, then, is vital to the success of your own advertising effort.

Advertisers do not approach competitors and ask them what kinds of advertising they are doing, because such data may give competitive leverage. Nor can advertisers monitor competitors' advertising and record what they do, where, how often and when, because such activity requires significant resources.

There are, however, syndicated research services that already perform this task. They observe the television, newspaper, radio, outdoor, and magazine advertising in major markets and in major media vehicles; they record when the advertising appears and for what products and services the promotion is intended. Sometimes they even estimate how much this advertising was likely to cost. They do this for many national advertisers in many product and service categories. They may observe your own advertising, as well as that of competitors. They tabulate all this information and make it available by subscription on a regular basis. Although the published data may not cover all advertising in all markets in all media vehicles, marketers learn about the most important and most prominent aspects of competitors' national advertising.

There is no single source to which you can subscribe that provides all the information you would like to have. The sources that provide information about advertising expenditures in several different media do not offer enough detail about the actual advertising; instead, they provide summaries of the expenditures in each medium. To learn about specific uses by your competitors within each medium you must consult a variety of sources.

Broadcast

Perhaps the best single source of competitive advertising activity in the broadcast media is *Broadcast Advertisers Reports*. This source is abbreviated as BAR, and it tells about competitive advertising in spot (i.e., local) television, network television, and radio. You can find the amount spent in each of those media per month for all major brand names. You can also locate the information for the parent companies, companies that have many brands. The information provided will tell you how many broadcast commercials were used, how long the commercials ran, on what programs the commercials appeared, and how much it is estimated that these commercials were likely to have cost. So BAR is a valuable source that will help you find out how your competitors are using television and radio, so that you can use that information in planning your own media effort.

There is also some broadcast competitive information available in sources that cover more than one medium, as you will see.

Print

For consumer magazines, the same kind of information can be found as BAR provides for broadcast media. Here, *Leading National Advertisers, Inc.,* prepares the information in conjunction with the *Publishers Information Bureau* of the Magazine Publishers Association. The title of this source is the Magazine Investment Analysis, but because it is a joint effort of Leading National Advertisers and the Publishers Information Bureau, the slang term in the advertising industry for this source is usually "LNA/PIB." It provides details on what magazines were used by various advertisers, the size of each advertisement, whether it was in color and whether it was printed right to the edge of the page as a "bleed" insertion, as well as an estimate of what the cost was.

The information for newspapers is also helpful. *Media Records* provides information on advertising in major newspapers around the country, with details on whether the advertisement ran in the morning or evening edition, how large the total amount of advertising space was, and summaries of how much advertising each newspaper carried for major categories of products or services.

Outdoor

Expenditures in outdoor (billboard) advertising are provided by Leading National Advertisers, Inc. This LNA source tells how much each advertiser spent on paper posters and how much on painted signs in each major market in the United States. It also summarizes the expenditures for each national advertiser for each 3-month quarter of the year.

Media Combinations

By now, you may have realized that it is cumbersome and sometimes confusing to have to search through so many sources for information on each advertising medium. It would be useful if there were a summary of competitive advertising expenditures for all media. Such a thing does not exist, but the *Multi-Media Report* from Leading National Advertisers, Inc., comes close. It provides an estimate of the amount of money that major advertisers spend in six advertising media: consumer magazines, newspaper supplements, network television, spot (local) television, network radio, and outdoor. There is no detail of how large or how long the advertisements were nor of the specific media outlets or vehicles that were utilized, nor the months when the advertising was carried; that information still must be located in the more specific sources that were described earlier. However, the *Multi-Media Report* is a very helpful summary that can give you a broad overview of how your competitors allocate their advertising budgets and the relative weights of advertising that would appear in each kind of advertising medium.

Part of the *Multi-Media Report* can also be purchased separately. It is called the *Ad $ Summary* and it tells how much money has been spent by major advertisers in all six of the media surveyed by Leading National Advertisers. It does not provide detail on how the advertising dollars were allocated to the various media, however.

Another useful source that can be helpful with several different media is published by *Trendex, Inc.* The Trendex data are prepared for specific product categories; an advertiser subscribes to only the information needed in a specific product category. A survey of consumers is made with questions that are quite specific about consumers' attitudes toward the advertiser's product and toward competitors' products, the kinds of stores that were shopped, who in the family made the actual purchase, and similar kinds of information. The Trendex information is quite valuable for marketing a product, even though it does not provide much detailed information about advertising media.

ESTABLISHING MARKET PROFILES

Now the important question that faces us is: how do you utilize all this information in media planning? It is fine to know where the necessary information is located and how to understand the materials, but how are they all put to work?

Looking at the market information sources will often provide some insights into favorable and unfavorable markets in which to sell your product and advertise your services. You may find that the demographic characteristics of the people who live in certain cities are not ideal for your marketing situation. If you are selling luxury automobiles; low-income markets may not be good locations, even if there are a few persons within those markets who can afford your wares. You can also find out if the populace seems willing to spend its income, and if so, is the money spent on your kinds of items?

More directly related to advertising media is the problem of the competition. You really cannot decide whether you want to face up to the competition and sell in the same kinds of markets and use the same kinds of advertising media until you find out just exactly what the competition has been doing. Obviously, you do not want to use certain advertising media just because your closest competitor is doing so; there should be a more sensible marketing rationale behind any decision you make. But this kind of analysis can indicate that the competition so outweighs you in advertising weight that you cannot possibly compete. Or you may decide that you can compete, but only in a small scale, such as in only part of the country or only in a few of the large metropolitan areas.

Product movement information can also help you understand more of what the competition is doing, and you can also try to trace correlations between the competition's advertising and the sales flow of the competitive product. The more comprehensive marketing and media sources can provide consumer profiles as well as market profiles, as we shall see in the next chapter, and some can also tell you how well the various advertising media and vehicles are received by various groups of potential consumers.

It probably makes most sense to start by defining the regions of the country that are most favorable to your product category, and also those regions that are not as favorable. You would do this even if you intend to plan a campaign that is national in scope, so that you can determine which regions should have the heaviest rates of advertising. If you have information about how your own brand compares with the generic category, you could also select favorable and unfavorable regions for your brand. Then you could compare your brand's regions with those of the entire product category and see if there are any differences that could possibly provide you with an advantage. This *regionality* decision process is only the initial step in establishing your market profiles, but it is a vital step.

Then you may want to start finding individual markets that offer opportunities for your product or service. These could be standard metropolitan statistical areas, or they could simply be cities or counties, or even just certain states. In some cases you might need to subdivide a market into parts, especially if there are widely differing demographic characteristics from one part of the market to another. Other possible market divisions will be discussed in the next chapter.

Finally, you will arrive at a listing of geographic territories that you believe will offer you the best opportunities. You may split up the country into markets in which you will advertise and markets in which you will not advertise, and you might do this even if you sell your item in the whole country, just to make your advertising more efficient and make your advertising budget provide enough advertising "weight." Another approach is to list certain markets that you think are your primary targets, those in which you know you will advertise and in which you will spend the greatest share of your budget. Then you may have another list of markets that you also think would be strong, but perhaps not as good as those in your primary list. These secondary markets may receive advertising if there is enough of the budget left from the primary markets, or they may simply receive less advertising weight than the primary markets. You may even make up a third list of tertiary markets that also might be considered for lesser amounts of advertising if the budget is adequate.

The task of establishing market profiles cannot be done without also considering the consumer profiles at the same time. The reasons for this is that some of the same sources of information must be utilized for both steps, and some of the information about where people live is obviously related to these people's other characteristics. In the next chapter, then, we shall go through the process of establishing consumer profiles.

QUESTIONS

1. What is the difference between a target market and a target group?

2. In what ways may demographic characteristics of a target group be more useful to a media planner than are geographic characteristics? What about psychographic characteristics?

3. How does using an index figure make market data easier for a media planner to use?

4. Why are competitive evaluations important in media planning? Why don't more advertisers and agencies conduct their own studies of competitors' advertising activities?

5. Why is the regionality consideration only an initial step in establishing market profiles?

4

CONSUMER PROFILES

Establishing consumer profiles must be done in conjunction with establishing market profiles because some of the same information sources must be used; both sets of profiles must operate in a coordinated fashion with one another; and parallel decisions are being made simultaneously.

The task of dealing with consumer profiles may be more difficult than that with market profiles, however. The consumer profiles may be used by the creative department to write copy and select the appeals that will be utilized in the advertising messages. The consumer profiles have more facets and more considerations than the relatively simple geographic considerations of the market profiles. The consumer profiles involve information about potential customers, about the general population, and about media audiences; all of these groups are constituted of people, but what we know about each group is slightly different so we must try to match up the information about all the separate constituencies.

You already know something about the problem of consumer profiles, because what you have read in the preceding chapter must necessarily overlap with this chapter, and because some of the important sources of consumer profile information, such as Target Group Index, were discussed in detail in that chapter.

GENERAL CONSUMER INFORMATION

The media planner starts with a general consumer profile and then makes the target more specific, so let us also start with general consumer information. There once were many sources of advertising information that gave general characteristics about consumers, but as advertising became more sophisticated and advertising and marketing research became more complex, we have slowly evolved into even more specific advertising source materials that tell us more about the characteristics of consumers of specific products and services. At the same time, we have fewer of the more general sources about consumers as a whole.

Much information still can be obtained from the census of the United States, which is compiled every ten years. There are many volumes of this kind of information, however, and it is difficult to delve through so much information to find the figures that are relevant to your particular situation or dilemma. Because the census is compiled only once a decade, the information in it may be dated when we want to use it, but this problem can be partially overcome by using a current version of the *Statistical Abstract of the United States,* which is an annual update published by the U.S. Department of Commerce. Again, however, the large amount of information and the fact that the information may not conform to the specific problem at hand may cause problems.

Some of the syndicated advertising and marketing research services do provide an overview of the U.S. consuming public. One of the best such sources is the *Profile of U.S. Consumer Market Segments* that is prepared by the well-known advertising research firm of Daniel Starch & Staff.

More useful, however, may be the specific information about the consumers of the product or service that is being marketed.

SPECIFIC CONSUMER INFORMATION

Information about the buyers or potential buyers of specific products and services would be more useful than general consumer information, of course, but researching and locating and utilizing such information may also be more difficult. There are some sources that will provide information about specific generic item categories, but they hardly include the entire range of available products and services. You may find the information you need about the consumers of one product, and then you may start another campaign plan and learn that no useful consumer information can be located.

The products and services that are widely used by all kinds of consumers are the ones for which there is most likely to be information about consumers, maybe even for your specific brand. If you are marketing packaged goods such as branded grocery products, laundry and household cleaning products, toiletries and cosmetics, and canned or bottled beverages, you probably will have a good deal of consumer characteristic information available. If, however, you are marketing products that are bought less frequently or that are not purchased by all socioeconomic groups of people, then the information will be less complete. Examples might be characteristics of people who purchase lawn mowers, sporting goods, shoes, and furniture. When you locate information about the consumers of these kinds of products, it is likely to be less specific, and there are fewer details on the purchasers of individual brands. Then, if your campaign is for products that are seldom purchased or that appeal to a narrow segment of the population, you may not find much useful consumer information at all. Marketers of typewriters, carpeting, pianos, and office furniture may have real difficulties in learning about their potential customers, at least from the syndicated research services.

What we have talked about so far has dealt mostly with consumer products and services. For marketers of industrial goods or of agricultural items, there may be even less information available. One reason is that there are no "ultimate consumers" for these kinds of goods: they are intended for sale to middlemen who will apply them or rework them or in other ways use them as a raw material. There can be no consumer characteristics for items that are not intended for sale to consumers. One advantage that industrial and agricultural advertisers may have, however, is that there are relatively few purchasers of their products and services and the buyers' interests are usually well known.

Most of the concern with consumer profiles concentrates on *demographic characteristics,* a term we have used before. Demography is the study of human populations, so demographic characteristics are those population characteristics that help us group people into similar categories.

In some cases, these kinds of demographic statistics can be generated by trade associations for certain industries. The member firms usually contribute their own figures and statistics, which are disguised so that no single company's results can be identified, then grouped and summarized for dissemination. The figures may only be distributed back to the member firms, or they may be made available publicly. In either case, there is no uniformity in the quality of the information: some trade associations do a very detailed and organized statistical search and analysis, while others simply supply haphazard information that may not be of much use, or no information at all. However, some advertisers and their advertising agencies may be able to acquire and use this kind of internal industry information to aid the advertising media plan.

Some publications for various industries may also have useful information. Trade publications in the grocery, pharmaceutical, automotive, and other fields can provide useful and specific information about the kinds of customers who may purchase these items, as well as information on competitive advertising, general sales and marketing trends, and economic outlooks.

There are also some more general business publications that still provide data on specific industries. *Business Week* gives an annual summary of the liquor industry, for example, and *Advertising Age* surveys several kinds of business fields. Another advertising publication, *Marketing and Media Decisions* (which was formerly titled *Media Decisions*), publishes an in-depth analysis of the advertising in a single industry in almost every issue, covering many consumer industry fields over the course of time.

Other sources of consumer information for certain product categories have already been described in Chapter 3. These include the drug and grocery sales audits prepared by the A. C. Nielson Company and others. Target Group Index provides detailed demographic information about the consumers for more than a hundred kinds of goods and services that are included in its semi-annual survey. You may want to refer back to Figure 3-1 to see the example of a small portion of the demographic information on people who do and who do not own life insurance coverage. Similar information, sometimes on individual brands of merchandise, is provided for many categories of items that are of interest to consumers and to advertisers and marketers who want to sell to those consumers.

To summarize, then, information about consumers may be available for some kinds of products and services and not available for other kinds. Industries vary a great deal, but in general, the more progressive and advanced the marketing style and approach used within an industry, the more detailed and complete will be the consumer information available.

AUDIENCE CHARACTERISTICS

We may know something about the kinds of consumers who have bought or who are likely to buy certain categories of products or services — or even certain brands of merchandise. But in dealing with advertising media, we also need to know about the characteristics of the people in the media audiences. You will remember from Chapter 2 that one of our approaches to selecting target groups is called the "demographic matching" method, in which we must determine the demographic characteristics of our potential consumers. That is what we have been doing so far in this chapter. But the second phase of the demographic matching approach is to determine the characteristics of the media audiences, so that eventually we can try to match up the consumers with the audiences. There are many sources of media audience information, and while the ones described here are the more popular, the list is not all-inclusive.

Television

The only continuous source of data about network television audiences comes from the A. C. Nielson Company. Because this audience service deals with what are known as television program "ratings," Nielson is usually referred to in the advertising industry as a "network ratings service."

Perhaps Nielsen is better known for network television ratings with its publication called Nielsen Television Index. American Research Bureau is known by its initials, A.R.B., and its ratings service goes by the trade name of ARBitron. In general, although there are some individual differences between these two services, they offer similar kinds of audience information about local television ratings.

Local television station advertising is usually referred to as spot television, and for each important local television market there are ratings services available from American Research Bureau and from A. C. Nielsen Company. The figures are similar to those used for network television.

Local broadcasting markets are unusual, however, because the stations' broadcast signals go out much farther than just the city or even the metropolitan area from where they originate. Advertisers want to know the total audience for each station, so the ratings services survey throughout the areas where the broadcast signal can be received well; this territory is called the Total Survey Area (by ARB) or the Station Totals (by Nielsen).

But on the fringe areas of reception, the residents usually can receive broadcast signals from some other market, and they may watch that market's stations more often. So the ratings services have devised a new kind of territory, which is constituted of all the counties where the residents watch more television from some certain market than from any other market. American Research Bureau calls this territory the "Area of Dominant Influence" (abbreviated ADI), and Nielsen uses a similar definition for its "Designated Market Area" (abbreviated DMA). Every part of the country, then belongs to an ADI (or to a DMA), because the residents of every county in the country watch television originating from some given market more than they watch television from the stations in any other market.

The television ratings for the areas of dominant influence or for the designated market areas are very useful, because those areas contain the bulk of the viewers for any city's stations. In fact, these concepts are so useful that even newspapers and other advertising media are starting to use them to talk about their audiences. Learn these terms well; you will often hear "ADI" and "DMA" mentioned in the advertising business.

Both Neilsen and ARBitron figures provide estimates of the numbers of people in various age groups who were viewing a given program, as well as trends so you can tell if the audience size for a program has been increasing or decreasing.

In addition to the ratings services, there are very complete television audience data available in special volumes of Target Group Index. This information is not a rating; instead, it offers detailed information about the demographic characteristics of various program audiences, as well as information on the amount of total television viewing and comparisons with the consumption of other media.

Radio

The same difference between network and spot broadcasting occurs in radio, but the heyday of network radio is past; spot radio dominates this particular medium. For spot radio, American Research Bureau surveys the larger radio markets and supplies information similar to the television reports.

NIELSEN DESIGNATED MARKET AREAS (DMA)

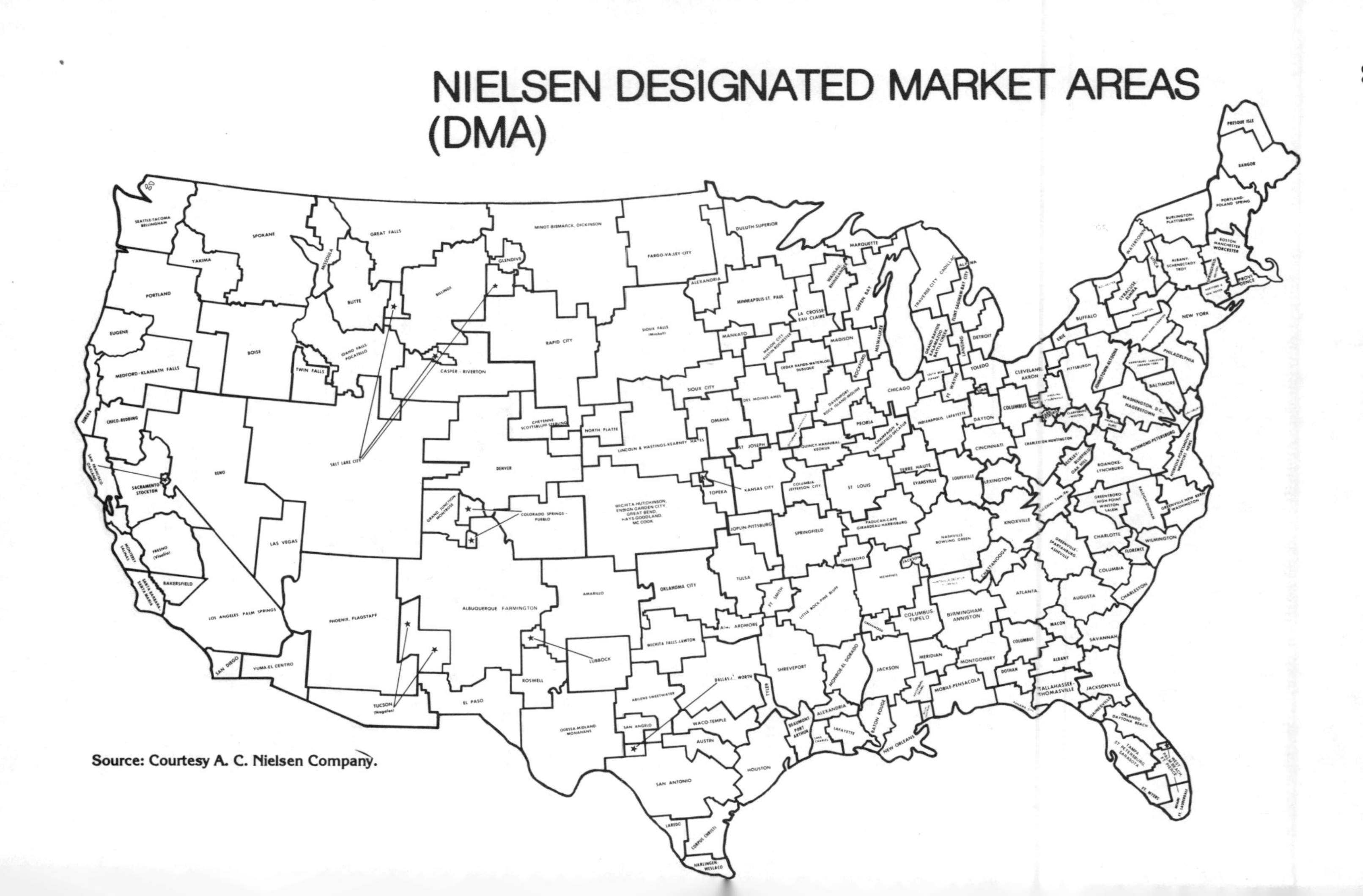

Source: Courtesy A. C. Nielsen Company.

Magazines

The magazine industry has been very progressive in research of its audiences, and perhaps there is more information known about magazine audience characteristics than about the audiences of any other medium. At one time, there were several syndicated services that reported on magazine audiences, but newer techniques were developed that made some of these services obsolete. Still, many magazines hire market research firms to study their audiences and find out the reactions to the magazine content; at the same time, this research often includes demographic and geographic information about these audiences. Of course, because these studies are authorized and subsidized by the magazines themselves, the information that results is often presented in a manner that is favorable to the publication. It may also be difficult to locate the research that is done for the magazines, or to learn if particular magazines even have such research, because the studies are conducted individually rather than by syndicated services on a regular schedule.

Once again, Target Group Index must be mentioned, because detailed audience information for magazines is available in certain special volumes of TGI. Target Group Index provides information on the demographic characteristics of many magazine audiences. It also tells which magazines are read in the home (as opposed to being read in offices or in waiting rooms or the like) and which audience members bought the magazine or subscribe to it, called the *primary* audience as opposed to the *secondary* audience of people who read "pass along" copies. There even is information on how many people read various combinations of magazines, so an advertising schedule that will be carried by more than one publication can be measured in how many repeat readers and non-repeat readers there are likely to be.

Incidentally, an *accumulative* audience (also called cumulative audience or just "cume") is all the different persons who saw an advertisement at least once when that advertisement was carried in more than one issue of a single magazine (or more than one broadcast of the same television program, and so on). An *unduplicated* audience is the total number of different persons who saw an advertisement at least once when it appeared in different vehicles, such as in two or three separate magazines, or on more than one program.
That is a fine difference in terminology that is often overlooked in the advertising business, but using each term carefully can help avoid confusion and mistakes. In TGI, the accumulative audience of more than one issue of a single magazine is just entitled "cumes" and the unduplicated audience of combinations of more than magazine is called "pairs."

Other Audience Information

For print media, the term "circulation" is important because it refers to the number of copies of a publication that are sold, compared to the number of persons who read those copies, the "audience." The

FIGURE 4-1

Example of Target Group Index Magazine Audience Information

C	TOTAL	PROFESSIONAL/TECHNICAL				MANAGER/ADMINISTRATOR			
	US	A	B	C	D	A	B	C	D
			%	%			%	%	
	'000	'000	down	across	index	'000	down	across	index
ALL ADULTS	145434	14350	100.0	9.9	100	19311	100.0	13.3	100
SOUTHERN LIVING	3728	605	4.2	16.2	164	853	4.4	22.9	172
SPHERE	745	*138	1.0	18.6	188	*143	0.7	19.2	145
SPORT	4134	456	3.2	11.0	112	449	2.3	10.9	82
THE SPORTING NEWS	3286	362	2.5	11.0	112	447	2.3	13.6	103
SPORTS ILLUSTRATED	9994	1748	12.2	17.5	177	1836	9.5	18.4	138
THE STAR	2698	*268	1.9	9.9	101	338	1.8	12.5	94
SUCCESSFUL FARMING	1738	* 45	0.3	2.6	26	*126	0.7	7.2	55
SUNSET	3577	771	5.4	21.6	218	759	3.9	21.2	160
TENNIS	1356	376	2.6	27.8	281	331	1.7	24.4	184
TIME	17614	3962	27.6	22.5	228	3142	16.3	17.8	134
TIMES MIRROR MAG NET (NET)	11882	2105	14.7	17.7	180	1925	10.0	16.2	122
TOWN AND COUNTRY	1219	*192	1.3	15.7	159	287	1.5	23.5	177
TRAVEL & LEISURE	2644	695	4.8	26.3	266	711	3.7	26.9	203
TRUE CONFESSIONS	2414	* 99	0.7	4.1	42	*180	0.9	7.5	56
TRUE EXPERIENCE	1422	* 47	0.3	3.3	33	*105	0.5	7.4	56
TRUE LOVE	1878	* 84	0.6	4.5	45	*130	0.7	6.9	52
TRUE ROMANCE	2425	* 68	0.5	2.8	28	*190	1.0	7.8	59
TRUE STORY	4764	*146	1.0	3.1	31	374	1.9	7.8	59
TV GUIDE	42441	4234	29.5	10.0	101	6192	32.1	14.6	110
TV MIRROR	3307	*108	0.8	3.3	33	331	1.7	10.0	75
TWA AMBASSADOR	931	*187	1.3	20.1	204	*267	1.4	28.7	216
U.S. NEWS & WORLD REPORT	7375	1577	11.0	21.4	217	1506	7.8	20.4	154
VOGUE	3843	746	5.2	19.4	197	703	3.6	18.3	138
WALL STREET JOURNAL	4929	1008	7.0	20.4	207	1325	6.9	26.9	202
WEIGHT WATCHERS	1974	303	2.1	15.4	156	327	1.7	16.6	125
WOMAN'S DAY	20498	2356	16.4	11.5	116	3345	17.3	16.3	123
WORKBASKET	3097	* 87	0.6	2.8	29	401	2.1	13.0	98
WORKBENCH	1325	*230	1.6	17.4	176	*220	1.1	16.6	125
WORLD TENNIS	1004	*193	1.3	19.3	195	*236	1.2	23.5	177
ZIFF-DAVIS NETWORK (NET)	9382	1579	11.0	16.8	171	1669	8.6	17.8	134
CBS AUTOMOTIVE GRP (GROSS)	4964	593	4.1	12.0	121	806	4.2	16.2	122
CONDE NAST MAG GRP I (GROSS)	25522	3707	25.8	14.5	147	4901	25.4	19.2	145
DELL MODERN GROUP (GROSS)	5502	398	2.8	7.2	73	606	3.1	11.0	83
FAM HEALTH/WGT WATCH (GROSS)	6181	1165	8.1	18.8	191	963	5.0	15.6	117
GOLF DIGEST/TENNIS (GROSS)	3689	827	5.8	22.4	227	932	4.8	25.3	190
HARPER/ATLA/NAT HIST (GROSS)	2543	708	4.9	27.9	282	414	2.1	16.3	123
KIWANIS/LION/ROTARIAN(GROSS)	1524	272	1.9	17.8	181	401	2.1	26.3	198
MACFADDEN WOMENS GRP (GROSS)	21503	1019	7.1	4.7	48	2035	10.5	9.5	71
PETERSEN ACTION GRP (GROSS)	13709	1747	12.2	12.7	129	1851	9.6	13.5	102
TIMES MIRROR MAG NET (GROSS)	13150	2368	16.5	18.0	182	2117	11.0	16.1	121
ZIFF-DAVIS NETWORK (GROSS)	11241	1846	12.9	16.4	166	1990	10.3	17.7	133

Source: Courtesy Target Group Index.

Audit Bureau of Circulations is the best known service that checks publishers' circulation figures for many consumer magazines and newspapers. The Bureau issues its ABC Blue Book of circulation figures, which may be of some use to media planners. There are other similar services for business publications and farm publication.

FIGURE 4-2

Example of Target Group Index Unduplicated Audience ("Pairs") Information for Magazines

	AMERICAN HOME '000	APARTMENT LIFE '000	BARRON'S '000	BETTER HOMES & GARDENS '000	BON APPETIT '000	BRIDE'S MAGAZINE '000	BUSINESS WEEK '000	CA '000
AMERICAN HOME	8417	7912	7266	25161	7394	7933	9727	7492
APARTMENT LIFE	7912	2292	2647	23879	2825	3201	5178	2780
BARRON'S	7266	2647	1516	23542	2111	2619	4201	2000
BETTER HOMES & GARDENS	25161	23879	23542	28680	23365	23758	25391	23767
BON APPETIT	7394	2825	2111	23365	1557	2863	4632	2264
BRIDE'S MAGAZINE	7933	3201	2619	23758	2863	2488	5187	2772
BUSINESS WEEK	9727	5178	4201	25391	4632	5187	5212	4608
CAR CRAFT	7492	2780	2000	23767	2264	2772	4608	1528
CAR & DRIVER	8682	4017	3325	24837	3577	4063	5787	3025
CBS AUTOMOTIVE GROUP (NET)	10479	5894	5219	26420	5425	5958	7647	4824
COSMOPOLITAN	13130	9156	8746	27270	8851	8995	11088	8887
CUE	7054	2379	1606	23358	1854	2369	4238	1751
CYCLE WORLD	7602	2916	2140	23823	2358	2898	4723	2081
DELL MODERN GROUP (NET)	10562	6432	5671	25879	5895	6217	8161	5798
EBONY	10409	5756	5147	26109	5336	5750	7543	5246
ESQUIRE	9973	5467	4709	25526	4931	5466	7013	4905
ESSENCE	8246	3621	2896	24321	3118	3581	5389	3025
FAMILY CIRCLE	23499	21425	21012	33243	20961	21307	23188	21211
FAMILY HEALTH INC TODAY HLTH	9915	5728	5065	25069	5268	5731	7579	5226
FAM HEALTH/WGT WATCHER (NET)	11328	7328	6731	26095	6869	7312	9149	6886
FAMILY WEEKLY	22181	18339	17656	35729	17854	18282	19884	17864
FIELD & STREAM	13311	8993	8204	28350	8504	8982	10392	8201
FLOWER & GARDEN	8914	4787	4133	23977	4280	4782	6547	4227
FORBES	8066	3490	2502	24080	2897	3478	4876	2870
FORTUNE	7916	3236	2388	23905	2731	3246	4697	2646
GALLERY	7719	2964	2241	23966	2469	2991	4773	2241
GLAMOUR	11101	6989	6550	25770	6629	6669	8947	6706
GOLF DIGEST	8626	4030	3222	24513	3459	3996	5647	3411
GOLF DIGEST/TENNIS (NET)	9760	5130	4413	25427	4633	5150	6747	4625
GOLF MAGAZINE	8175	3504	2695	24125	2957	3499	5196	2842
GOOD HOUSEKEEPING	23008	21245	20794	32963	20779	20982	22894	21031
GOURMET	7816	3236	2554	23677	2589	3221	5055	2704
GRIT	10311	5897	5063	26000	5335	5845	7616	5219
GUNS & AMMO	8617	3963	3214	24699	3449	3954	5692	3267
HARPERS/ATLAN/NAT HIST (NET)	8314	3839	3191	24234	3358	3899	5632	3325

Source: Courtesy Target Group Index.

Another publication is simply called *Circulation,* and although it has so many items of information that it may occasionally be difficult to digest, it provides an idea of print media *penetration* into markets. That means that the percentage of the population that reads a given newspaper or several different magazines will be indicated in this source. In a way, the percentage figures almost make this a ratings service for print media, so it is a very helpful information guide.

And still again we must mention Target Group Index, this time for the "product user" approach to defining target groups that we mentioned in Chapter 2. For the product user method, the concern is not with the demographic characteristics of a product's consumers, but rather the media habits of those consumers. Target Group Index gives detailed media habit information for all the product and service categories that it surveys and reports, so it is an essential tool for media planners who want to use the product user approach. The fact that there need not be complicated attempts to match up demographic groups makes the product user approach very attractive and that there is no loss of detail by trying to make demographic matches has brought widespread use of the product user approach in modern advertising practice. In turn, these trends to the product user approach have brought greater need for media audience information about the purchasers and potential purchasers of goods and services, which puts still greater emphasis on a comprehensive service such as that offered by Target Group Index.

Another note about Target Group Index, for which you may wish to refer back to Figure 3-1 in Chapter 3: for the specific advertising media of daytime television, "prime time" (evening) television, magazines, radio, newspapers, and outdoor, the likelihood of consumers being exposed to any of these media is expressed in *quintiles*. This kind of distribution divides the population into five equal-sized groups, each group constituting 20 percent of the population. Quintile I is those 20 percent of the people who are most exposed to each of these advertising media; Quintile II is the 20 percent who are next "heaviest" in their exposure to each medium, and so on down to Quintile V for the 20 percent of the population that is exposed very little or not at all to each medium.

Then Target Group Index goes on to provide detailed information about which magazines these consumers read, what times they listen to radio on weekdays and on weekends, the kind of radio programming they prefer, when they view television on weekdays and weekends, the kinds of televised sports they watch, the specific network television programs they tune in, the days they read newspapers — even if their amount of magazine reading matches up with their television viewing.

You can see from this summary that there is a wealth of information in Target Group Index. It is perhaps the most valuable single source of information for the media planner. There is a problem, however, when so much information is packed into a single source. It may seem like the answer to any question, and it may be — but the right question must be asked. The media planner cannot just hope that TGI is going to provide the direction for an advertising campaign. Instead, specific questions must be asked *before* these information sources are consulted. A general question such as, "Where do our best prospects live?" cannot be asked, because there is so much information that no single solution can be found. A specific question is better such as, "Where do people live who can afford to buy our product, and where the competition has not yet pre-empted a large share of the market, yet where the rest of our product line has a favorable image, there is adequate media exposure, and we have not already achieved most of our total market potential?" That is a complicated question, and it can lead to complicated answers.

ESTABLISHING CONSUMER PROFILES

In our application of consumer profiling, we are trying to match up product purchasers with media audiences. If we are using the demog-

FIGURE 4-3
Example of Target Group Index Media Usage and Exposure Information

6	TOTAL	ALL USERS				HEAVY USERS			
	US '000	A 000	B % down	C % across	D index	A '000	B % down	C % across	D index
ALL WOMEN	76597	29642	100.0	38.7	100	3515	100.0	4.6	100
RADIO WKDAY:6:00AM - 10:00AM	18512	7184	24.2	38.8	100	958	27.2	5.2	113
10:00 AM - 3:00 PM	13040	5426	18.3	41.6	108	617	17.6	4.7	103
3:00 PM - 7:00 PM	12857	5860	19.8	45.6	118	769	21.9	6.0	130
7:00 PM - MIDNIGHT	8764	4258	14.4	48.6	126	534	15.2	6.1	133
MIDNIGHT - 6:00 AM	2973	1224	4.1	41.2	106	*163	4.6	5.5	119
RADIO AVERAGE WEEKDAY CUME	63862	25665	86.6	40.2	104	2951	83.9	4.6	101
RADIO WKEND:6:00AM - 10:00AM	11831	4573	15.4	38.7	100	704	20.0	5.9	130
10:00 AM - 3:00 PM	12547	5452	18.4	43.5	112	624	17.8	5.0	108
3:00 PM - 7:00 PM	10795	4888	16.5	45.3	117	583	16.6	5.4	118
7:00 PM - MIDNIGHT	7216	3445	11.6	47.7	123	510	14.5	7.1	154
MIDNIGHT - 6:00 AM	2697	1347	4.5	49.9	129	*194	5.5	7.2	156
RADIO AVE. WEEKEND DAY CUME	48572	20517	69.2	42.2	109	2398	68.2	4.9	108
RADIO TYPES:PROGRESSIVE ROCK	9918	4682	15.8	47.2	122	543	15.4	5.5	119
TOP HITS	19742	9387	31.7	47.5	123	1204	34.3	6.1	133
GOLDEN OLDIES	10660	5275	17.8	49.5	128	779	22.2	7.3	159
POPULAR CURRENT HITS	15643	6994	23.6	44.7	116	807	23.0	5.2	112
SOFT MUSIC	15553	6668	22.5	42.9	111	568	16.2	3.7	80
CLASSICAL & SEMI-CLASSICAL	5448	1989	6.7	36.5	94	*152	4.3	2.8	61
COUNTRY MUSIC	14894	6290	21.2	42.2	109	636	18.1	4.3	93
TELEPHONE TALK	6024	2566	8.7	42.6	110	*271	7.7	4.5	98
TALK	6209	2580	8.7	41.6	107	297	8.5	4.8	104
NEWS	18929	7245	24.4	38.3	99	757	21.5	4.0	87
BLACK	2921	1431	4.8	49.0	127	383	10.9	13.1	286
SPORTS	3464	1471	5.0	42.5	110	*179	5.1	5.2	113
ABC CONTEMP-AVE.WEEKDAY CUME	6965	3034	10.2	43.6	113	491	14.0	7.0	154
ABC ENTERTAINMENT	5660	2515	8.5	44.4	115	280	8.0	4.9	108
ABC FM	2346	1167	3.9	49.8	129	* 76	2.2	3.2	70
ABC INFORMATION	5193	2176	7.3	41.9	108	*214	6.1	4.1	90
CBS	7924	3252	11.0	41.0	106	341	9.7	4.3	94
MUTUAL	4295	1925	6.5	44.8	116	*237	6.7	5.5	120
NBC	6671	3019	10.2	45.3	117	*239	6.8	3.6	78
TV WKDAY: 7:00 AM - 10:00 AM	9130	3647	12.3	39.9	103	578	16.4	6.3	138
10:00AM - 1:00 PM	12221	5041	17.0	41.2	107	764	21.7	6.3	136
1:00 PM - 5:00 PM	15345	6480	21.9	42.2	109	811	23.1	5.3	115
5:00 PM - 7:30 PM	18445	7834	26.4	42.5	110	940	26.7	5.1	111
7:30 PM - 11:00 PM	39128	16298	55.0	41.7	108	1612	45.8	4.1	90
11:00 PM - 1:00 AM	15458	6933	23.4	44.8	116	831	23.6	5.4	117
TV AVERAGE WEEKDAY CUME	65070	26141	88.2	40.2	104	3010	85.6	4.6	101
TV WKEND: 1:00 PM - 7:30 PM	11314	4861	16.4	43.0	111	549	15.6	4.8	106
7:30 PM - 11:00 PM	39670	16463	55.5	41.5	107	1779	50.6	4.5	98
11:00 PM - 1:00 AM	16934	7954	26.8	47.0	121	917	26.1	5.4	118
TV AVERAGE WEEKEND DAY CUME	60056	24669	83.2	41.1	106	2741	78.0	4.6	99
TV SPORTS: AUTO RACING	3198	1483	5.0	46.4	120	*210	6.0	6.6	143
BASEBALL	6342	2851	9.6	45.0	116	349	9.9	5.5	120
BASKETBALL - COLLEGE GAMES	3586	1746	5.9	48.7	126	*166	4.7	4.6	101
BASKETBALL - PROF. GAMES	3859	1958	6.6	50.7	131	*254	7.2	6.6	143
BOWLING	4170	1880	6.3	45.1	117	*146	4.1	3.5	76
FOOTBALL - COLLEGE GAMES	5404	2522	8.5	46.7	121	*263	7.5	4.9	106
FOOTBALL - PROF. GAMES	7021	3044	10.3	43.3	112	420	12.0	6.0	130
GOLF	3261	1430	4.8	43.8	113	*131	3.7	4.0	87
HORSE RACING	2956	1339	4.5	45.3	117	*168	4.8	5.7	124
ICE HOCKEY	2463	1127	3.8	45.8	118	*117	3.3	4.8	104
POST-SEASON COL. FOOTBALL GM	3807	1742	5.9	45.8	118	*234	6.6	6.1	134
POST-SEASON PROF. FOOTBALL	4828	2124	7.2	44.0	114	*252	7.2	5.2	114
TENNIS	3952	1890	6.4	47.8	124	*209	6.0	5.3	115

6037F

Source: Courtesy Target Group Index.

raphic matching approach, then we must determine the demographic characteristics of the people who purchase (or whom we would like to encourage to purchase) our product or service. Then we try to find a medium or a combination of media whose audience members have demographic characteristics that will match up with those of the purchasers. As we have stated before, there may not be complete agreement or perfect matches on both sides, and this kind of matching process can also "lose" some information or detail in the "translation" process.

If there is information available about the media habits of the product or service purchasers, then perhaps the demographic matching process can be bypassed and the product user approach can be implemented. Here, as you already know, the media audiences are selected on their usage of the items that is to be advertised. In effect, the audience of each medium and vehicle is being converted into users of the product. We no longer think of four million readers of a magazine; instead, the audience is pictured as 1,850,000 purchasers of our product, or maybe even as 10,000,000 units of the products consumed within a given year.

Using demographic characteristics such as age, gender, income, educational level, employment status, number and ages of children, and other categories can help us in establishing our target groups, that is, in defining the kinds of people to whom we most want to direct our marketing and advertising efforts. Then we may also outline the next most important kinds of people (our secondary target group) and perhaps even a tertiary (third-level of importance) target. This helps us to be certain that the bulk of our advertising is aimed to reach the best or most likely prospects, but that other less-likely prospects may still get some advertising impact.

We may also attempt to outline *target audiences,* rather than stopping with target groups. In this phase, we would determine the specific media or even specific vehicles, times, advertisement sizes or lengths, and other advertising unit information that best seems to reflect the purchasers or potential purchasers of our advertising item.

The task is not always an easy one. Remember from the example of Target Group Index data in the preceding chapter (Figure 3-1) that about three-fourths of all men own life insurance, but comparatively few women have such coverage. Does that mean that life insurance should be targeted toward women, because they have so much market potential left in this particular line? Or would that be more difficult because it is contrary to the natural tendency of people to insure the male of the household more heavily and carefully than is done for the female? Obviously, either approach could be correct, depending upon the specific objectives of the particular marketer involved.

QUESTIONS

1. What is the difference between potential customers (prospects) and audience members?

2. Why is it difficult to get information about radio audiences?

3. What is the difference between an accumulative audience and an unduplicated audience?

4. How does the use of quintiles make consumer profile information more understandable and usable?

5. What is the difference between a target group and a target audience?

5

GEOGRAPHIC AND TIMING CONSIDERATIONS IN MEDIA PLANNING

Even for the so-called "national advertiser" there are considerable fluctuations on selling a product or service across the country. Fluctuations reflect the buying habits in each area or region. As marketing data feedback from the field has improved, marketers have learned of significant differences in sales flow between markets and regions. If these differences in sales position, distribution, seasonal buying trends, etc., are substantial, marketers must adjust advertising plans accordingly. These geographic and temporal shifts have a profound emphasis in media planning because they dictate certain strategies in selection of media and allocation of advertising dollars.

This chapter concerns answering the questions of where to spend and when. True, these are marketing decisions, but they have so much influence on media that it is essential to have knowledge of how marketing information directs media choices. It is not our purpose to exhaust the subjects of market sales analysis or sales season evaluation, but there will be sufficient illustration for you to see how marketing information guides media planning. This is best done by showing the problems of products in national distribution.

GEOGRAPHIC SELECTION

The threshold question for national marketers is whether to support sales with a national (all market) effort, a major market emphasis (regional activities) or a combination of both. Here is a summary of the factors that might influence the decision.

NATIONAL MARKETING EFFORTS

There are conditions in which a national advertising program is preferable. New products or services seeking a quick introduction to the public will adopt a national effort. With no instructive sales history, the firm may wish to use the first year to gain as much market reaction as possible. Other corporations may, for reasons dealing with distribution channels, wish to simplify procedures by guaranteeing advertising coverage of every dealer/distributor's area with national spending. There are still other situations favorable to pure nationwide efforts. These include advertisers who can't afford to buy individual campaigns for each market and advertisers who have relatively proportional or stable sales patterns.

For all these circumstances there are some advantages to national advertising as well:

Cost. Purchasing advertising or promotional activity on a national or volume basis can represent significant cost savings in time or space. Though the out-of-pocket costs seem high, the national purchase has serious cost leverage over market-by-market buying. Here is a television example.

The cost of one rating point (one per cent of the television households) in daytime network television was recently estimated at $1,200 for a 30-second announcement. This means that for each $1,200 (on a national average) the company can buy a percentage of viewing homes in each of more than 200 television markets. Now observe how much the $1,200 will buy on a market-by-market basis. The following is the estimated cost of purchasing a daytime 30-second rating point on a market-by-market basis.

Markets*	% U.S. TV HH**	Cost/Point
1-20	46	$ 600
1-50	69	915
1-100	86	1,190
1-200	100	1,400

*Ranked by HH in Market Area
**HH is a standard abbreviation for "households"

For $1,200 spent in network, the company could buy slightly more than 200 markets. Another way, by using equal dollars, the network gives the advertiser nearly 100 markets more or nearly 14 percent of U.S. homes *for nothing*. This same relationship exists to varying degrees between network and spot radio, national and regional space in magazines and between local newspaper and Sunday supplements bought on full-network basis. Unquestionably there are economies of scale in mass media advertising, if the company can afford advertising on that scale.

Selective Content. Advertisers using national media have much more control over the programming or editorial value. The sponsor of a network television special or mini-series has a consistent program environment not available on market-by-market basis; the firm participating in a network radio drama cannot expect such programs market-by-market. The advertiser seeking a special editorial topic in a magazine might not be able to schedule his message in that same way on a regional basis.

Simplified Logistics. Any production department or media traffic section will tell you how much simpler it is to meet deadlines of a network or one publication that to deal with all on a market basis.

MARKET-BY-MARKET EFFORTS

The use of customized marketing efforts is primarily a reflection of the unevenness of consumer buying habits. For numerous reasons, brand sales activity will deviate from market-to-market; brands as a top seller in one market will be only mediocre in others. Companies wishing to match promotional efforts with sales development have had to rely more and more upon individualized market promotion. Marketing plans that flex according to regional strategies provide the efficiency sought by management. Some promotional advantages will illustrate.

Adjustment of Advertising Weight. Just as the one-size sock "fits all," national advertising operates in the same way. Unfortunately the avertising pressure given by national vehicles may be too great in very weak sales areas, too high where sales are near optimum levels, and too low in developing markets. If a marketer is seriously intent upon tuning advertising pressure according to growth (development) and/or maintenance (performance) he is well advised to consider market-by-market activity.

Uneven Media Performance. Marketers who claim a proportional contribution of sales to justify national activity have been advised to verify audience performance to be sure advertising weights are evenly distributed. Once the media audiences are examined on a regional area basis one can see skews (trends) that are not proportional to the population distribution. The following table illustrates a sample of media vehicles and how they perform regionally versus a national average.

If we assume that an advertiser was receiving sales in near proportion to the population, none of the above media opportunities would match. For example, ABC Football delivers more impressions than needed in the Pacific (142) and too few in the Northeast (86). These examples are representative that there are few (if any) national media opportunities that distribute advertising impressions in the same proportion as households. To rectify these imbalances, firms use some of the national allocation to purchase impressions on a regional or market-by-market basis. This flexibility is essential to many consumer-goods firms.

% Share U.S. Pop	North East 25.1%		East Central 15.5%		West Central 17.7%		South 26.3%		Pacific 15.4*R*	
Media Vehicle	%* Aud.	Index **	% Aud.	Index	% Aud.	Index	% Aud.	Index	% Aud.	Index
NBC-Tonight Show	22.2	88	17.2	111	26.5	150	21.6	82	12.5	81
People Weekly Mag.	21.7	86	17.3	112	11.4	64	24.5	93	17.4	113
ABC-Mon NFL Football	21.6	86	11.5	74	19.5	110	25.5	97	21.9	142
Time Magazine	27.8	111	18.5	119	12.9	73	24.3	92	16.3	6

* Audience: TV-% HH Viewing; Mag. – Circulation
** Index: Audience/Region ÷ Region Share of Population

Adjustable Scheduling. There are many products and services that depend upon weather and other seasonal considerations for sales. Those advertisers wishing to time promotional efforts with seasonal changes are often frustrated when they try to use national promotions. The national medium cannot be scheduled to take maximum advantage of regional differences.

COMBINING NATIONAL AND MARKET-BY-MARKET EFFORTS

The particular advantages of national and market-by-market promotion has prompted many advertisers to utilize both spending approaches in the same campaign.

A layer of national activity assures that all markets (distribution outlets) will receive some advertising. It also means efficient advertising and an opportunity to utilize the prestige that follows certain national vehicles.

The market-by-market approach fills in the weaknesses and voids of national efforts. It gives the marketer the flexibility to concentrate advertising impressions, set timing to regional patterns, and balance national advertising.

METHODS IN MARKET RANKING

Since market-by-market spending is involved in two of the three approaches of geographic spending strategy there should be consideration of how to arrive at a market ranking. What makes one city more valuable than another? Why does a market smaller in population size rank above others in spending priority? Media people do not set the rules of market evaluation but they need to understand how the marketer arrived at the priorities.

Ranking factors are often divided into two dimensions: market opportunity factors and market performance factors. The opportunity means sales potential and includes the size of the market, the number of prospects, the total sales activity in the product area and any other factor that would assist the marketer in measuring the *degree* of sales opportunity. Market performance includes brand-directed factors such as sales history for the brand or, if a new brand, the history of other brands of that marketer, how well the product is distributed (degree of retail coverage) and any other measure that indicates the consumer and trade acceptance of the brand. The following discriptions identify how some of these factors are utilized to order and rank market contributions.

MEASURES USED IN MARKET PERFORMANCE

Many firms are pragmatic about promotional spending. They spend advertising dollars wherever they are reasonably sure sales will result. Some marketers use a simplified set of data to determine how much better one market is than another.

Sales Data. The common denominator is the annual sales figures of a brand for each market, expressed in units or sales dollars. For comparability, each market's sales is taken as a percentage of the total sales for the brand:

$$\frac{\text{Market's Brand Sales}}{\text{Total U.S. Brand Sales}} = \text{Market's Share}$$

For illustration, the table below is an excerpt of a company's market-by-market (in this case a geographically larger or district) sales report for the past year.

Sales District	Last Year Sales (Units)	% U.S. Sales (Units)
Chicago	380,400	8.5
Denver	300,000	6.7
Dallas	225,000	5.0
New York	187,000	4.2
Seattle	98,000	2.2

Certain firms would go a little further to rank and allocate, arguing that the largest sales markets are best able to respond to advertising pressure. The result would see Chicago receiving the primary share of dollars of this market list. This is not a sophisticated method since it rewards markets solely on units sold in the past period.

Sales Data with Market Factors (BDI). Some firms would reject ranking purely on sales because the sales history does not reflect the size of the market. Arguably, larger cities (or districts) in population *should* be greater in sales simply because of more prospects and customers. However, there may be smaller markets in size where per capita consumption is higher than in the larger markets. Such a reflection indicates efficiency and is done by comparing the market's percentage of U.S. population with its percentage of sales. This gives some indication of growth or possibility of higher than average increase. When multiple market performance factors are used it is called a *brand development index* (BDI).

A reminder about indexing before we examine brand development. An index is a figure showing the relationship between two whole numbers or two percentages. The comparative relationship can be done for each two sets *or* by using an average factor (e.g., average U.S. sales) to compare with each market.

If the five districts shown earlier are compared with their populations in percentages we can divide the two for a comparative index or

$$\text{Market Sales Index (Brand Development)} = \frac{\text{\% U.S. Sales (Units)}}{\text{\% U.S. Population (HH)}}$$

Sales District	% U.S. Population (Households)	% U.S. Unit Sales	BDI
Chicago	3.8	8.5	224
Denver	1.0	6.7	670
Dallas	1.5	5.0	333
New York	8.8	4.2	48
Seattle	1.2	2.2	183

Reranking the markets on BDI would put Denver in first position and New York a very poor last. Remember, the greater an index is over 100, the more favorable it becomes; the lower (or under 100), the worse. New York's 4% percent sales is impressive by itself but in comparison to the New York population it is unlikely to receive special effort.

Another important performance factor is distribution. Finding and keeping the necessary retail outlets is a continual struggle for consumer product marketers. Shelf space (or floor space) is enormously scarce and sales potential may rise and fall on the degree to which the product appears in the market. The simplest manner of showing distribution is as a percent of total market distribution. A market or district with a distribution grade of 50 means that the product is sold in stores that account for 50% of the market's retail sales. Is 50% good or bad? Certainly the fact that half of the market cannot purchase the brand at their store is not good news. However, if the marketers believed something could be done to increase distribution the market might be valued more highly. In our example, the distribution is thought to be static with little movement (increases) possible within a year. In such circumstances the higher the distribution the better the ranking. Here is a typical method of modifying a BDI with distribution factors:

$$\text{Market Brand Development} = \frac{\text{\% U.S. Sales} \times \text{Distribution Factor}}{\text{\% U.S. Population}}$$

From our example, if Chicago had a .70 distribution factor, here is its new BDI:

$$\frac{8.5 = .70}{3.8} = \frac{5.95}{3.80} = 157$$

Here are all the districts reordered with distribution factors added.

Sales District	**% U.S. Pop.**	**% U.S. Sales**	**Distribution Factor**	**Brand Development**
Denver	1.0	6.7	.80	536
Dallas	1.5	5.0	.65	217
Chicago	3.8	8.5	.70	157
Seattle	1.2	2.2	.50	92
New York	8.8	4.2	.45	22

The complexity of brand-market indexing is a matter of choice. A firm or an agency may use five or more factors to calculate rankings.

MEASURES USED IN MARKET POTENTIAL

A brand does not exist in a vacuum. There are competitors and competitive products and advertising campaigns. As important, then, as the brand's development is, there is a potential or opportunity to gain additional sales from wringing customers from competitors.

Industry Sales Data. In chapter three we learned that for most consumer goods there are independent research firms that monitor all brand activity on a regional or market basis. Through audits, research firms are able to estimate the total sales of all brands or companies in a particular product category by market, by region, and as a national total. Companies needing a close observation of sales activities purchase the sales audits to give a total picture of a region or market. This is called industry, or more popularly, *category development.* Advertisers will use cateogry sales information to create an index for market potential — the category development index. The logic is simple, if the total sales of all brands in a market is good, there is an opportunity to gain increased sales from competitors. Thus, even if a brand isn't performing well, the company may invest in a heavier advertising effort because the potential for sales is available. Here is the description of the formula.

$$\text{Category Development Index} = \frac{\text{Market's Sales (all brands)}}{\text{Total U.S. Sales} \div \text{¢Districts in U.S.}}$$

In this index procedure we are using the raw number of sales compared to the U.S. average sales. Here is how the data might look for our example:

Total U.S. Unit Sales (all brands)	25,000,000
U.S. Sales Districts	20

District	Sales Units (Category)	Category Development Index (CDI)
Chicago	1,870,000	150
Denver	620,000	50
Dallas	986,500	79
New York	2,540,000	203
Seattle	1,500,000	120

Average District = 25,000,000 ÷ 20 Districts = 1,250,000 Avg. Units

$$\text{Chicago CDI of 150: } \frac{1{,}870{,}000}{1{,}250{,}000}$$

The category development index can tell a marketer the relative sales health of each market. Aggressive marketers look for potential sales in this way. The CDI indicates those areas where opportunity growth could come from.

COMBINING BRAND AND CATEGORY DATA

It should be obvious by now that both the brand and category are valuable for market ranking. The brand data measure how well the brand is performing while category data show potential. Many marketers blend these two sets of data by giving each measure a weight of priority or importance.

Statistical weighting is little more than a numerical basis for assigning priority or emphasis. If items or factors are not equal in importance to a marketer, then the weighting concept allows a statistical means to influence the data. The combining of performance and potential factors for market evaluation is a typical problem for a weighting solution.

For our illustration, the marketer has already computed BDI and CDI indices for the five districts (see pages 00 and 00). Remember, the BDI reflects the brand's performance while the CDI indicates all brands or category activity. Here is a summary.

District	BDI	Rank	CDI	Rank
Chicago	157	3	150	2
Dallas	217	2	79	4
Denver	536	1	50	5
New York	22	5	203	1
Seattler	92	4	120	3

The assignment of weights follows no formula but reflects the judgment of the marketer in each brand situation. Each time the question is asked, How important is one set of data in relation to another? Is BDI more important than CDI in suggesting market concentration? How much more important than CDI? The judgment incorporates all the marketing intelligence that can be brought to bear. Pricing, brand distribution, advertising and sales promotion activity, trade relations, and shipping are only a few factors that could enter in. To illustrate the procedure of weighting, we assume that the BDI has been assigned a substantial priority in a year of brand retrenchment. The BDI is given a weight of .70 (on a scale of 1.00) or more than twice the emphasis of CDI .30. The computation simply then requires the weights to be multiplied by the indices and the products added to form a weighted index. Here is Chicago as an example.

$$\text{Chicago} = \text{BDI } 157 \times .70 + \text{CDI } 150 \times .30 =$$
$$109.9 + 45.0 = 154.9 \text{ or } 155$$

Once the weighting is completed, we have a list of indices and a new order to the districts on a weighted BDI-CDI Index:

District	BDI-CDI Combined Index	Mkt. Rank
Denver	380	1
Dallas	177	2
Chicago	155	3
Seattle	100	4
New York	76	5

Weighting can be done with any type or number of factors. Marketers who are faced with new product types cannot rely upon previous brand or category experience are representative of groups using other factors. Weighting in such a case could use population demographics or composite sales activity — e.g., retail sales, automotive products, clothing, etc. The principle of weighting remains: identify the factors, assign weights, compute weighted values, and sum to find each market's comparative rating.

HOW MARKETING RANKINGS ARE UTILIZED IN MEDIA PLANNING

Once the performance and opportunity factors have been manipulated to create a rank order of markets, the budget allocations can begin. If the company is in a restricted budget period or if the firm is using primarily a national media campaign, it is unlikely that each ranked market will receive special media funding. Typically, markets at the bottom of such a list are eliminated from special dollar attention. The following are other methods employed with ranked market lists.

Allocating Media Dollars by Coverage of Sales. Some market lists are made to cover a certain percentage of a company's sales. Once markets are ranked, a decision is made to cover a proportion of sales and media planners move down the markets until the predetermined sales coverage is achieved.

Allocating Media Dollars at Common Levels of Advertising Weight. When the best performing markets are only slightly separated in BDI or CDI value, they can be selected by the limit of the budget. In such a situation, marketing may decide not to treat similar sized markets with different advertising weight levels. Instead, the same level of activity would be costed in the best market, then the next best and so on until the budget is expended. Each market included would receive the same number of insertions or rating points.

Allocating Media Dollars by Market Grouping. When a ranking of market districts shows wide disparity of performance, marketers are inclined to collect markets into groups and treat them alike. In this way a group of the top BDI markets would receive especially aggressive activity, while markets group in a lower BDI range might receive only modest schedules.

TIMING (Seasonal Influences)

Most companies cannot afford to purchase substantial media schedules each week throughout the year, even if it was desirable to do so. Rather than spread out advertising activity thinly to cover each week, marketers design schedules to concentrate advertising during certain periods and eliminate spending at other times. The marketers' decision for emphasis is guided by a number of considerations including sales or consumption patterns (seasonality), product/service turnover ratios, promotional plans and competitor's activity. In the discussions that follow, these timing influences will be explained and illustrated.

SEASONAL SALES PATTERNS

Products have consumption cycles and these patterns often cause uneven sales. Some products are highly seasonal (antifreeze, snow tires, and lawn equipment), others have peaks established by weather (beverages, recreation products), and still others have high sales periods dictated by holidays (toys and food, for example). Even products with no predictable season have cycles of high and low sales activity that reflect changes in buyer interest.

Companies recognize the peaks and valleys and try to coordinate advertising plans to accommodate the cycles. To install a seasonal spending strategy it is necessary to plot sales trends by month or by quarter. Certain firms are able to monitor their own sales flow from monthly inventories, while others purchase consumption data from syndicated research firms that maintain store audits. Also available are national panel reports that give usage or consumption trends for a product. The data usually begin in raw numbers, reflecting perhaps no more than inventory withdrawals. Here is an illustration based on a cold cereal company.

Product: RTE Cereal Brand
Units: Cases
Area: U.S.

Month ending:		Cases Sold (Warehouse) '000
January	31	11.4
February	28	27.8
March	31	32.4
April	30	39.4
May	31	42.5
June	30	41.9
July	31	39.8
August	31	45.2
September	30	47.4
October	31	25.0
November	30	18.0
December	31	9.3
Total		380.1

For marketing purposes it is advantageous to simplify the data. In this illustration the units were converted into share of the total by quarter of the year with these results.

Quarter	Total Units (000)	%Year Consumption
1st (Jan-Mar)	71.6	18.8
2nd (Apr-Jun)	123.8	32.6
3rd (Jul-Sept)	132.4	34.8
4th (Oct-Dec)	52.3	13.8
	380.1	100.0

Should the marketer be interested in creating an index of sales, he would divide total sales by 12 (months) and divide the average month by sales into the actual sales per month.

$$\frac{\text{Total Sales 380.1M}}{\text{12 months}} = \text{31.68M Units/Month Sold (Average)}$$

With 31.68 as divisor, each month can be indexed; months selling above 31+ will be 100+ (or above average), and those selling below 31+ will be below average. On that basis, September has the highest index of 149 and December the lowest with 29.

Once the sales data are ordered, it is necessary for the marketing management to decide if advertising levels will proportionally reflect sales trends or not. In most situations advertisers will spend proportionally to sales. That is, the highest sales months will receive the highest dollar investment. There are, however, some exceptions worth noting.

New Product Introductions. Those companies facing the public introduction of a brand understand that it is vital to make an impression on consumers and the trade. This usually calls for heavily disproportionate spending prior to peak demand periods. Early spending is needed for the distribution channels to assure adequate shelf or floor space. "Start up" spending is also needed to create consumer brand awareness *before* peak usage sets in.

Countering Competitive Spending Plans. If a large firm follows the seasonal patterns, most competitors are likely to do so. The cumulative effect of many brands all competing for buyer attention at the same time could be troublesome for smaller brands unable to spend equally with the major brands. Off-peak spending is possible and advisable as long as the goal of avoiding competitors does not move the smaller company too far from a time period of primary usage.

Product Turnover (High Ratios). The more often a product or service is consumed, the more often the user is a prospect. Frequency of use dictates the purchase rate. Companies who sell products with a daily or weekly purchase rate do not feel comfortable with disproportionate promotional activity. They cannot afford to trade one season for another. If a company has to cover the major part of a year with advertising, it means either larger budgets or low advertising levels each week. Actually there is an alternative called "flighting" by some and "wave" strategy by others. Simply stated, this is advertising on-and-off with the "off" periods limited to less than a month if at all possible. Flighting allows coverage of long selling periods without having continuous schedules. The "off weeks" allow the flight periods to be of greater intensity. The risk is that increased advertising will gain awareness that will not completely erode (memory decay) before the next flight. Careful scheduling has reduced this risk and made firms with high turnover goods more capable of scheduling year-long promotion needs.

QUESTIONS

1. Discuss how the BDI and CDI indexes complement each other in market evaluation.

2. The network television program's NTI rating is a national average and does not indicate the program's selective market performance. Explain.

3. Most advertisers spend promotional dollars proportionally with seasonal sales patterns. However, there are situations when so-called off-peak spending is used. Identify and discuss these situations.

SECTION III
MEDIA PLAN ANALYSES

INTRODUCTION TO SECTION III

The next portion of the text concerns those aspects of the media that planners use to make their selections for each campaign. It covers each segment of the decision process on the way to developing a cohesive media plan that attempts to achieve advertising's role in the marketing objectives.

Chapter 6 discusses the general frame of reference for media differences. It explains the characteristics of each communication experience and how a media planner utilizes the advantages of each medium. Chapter 7 covers the role of cost in media planning. It demonstrates how planners estimate audience levels within budget constraints. The crux of current media selection is audience value, and Chapter 8 discusses the many measures used to identify size and prospect qualities of the audience. Chapter 9 concerns the use of "cost per thousand" analysis to select media vehicles. This critical selection procedure is used throughout the planning and buying process, and each stage of the "cost versus audience decision process" is illustrated. This section ends with coverage in Chapter 10 of those factors important in the selection process that seldom have finite value. Yet, even without specific measures, these media qualities often have significant influence upon planning decisions.

In Section III, the reader is exposed to the full selection process that reflects the marketing development that was covered in Section II. Mastery of the techniques included will satisfy all but the most demanding planning sequences.

6

MEDIA CHARACTERISTICS

It is a common practice for each media industry or organization to publish a list of the principal advantages of using its medium as an advertising outlet. The problem with such lists is that the individual who is planning or buying advertising media does not usually look at each medium's characteristics and then match those to the desirable and needed characteristics. Instead, the media planner will compose a list of necessary attributes to be sought in the advertising media selection, and then will review the various media available in an attempt to find those media that best match those attributes.

With this process in mind, the sensible approach to the characteristics of various media is to outline the qualities that may be considered by the media planner, and then to determine how each medium matches those attributes.

Media characteristics can be organized under certain general topical headings. These topics include audience characteristics, timing characteristics, geographic characteristics, creative considerations, competitive considerations, control characteristics, production and mechanical characteristics, and financial characteristics.

AUDIENCE CHARACTERISTICS

The *quality* of a medium's audience is a term that is used too freely in the advertising business. There are, of course, many qualities within any audience, and the qualities that are of concern to a media buyer will vary according to the goals of the advertising and the approaches to be used. Certain magazines, for example, may claim that their readers constitute a "quality" audience, the implication being that the readers are upperclass individuals with a lot of money to spend. Selling a general-appeal product such as detergent, however, may not require such qualities in the media audience, because the advertising for such products probably will be aimed at all types of people, not just those in the higher socioeconomic categories.

More important audience qualities would include such things as audience *attentiveness* and *interest,* either in the medium's content or in the advertisements. Certainly a reader of a magazine pays close attention to that publication, usually because of some interest in its content. Publishers of magazines have for years tried to establish the fact that magazine readers are more attentive to the medium and more interested in its contents than the audience of, say, television may be interested in the programs that are offered. In the case of interest in the medium's offerings, this kind of comparison may be true, but to say that the television audience does not pay attention to what appears on the screen is an exaggeration. Any advertiser who has received bags of mail protesting some program that carried a commercial for one of his products can testify that the television audience is very attentive — and very responsive.

Of course, there are advertising media that do not inherently attract a great deal of attention or build much interest on the part of their audiences. Outdoor advertising, point-of-purchase materials, and many specialty advertising items may fit into this categorization. The attention and interest to the broadcast media of television and radio relate directly to the specific programming and to the specific nature of the commercials that are offered. In the same way that an audience relates to only part of the programming on radio and television, it may relate to only part of the content of a daily newspaper, such as to certain sections or features. Similarly, an audience will pay attention to certain magazines, or only to certain sections of a magazine, ignoring or only glancing at other sections that do not seem to be of interest.

This kind of audience *selection* process is also important to advertisers. Today's audiences are bombarded with all types of media every day, and each individual member of the audience must make a selection of which media vehicles he will read or watch or look at, and how much time he will spend with each one. Within certain media, such as most print media, the reader also selects the sections to be read, the pages that will be turned to, and the specific articles and features and advertisements on each page that will be studied. This same selection process occurs when an individual member of an audience selects a program or station on television or radio, but once the receiving set is turned on and a station is selected, much of the control is out of the hands of the listener. To avoid being exposed to an announcement or a commercial involves a great deal more effort for a broadcast audience (turning off the set or changing the channel or turning down the volume) than it does for a newspaper or magazine reader simply to turn the page. In most cases, the better the advertisement or commercial, the less inclined the audience will be to avoid the advertising message. The inherent quality of the advertisement, then, can compensate for or overcome some of the selection process of the audience members.

The audience term that is similar to selection on the part of the audience is audience *selectivity,* but the concept of selectivity is very different from that of selection. In audience selection, the decisions were made by the members of the audience; in audience selectivity, the decisions are made by the media planner. Some media offer a great deal of selectivity of certain kinds of people or certain subgroup audiences. An advertiser who sells sports equipment might not want to use a mass-appeal medium such as television unless there is some specific programming that offers greater selectivity: golf equipment, for example, is often advertised during televised golf tournaments. If winter sports equipment is involved, advertising in a magazine such as *Skiing* may offer the greatest possible selectivity. In general, television and newspapers do not offer as much audience selectivity; they tend instead to reach large, general audiences. Magazines offer much selectivity, and some magazines now offer special "demographic" and "professional" editions, so that advertising can be directed only toward certain segments of the magazines' audiences.

Related to selectivity is the concept of *waste* circulation. A medium that reaches many persons who are not considered prospects for the product or service offers "waste" audience — persons not desired but still paid for. In the audience for a televised golf match are many people who do not plan golf and who are not prospects for buying golf equipment, so there is some waste involved. By comparison, there are few readers of *Golf Digest* magazine who are not golfers, and there is likely to be less waste in that situation. Similarly, advertisements for disposable diapers in *Reader's Digest* may reach a very large audience, but a sizeable portion of the readers probably are not in the market for buying this kind of product; parents with infants might be reached more efficiently with a magazine such as *American Baby,* and the amount of waste would be reduced. At first glance, the high cost of an advertisement in *Reader's Digest* can seem to be offset by the enormous size of the audience, but when waste is included in the analysis, *American Baby* probably is much more efficient if the aim is to reach buyers of disposable diapers.

The readers of *American Baby* may also be more *involved* with the contents of the magazine than are the readers of *Reader's Digest.* Articles about child care and development are of prime importance to new parents, whereas the human interest features in a more general publication may be quite interesting but probably are not as vital to the audience members. This kind of audience involvement is another important audience characteristic that media planners and buyers must consider.

The greater the involvement with a medium on the part of the audience, it is less likely that *distraction* will be a factor. Readers of a magazine or newspaper can be distracted by nearby noises, conversations and requests, competing media messages, or numerous other external events. Similarly, broadcast audiences can be distracted. An automobile driver who is listening to the radio may be distracted by other traffic, by billboards along the road, or by the necessity of searching for a parking place. The more involved that the audience member is with the medium's content, however, the more difficult it is for that person to be distracted, as any parent already knows who has tried to talk to a child while the child is engrossed in a comic book.

The audience may also resist receiving the message that the advertising is attempting to convey, just as customers may resist buying a product or using a service. This *audience and customer resistance* can affect the success or lead to the failure of any advertising. It may be that the customer is dissatisfied in some way with the product, brand, or company, perhaps because of unsatisfactory experiences in the past or even because of the distaste for the advertising for the item. Resistance may also result from a product being compared to a competing product that for some reason better meets the customer's needs or expectations. One of the most common reasons for resistance, of course, is lacking the necessary funds to purchase the item.

This kind of audience and customer resistance can occur with any medium, although it has been charged that resistance due to irritation with past advertising is more likely to occur in television than in the print media where it is easier for the audience member to avoid unwanted messages.

Resistance to advertisements may in turn affect the *impact,* the intrusive force of a message in the minds of the audience. The impact of an individual advertisement may, of course, be a factor of the size of an advertisement or the length of a commercial, the use of color vs. black-and-white, the use of bleed in a magazine advertisement or of sound effects in a radio commercial, and similar specifications of the advertising unit.

Each individual medium also has an effect on advertising impact. The combination of sight and sound that is available in television provides a unique opportunity to impress a message on an audience, increasing the impact of the advertising message. In a similar way, a spectacular lighted outdoor display in New York's Times Square may have more impact on the audience than a regular illuminated billboard. Providing news or entertainment matter as part of a medium's offerings may also increase the amount of impact on that medium's audience, including the impact of the advertising matter.

Certain magazines also seem to have more impact on their audiences than do other magazines, and this kind of impact is often due to the *prestige* of one publication compared to the prestige of another. Certain media also seem to confer prestige on their audiences and on the materials contained within those media. At one time, advertising on television brought prestige to the advertiser who could afford to use that then-new medium. More often, magazines are considered to have more prestige than do newspapers or broadcast media, and even lower on the prestige scale would be media that do not offer news or entertainment or information to accompany the advertising matter; these lower-prestige media would include direct mail, outdoor, transit, point-of-purchase, and specialty advertising.

Prestige is a personal factor, one that cannot be found in a source of advertising media information. There is no reference book that lists the relative prestige of each of the available advertising media, and as a result the evaluation of the prestige of each medium and each vehicle is a personal judgment on the part of the media planner and buyer.

Most information needed in the advertising media evaluation process can be found in published sources, however, and there is a difference in the *quality of audience data* available for the various media. Magazines, both consumer and business publications, claim to offer the most complete information about their audiences. For many magazines, complete breakdowns of demographic and psychographic characteristics of readers can be found, along with very specific information on readership, goods and services purchased, reactions to editorial material, and what other magazines are also read. In recent years, television and radio have been able to offer more detailed information than simply ratings, and lately the data for television are beginning to become very competitive in terms of completeness and availability, approaching the data for magazines in their scope, timeliness, and reliability.

Several types of media still can only describe their audiences in rather general terms. Outdoor, transit, point-of-purchase, specialties, and similar media have more transient audiences that are hard to research and even more difficult to define in detail, so the information available on those kinds of media are not as complete nor as refined as are the data for some other media. Newspapers are in the process of trying to improve the quality of the audience data, but with so many localized publications involved it is a very difficult task.

TIMING

Another media consideration of importance to media planning is the timing characteristics of each medium. Certainly, factors such as when an advertisement is to run and meeting the deadline for insertion must be considered in the planning and buying processes. Timing alone is too general a term to use to describe the myriad of functional considerations that can be included under such a heading.

The *repetition* of an advertisement, that is, using the same message over and over again without change, may be very desirable. Not changing a message can save money; avoiding the necessity of producing new advertisements and coordinating new campaigns makes the advertising process easier and less costly. Some media lend themselves to repetition of advertisements more than do others. On television, for example, the repetition of a commercial may cause the message to become stale and a commercial may "wear out" because of repetition. In magazines, on the other hand, repetition may not be as much of a problem and, in fact, repetition may be desirable in magazines. In consumer magazines, for example, studies have shown that repeating an advertisement contributed to increases in reach, readership, recall, and sales, and that repetition of the same advertisement six, seven, or even more times need not necessarily be detrimental to advertising communication success. Similarly, in business publications, readership of strong advertisements does not seem to drop off just because the same advertisement is used repeatedly, and recognition of corporate and brand names, recall of copy points, and actual brand preference can result from repetition of an advertisement.

One of the drawbacks of repetition of an advertisement is that the audience may eventually become irritated with that message. This *irritation factor* is another important media selection consideration. Many advertisers want to be sure to avoid irritating prospective customers, and thus they may also avoid repeating advertisements excessively or schedule their messages to run on a variety of media so the chances of a message repeatedly reaching the same people may be reduced. Some advertisers, though, may intentionally repeat an advertisement to create irritation among the audience in the belief that irritation helps create recall and makes the advertising message and the brand name more memorable. The audience may forget that it was irritated, but the brand name may be more recognizable, say, when it is seen on a package on a store shelf, because the name has been impressed more firmly into the audience members' minds.

Another method of gaining some of the benefits of repetition without confronting many of the concomitant disadvantages is to use a variety of advertisements for a product rather than repeating the same message. In this way, *schedule frequency* can be obtained without the necessity of repetition. Schedule frequency is achieved by advertising often, whether a single advertisement is used over and over or with a different advertising message for each insertion. Repetition, on the other hand, is using a message more than once, whether or not it is run frequently. For example, each year during the Christmas season the New York Life Insurance Company inserts a Christmas prayer advertisement in magazines, and as the same message appears each year, repetition is involved, even though running an advertisement once a year can hardly be considered as frequent advertising.

Another characteristic of frequency is the *frequency of issuance* of a medium or vehicle. The more often that a medium is issued, the more *flexibility* in scheduling advertisements. A magazine that is issued weekly permits a Christmas season advertisement to be scheduled early in the month of December, whereas a monthly magazine's December issue may not come out until too late in the shopping season, forcing a Christmas season advertisement to be placed in the November issue, which in turn may be too early for many shoppers. Daily newspapers, of course, offer even more flexibility because they are issued more frequently, and broadcast media, with their continual issuance, provide even more scheduling opportunities.

The frequency of issuance, in turn, affects the *exposure life* of a medium. Advertising that is carried on broadcast media is relatively transient, with the message lasting only for a short period, then the programming moving on to something else. Printed advertisements may last longer and also be available for reference. For many media, the life of each issue lasts only until the next issue, so the life for a daily newspaper would be about a day, and the life of a weekly magazine would be about a week, but the life of a monthly magazine would probably be about a month. In the case of business publications and some consumer magazines, the life of an issue may be much longer. A business publication's life often runs until the complete issue is read, rather than being affected by the next issue, and publications such as *National Geographic* may have a much longer life than a month because they often are retained within the household for many months or even for years.

The *mortality rate* of advertisements may be related to the life of the medium. An advertisement that runs only once may lose its effectiveness when the life of the issue is over, because the advertisement no longer has the ability to communicate a message. Mortality also may result from running an advertisement repeatedly, very often, so that its ability to communicate is diminished by the audiences' refusal to pay attention to it any longer. This *perishability* of an advertising message is related to the mortality rate, but also to repetition and frequency considerations.

A final important timing consideration is the *length of the message,* at least insofar as broadcast media are concerned. At one time, the standard length of a broadcast commercial was a minute, but costs for television time have increased and the competition for buying television advertising time has stiffened, so that the standard length for a television commercial today is thirty seconds. One outcome of these shorter television commercials was the use of *"piggyback"* commercials, when two shorter commercials for two of a sponsor's products are run back-to-back within a one-minute time period. Shorter commercials allow broadcasting stations to sell, say, six 30-second commercials within a 3-minute block of time, resulting in *multiple spotting* of more than two commercials in a row. The increasing number of commercials can result in problems of *product protection;* an advertiser's commercial may not have much time separating it from a competitor's commercials. The clusters of several commercials in succession also make it difficult for the audience members to recall any one commercial message.

GEOGRAPHIC CONSIDERATIONS

Geographic considerations are an obvious media decision, but there are some aspects of geographic considerations that may not be as simplified as they might seem as first glance. Where the advertising is to be run must match up with the planning goals and objectives. Finding media that have circulation in those regions or areas is an obvious task. Similarly, if the media plan calls for advertising to appear in specific markets or metropolitan areas, it is then necessary to search for media that allow those kinds of arrangements. Many of these considerations have already been discussed in earlier chapters, and they will be examined in more detail in the next chapter.

There are, however, some less obvious media characteristics that must be taken into account when media types and vehicles are being selected.

The *geographic selectivity* of an individual medium may influence the selection of which media are to be used, as well as which specific vehicles are selected. Some media, such as newspapers and spot television and spot radio, offer a great deal of regional or market-by-market selection. The same is true of outdoor, transit, and direct mail advertising. Network television now also offers geographic selectivity; governmental regulations of broadcast media have encouraged networks to make portions of the country available to advertisers who advertise regionally, although individual markets still cannot be reached efficiently with network advertising. Magazines also have initiated advertising arrangements that allow for advertising in certain regions and markets. Some magazines offer "metropolitan" editions that allow advertising to be directed at readers in and near large cities, and many magazines now permit "regional" editions that cover individual states or combinations of states that are geographically proximate.

Some media stress their availability close to the point of sale of merchandise. This *proximity to point of sale* characteristic is important for outdoor advertising, where billboards can be located along the shopper's route to the shore or actually in the parking areas of shopping certers. Point-of-purchase materials are located at or near the point of sale, allowing an advertiser to communicate a sales message to customers who are already in the mood and position to buy and who may be in the process of making actual buying decisions.

Media decisions must also take into account the possible need for inserting the names and addresses of local dealers of merchandise or services. Including *local dealer "tags"* is common when a regional or national advertiser buys advertising in newspapers. Many radio and television commercials on broadcast stations will allow time for an announcer to include information about a few of the area dealers on a rotating basis, so that even though only a couple of dealers may be mentioned each time the commercial is broadcast, every dealer who cooperates will have an opportunity to be included in a proportionate share of the commercials.

CREATIVE CONSIDERATIONS

The creative appeals to be employed in the advertising and the specific copy and layout to be used must match the media that are selected. It would do no good to write a series of television commercials if television is not a medium to be used in an advertising campaign. The logical process would be completing the gathering of necessary information and conducting needed research that could aid both the media and the creative portions of an advertising effort. Then media planning could take place and media types could be determined, so that the copywriter and artist would know for what media they are preparing the creative effort. In practice, however, the creative decisions may be made prior to the completion of the media selection, and the media planner or buyer may be instructed to select media that match these creative considerations. The ideal practice probably is for the research, media, and creative functions to operate cooperatively so that the entire advertising campaign is a coordinated and sensible approach.

If the creative department has determined that *demonstration* is necessary to communicate the advertising message to the appropriate audience, then the media selection will necessarily include television, in all probability, perhaps not because of television's other media characteristics as much as for the reason that television is the medium that best lends itself to a combined sight-and-sound demonstration. The need for demonstration, especially for services and for new products, often affects the media plan and the media to be selected for the advertising campaign.

Certain kinds of creative *impact* also may need to be considered. If a copywriter needs alot of copy to explain a process fully, to justify a copy claim, or to provide evidence of some purported product superiority, a very small newspaper advertisement simply will not be adequate for this purpose. At the same time, a magazine advertisement for a food product may need to show a product in full color, which will in turn limit the choices of the media buyer. Sometimes media production limitations may be considered as creative considerations; many television set manufacturers do not like to advertise their products on television because the people who are in the market for a new receiving set probably cannot appreciate the clarity of the picture and the correctness of the color available from a new set when it is shown to them on their old set.

Inserting an advertisement in a publication or on a broadcast station may affect the *relationship to editorial material*. A department store advertisement for sporting goods may be more effective if it is placed in the sports section of a newspaper, while the same store's advertisement for housewares may benefit from a location in the society or women's section. There are cases of television advertisers becoming unhappy because their commercial for ketchup ran immediately after a bloody murder scene, or because a program that had a young boy making a ham sandwich was followed immediately by a commercial for peanut butter.

COMPETITIVE CONSIDERATIONS

Considering what competitive manufacturers or advertisers may do will affect many aspects of the media planning and selection effort. Only in certain instances will the characteristcs of the media themselves influence these competitive considerations.

The media that a competitor uses can affect an advertiser's media selection. Some advertisers may, for a very good reason, want to avoid using the same types of media or especially the same vehicles that a competitor's advertising uses. On the other hand, some advertisers figure that they should be in the same media as their major competitors. The specific decision in these instances will be the result of personal preferences as well as the relative competitive situation that the advertiser is in and the goals and objectives of the advertising campaign. Sometimes an advertiser who is not in the leadership position within an industry can run advertising in media other than those used by the industry leader, thus reaching a different audience and making the audience believe that his product holds a premier position. Sometimes an advertiser who does not have as much money to spend for advertising as his major competitors will avoid head-to-head competition with the competitors' advertising simply because of the unlikelihood of winning such a head-on battle. Other advertisers in similar positions will want to spend the bulk of the advertising budget in the competition's primary advertising medium in an attempt to demonstrate that the product is "just as good" or that the company is "just as big" as the competition, even though it may result in very little money being available for allocation to any other advertising media.

Advertisers may also select a certain medium or a certain vehicle because of the absence of other advertising, in the belief that the message will communicate more effectively if there is a lot of other advertising competing for the audience's attention. The other advertising in a vehicle may not be from direct competitors; it might just be other advertising that may not be selling the same kind of product or service at all. The view in this case is that all advertising competes for the audience's attention, and there is only a limited amount of time that the audience member can spend with a media vehicle, so the absence or reduction in the amount of other advertising will enhance the selection possibility for one's advertisement. Reducing the number of advertisements may also allow the audience to remember an advertiser's message and brand name more easily and clearly. Some FM radio stations find that they can operate relatively inexpensively and thus are able to offer advertisers only a limited number of commercials during each programming period, a factor that many advertisers appreciate.

CONTROL

At one time, advertisers actually produced many of the programs that were carried on network radio. In that situation, the advertiser had full control over programming content and could schedule advertising for his products as part of the program or compatibly with the program. Advertising agencies found themselves in the role of radio program producers; entertainers often were hired by advertisers to appear in programs; stations and networks served only as brokers of time that they had available to sell to advertisers to use as they wished.

With the advent of television and with inflation, the costs of controlling entire programs became too great for most advertisers. Now, television producers try to sell programs to networks and stations, who in turn try to selling participating announcements to advertisers. The advertisers seldom sponsor an entire program, preferring instead to buy their television advertising time as participations in a number of programs, thus increasing the reach while not significently reducing the frequency of their advertising. With this change, the amount of control that advertisers and their agencies once had over programming has been reduced to the point that the programming first is scheduled by the stations and networks and only then do advertisers have an opportunity to purchase advertising within the body of the established programs.

Still, advertisers find it necessary to retain some sort of control over the messages that may surround their advertising. In television, some large advertisers may negotiate to be able to read the scripts of programs or to preview the actual programs before they are aired to be sure that the subject matter of the program does not conflict with advertising goals and messages. A more common practice is for advertisers to establish a list of rules or practices that the station or network may agree to follow. For example, when cigarettes contributed large amounts of money for television advertising, it was a common practice for networks to agree that cigarettes would not be extinguished by being ground out in ashtrays or stepped on under a shoe heel; villains often were shown smoking cigars and pipes, while heroes could only be shown smoking cigarettes. Some large advertisers have long and complex sets of rules that apply to any programs on which their advertisements appear; this practice may be responsible for television network programming that is intended to avoid offending any audience member because the advertisers want to be certain not to lose any prospective customers.

This type of *control of the message* is less common in print media. There have been attempts by advertisers to "sponsor" certain articles or sections of magazines, but criticism of such practices has largely halted them. There are instances where advertisers may sponsor regular features within publications, but these are usually limited to series of public service advertisements or to advertisers "sponsoring" weekly predictions of football scores.

Despite the lack of control over nonadvertising material in the mass media, advertisers are concerned about the *environment* in which their advertisements appear. As a result, some general advertisers have avoided running advertisements in "pulp" magazines, even though the audiences of such magazines might be potential customers for the advertisers' goods, simply because the environment was not considered apprпохpiate in such publications. Other advertisers manage to influence the environment by sponsoring television "sepcials" that they feel are suitable for their corporate or product images; companies such as Xerox, American Telephone and Telegraph and IBM have utilized this practice, in part because it permits them to maintain an aura of quality that may be missing from the general run of television programming.

These same concerns may lead advertisers to try to *control locations* of their advertisements in print metia. Newspaper advertisers may request that their advertisements appear in certain sections of the newspaper, or on or opposite certain pages within the newspaper. Many newspapers will try to cooperate with advertisers' requests for certain locations, especially for large and important customers who advertise regularly, although in some cases the advertiser may have to pay a premium charge for the special location. Magazines regularly charge extra for advertisements that appear on an inside or back cover of the publication, although regular advertisers may be able to arrange special location considerations. Magazines may also permit advertisers to request that their advertisements be run in or near certain sections of the issue, although the purchase of a certain minimum amount of space may be required.

In broadcast media the problem is not so pronounced, because almost any advertiser who wishes to pay the full price for a certain time segment can buy it as long as it has not already been sold. Advertisers who buy combinations of times for reduced prices or who buy certain *packages* or groupings of times may find that their control over the location of their commercials is reduced. Many stations offer *orbits* that allow the advertiser to purchase several commercials that run on a series of daily programs; the exact time that the commercials will be aired is up to the station, but the advertiser knows in advance the approximate time and kind of programming that will be involved. Some stations offer *scatter packages* so advertisers can save money by buying multiple commercials and may have some decision as to when the individual commercials will run within the time segments being purchased. Other stations are taking over more of the actual time specification decision making by selling broadcast time with a guaranteed audience level for a certain number of commercials with the station running the commercials during times it has available, similar to the way that magazine space is sold with a guaranteed circulation minimum but without the option of specifying location. This *magazine concept* of broadcast advertising permits the station more flexibility in its scheduling of commercials while assuring advertisers that their commercials will not all fall into undesirable or low viewing times.

Another kind of control that affects media selection is *governmental regulation* of media and advertising as well as *public policy* considerations. A distiller of liquor does not have the option of advertising his wares on television and radio, because the liquor industry has agreed that broadcast media are not an appropriate location for such advertising. Cigarette advertisers experience similar restraints on using broadcast media, but in their case it is a result of a federal legislative ban on cigarette broadcast advertising. Certain broadcast stations or networks may prohibit advertising for certain kinds of personal products from being carried, and some magazines and newspapers similarly exclude advertising for some products and services that they feel might not be appropriate for their audience.

Some categories of advertisers may find that they must follow other kinds of restrictions, even though they may be allowed to advertise. It is a common practice for newspapers and broadcast stations to demand payment in advance for political advertising, because of past poor payment records of unsuccessful candidates. Theater advertising may also be on a "cash-in-advance" basis. Most political advertising must be clearly identified as such, to avoid possible misconceptions among the audience that the medium is endorsing a certain candidate or issue. Many media also retain the right of prior censorship of advertising to be certain that the advertisements themselves meet the medium's standards for good taste, honesy, or ethics. In some cases, such as with *Good Housekeeping* magazine's seal of approval, the advertiser may benefit from the vehicle's guarantee to stand behind all advertised claims.

MECHANICAL AND PRODUCTION CONSIDERATIONS

Even though a medium's audience may match up quite well with the desired buyer prospect whom an advertiser wants to reach with advertising, certain mechanical and production problems may interfere.

In some cases the *ease of insertion* of advertising material is important. In recent years, magazines have become more standardized in their page sizes, so that advertisers now have fewer problems in preparing advertisements for varying requirements. With the help of the American Association of Advertising Agencies, the printing ink colors in magazines also have been standardized so that a color advertisement in several publications will appear much the same in all of them.

The length of commercials is becoming fairly standardized in broadcast media, and the ability of most networks and stations to handle commercials in a variety of forms (such as on videotape, film, or produced by the station) has also helped. The complex rate structure and the confusing numbers of broadcast packages available, along with the negotiation process for buying broadcast advertising time, make inserting commercials a complicated process.

Most local advertisers find it a simple task to insert an advertisement in the local newspaper, but regional and national advertisers have found the wide variation in newspapers' column widths and page sizes a handicap in placing advertisements in a variety of newspapers. To counter this problem, the newspaper industry has reduced the number of variations of advertising sizes in newspapers, so that most newspapers can accept and run one of six standard advertising formats for each common size of advertisement, greatly reducing the need for advertisers and agencies to product dozens of different sizes of advertisements to appear in various newspapers.

Another potential production problem has been the *reproduction quality* available from the medium or vehicle. Newspapers have varied widely in their ability to reproduce illustrations and color in advertising, but the trend toward printing with offset presses has improved the quality of newspaper production. Magazines usually offer very high qualities of reproduction, although some publications use cheaper paper which prevents good color and illustration reproduction. Direct mail production is under the direction of the advertiser, so the quality of the finished advertising material can be completely determined without relying entirely on outside control. Outdoor posters that are produced in a central location and then sent to the outdoor advertising operators will have a uniform quality, but the ability of a painter to reproduce the planned advertisement on a billboard may vary greatly from one place to another, even within the same firm.

A *flexible format* may be desired by some advertisers. Some magazines, for example, permit insertion of business reply postcards or of entire sections of advertising. Color, various sizes and shapes, foldout pages, and even smells are available to today's magazine advertisers. Direct mail also offers a choice of formats, including pencils and gifts to induce audience cooperation. Newspaper advertisers may also insert special advertisements, and new shapes of advertising are available with FlexForm, which allows the advertiser to run a newspaper advertisement of almost any shape on the page, with the newspaper using the surrounding area for editorial matter.

Some media are subject to *vandalism,* and outdoor companies may offer services so that torn or damaged billboards are replaced or reapinted. Transit advertising in stations or inside trains and buses is particularly subject to vandalism, and frequent replacement of advertisements may be necessary.

FINANCIAL CONSIDERATIONS

Selection of advertising media must of necessity match the financial capabilities and expectations of the advertiser. Almost any advertiser will be aware of the total cost of his advertising efforts, and will be cautious about exceeding his established total advertising allocation without good reasons for such excesses.

Advertisers also need to be aware of the relative costs of their advertising. A knowledgeable advertiser will know the approximate proportions of his advertising budget that each medium accounts for, and he will know at any time the approximate percentage of his budget that has been expended in that advertising period.

Financial considerations also must take into account the relative costs of media, either in comparison to other media or to other vehicles within a medium. There are a number of methods available that permit evaluating the relative *efficiency* of advertising in certain media or vehicles. The cost of advertising to each thousand audience members permits a relative evaluation of advertising media expenses and efficiencies. This comparison is known as *cost per thousand* and it was discussed in Chapter 2.

The importance of comparing cost efficiencies can be seen in the case of direct mail. Whereas another mass medium may be able to reach a thousand audience members for only a few dollars, to achieve the same audience size with direct mail may cost a hundred dollars or more. The ability of direct mailing address lists to include only prospective customers may eliminate waste circulation, however, and the comparative cost of reaching actual prospects may eventually turn out to be less using direct mail than with the other media that may have appeared less expensive in the first analysis.

Price Information

Before it is possible to compare price information, of course, one must first find out what the advertising rates are for the various media vehicles. For most media, the *Standard Rate and Data Service* provides this information. It publishes separate advertising rate volumes for daily newspapers, weekly newspapers, consumer magazines and farm publications, business publications, direct mail, spot radio, and spot television. It also provides some information about network broadcasting, but the actual advertising rates for networks must be found through direct contact with the broadcasters.

The only important advertising medium that is not covered by Standard Rate and Data Service (known as SRDS) is outdoor advertising, and for outdoor there is a publication called simply Outdoor Advertising Rates.

By referring to SRDS and the outdoor rates, the national advertising rates can be located for most of the important media vehicles. Some media, such as newspapers and local broadcasting stations, may have less expensive advertising rates for local advertisers, and these local rates will not be shown in SRDS, which covers only the rates that large national or regional advertisers might pay. Each media outlet usually has its own printed *rate card* that may duplicate the SRDS information, but the rate card may also have the special local advertising rates and be provided only to local businesses that are located near the media outlet offices.

THE EVALUATION PROCESS

Knowing the characteristics of the media in general is not enough. The media planner and buyer must also be able to evaluate how these characteristics relate to the specific needs of the current advertising effort. The characteristics of a particular medium may be considered assets in some situations and detriments in other settings. Some advertisers may feel that irritating customers with repeated television advertising will hurt the success of the advertising campaign, for example, but for a packaged good without many differentiating characteristics the irritation factor may be used to increase brand identity.

There are many approaches that can be used to evaluate the characteristics of the media and their applicability to the particular advertising problems at hand. Eventually, a skilled and experienced media planner may know inherently which media fit the requisites for an advertising program. For the novice media planner, however, it may be useful to rely on a more formal evaluation in written form. In Table 6-1 a comprehensive evaluation of most of the standard media shows how such a written format can detail the advantages and disadvantages of the various media to permit careful comparisons between them. This particular evaluation will not apply to all cases, of course, because the specific needs and objectives of each individual advertising campaign will vary, creating a need for a specific evaluation of the available media within the framework of the needs and contraints of that particular advertising effort.

Notice how none of the evaluations in Table 6-1 is negative; rather, each medium has been assigned a positive score in each category, with varying degrees of this positivity. The novice media planner may make the mistake of giving some medium or vehicle a negative

TABLE 6–1.
Sample of Comparative Evaluation of Available Media.

	Spot television	Network television	Spot radio	Network radio	Consumer magazines	Business publications	Farm publications	Sunday supplements	Daily newspapers	Weekly newspapers	Direct mail	Outdoor	Transit	Point of purchase
AUDIENCE CONSIDERATIONS														
Attentiveness of audience	++	++	++	++	++	++	++	++	++	++	++	+	+	+
Interest of audience	++	+++	++	++	+++	+++	+++	+++	+++	+++	+	+	+	+
Avoids excess selection by audience	++	++	++	++	+	+	+	+	+	+	+	+	+	+
Offers selectivity to advertiser	+	+	++	++	+++	+++	+++	+	+	+	+++	+	+	+
Avoids waste	+	+	+	+	+++	+++	+++	++	+	+	+++	+	+	+
Offers involvement	++	+++	++	++	++	+++	+++	++	++	++	+	+	+	+
Avoids distraction	++	+++	++	++	+++	+++	+++	++	++	++	+++	+	+	+
Avoids resistance	N	N	N	N	N	N	N	N	N	N	N	N	N	N
Provides impact	V	V	V	V	V	V	V	V	V	V	V	V	V	V
Offers prestige	++	+++	+	++	+++	+++	++	+++	++	+	+	+	+	+
Good quality of audience data	++	++	++	++	+++	+++	++	++	++	+	++	+	+	+
TIMING FACTORS														
Offers repetition	+++	+++	+++	+++	++	++	++	+	++	+	V	+++	+++	++
Avoids irritation	+	+	+	++	++	++	++	++	++	++	++	++	++	++
Offers frequency	+++	+++	+++	++	++	++	++	+	++	+	++	+++	+++	++
Offers frequency of issuance	+++	+++	+++	+++	V	V	+	+	++	+	V	N	N	N
Offers flexibility in scheduling	+++	+++	+++	+++	V	V	+	+	++	+	V	N	N	N
Long life	+	+	+	+	+++	+++	+++	++	+	++	+	+	+	+
Low mortality rate	+	+	+	+	+++	+++	+++	++	+	++	+	+	+	+
Avoids perishability	+	+	+	+	+++	+++	+++	++	+	++	+	+	+	+
Allows long message	++	++	++	++	+++	+++	+++	+++	+++	+++	+++	+	+	+
Provides product protection	V	++	V	++	++	++	++	++	V	V	+++	+	+	++
GEOGRAPHIC CONSIDERATIONS														
Offers geographic selectivity	+++	+	+++	+	++	++	++	+++	+++	+++	+++	++	++	+++
Offers proximity to point of sale	+	+	+	+	+	+	+	+	+	+	++	++	++	+++
Provides for local dealer "tags"	++	+	++	+	++	++	++	++	+++	+++	+++	++	++	+++
CREATIVE CONSIDERATIONS														
Permits demonstration	+++	+++	+	+	++	++	++	++	++	++	+++	+	+	+++
Provides impact	+++	+++	++	++	++	++	++	++	++	++	+++	+	+	++
Permits relation to editorial matter	++	++	+	++	+++	+++	+++	++	++	++	+++	N	N	N
COMPETITIVE FACTORS														
Light use of medium by competitors	+	+++	+	+++	+	+++	+++	++	++	+++	++	++	+++	+++
Low amount of total advertising	+	+	V	+++	++	V	+++	++	++	++	+++	++	+	+++
CONTROL CONSIDERATIONS														
Advertiser control of media content	+	++	+	++	+	+	+	+	+	+	+++	N	N	N
Favorable environment	+	++	+	++	+	+	+	+	+	+	+++	+	+	+++
Advertiser control of location	V	+++	V	+++	++	++	++	+	+	+	+++	+	+	++
Amount of governmental regulation	+	N	+	N	N	N	N	N	N	N	+	+	N	N
Number of other restrictions	+	+	+	+	V	V	V	V	V	V	+	+	+	+
MECHANICAL AND PRODUCTION FACTORS														
Ease of insertion	++	+++	++	+++	+++	+++	+++	++	++	+	+++	++	++	+
High reproduction quality	++	++	++	++	+++	+++	+++	+++	V	V	+++	V	V	+++
Flexibility of format	++	++	++	++	+++	+++	+++	+	+	+	+++	++	+	+
Avoids vandalism	N	N	N	N	N	N	N	N	N	N	N	+	+	+
FINANCIAL CONSIDERATIONS														
Low total cost	++	+	++	+	+	+	+	++	+++	+++	+	++	++	++
High efficiency	++	+++	+++	++	++	++	++	++	++	+	+++	+++	+++	+

N = not a factor for this medium.

V = varies from one vehicle to another within the medium.

evaluation at some time, and then find later that this negative assessment will prevent an advertiser from considering that same medium for some completely different purpose when, in fact, the medium under consideration may be quite appropriate. To avoid this problem, the simplest solution is to avoid ever degrading or "bad mouthing" any possible medium, because there will eventually come a time when that same medium will hold positive attributes for some other situation's requirements.

Within the process of evaluation, a common approach to selecting the eventual media to be used is one of elimination. Using a matrix format similar to that in Table 6-1 the media planner can begin to eliminate some media that simply do not match up in any or many ways with the objectives at hand. This elimination allows the list of media under consideration to be reduced to perhaps four or five types of media. Then some sort of numerical value may be placed on each of the characteristics for each remaining medium, with "weights" added by multiplying the appropriate score by 2 or 3 for characteristics that seem particularly important for the task at hand. For example, a value "1," "2," or "3," could be assigned corresponding to the number of "plus" (+) signs that have been previously assigned to each medium and each characteristic. Then, to continue the example, if attracting the attention of the audience is a vital factor in the use of the media, each medium's score for that trait may be doubled. Similarly, if repetition is considered the most important single consideration, those scores may be tripled. Eventually, totalling the scores for each medium will provide a concrete method of comparing the media that still are under consideration. The medium with the highest score may receive the bulk of the advertising effort, with the others falling somewhat behind. A medium with a relatively low total score may be eliminated from further consideration or, at the least, be reserved for use only if the available budget allows it to be included in the eventual media plan.

The key to the process, then, is to evaluate each medium's strengths in relation to the requirements at hand, and to assign lower positive values, rather than negative evaluations, to weaknesses of a medium.

SUMMARY

Although it is a common practice to provide lists of the strengths and weaknesses of each medium as it might be utilized by an advertiser, the media planner and buyer must reverse that process to determine how the characteristics fit into the planned advertising project or campaign, and then, after determining the necessity or desirability of certain characteristics, to find the media that offer these traits in the best possible combinations.

Another important factor to keep in mind is that there is no single nor any perfect solution to the problem of selecting media. Given the same requisites for a media selection problem, two media planners may derive separate and distinct solutions that may be far from identical yet both of which may meet the stated requirements. There is no easy nor "right" solution, but there are many wrong solutions that do not serve well to further the effectiveness of the advertising process. Each problem is unique, and each solution may also be unique. The key to remember is that the solution must, in fact, meet the stated objectives and operate within any limitations that exist.

QUESTIONS

1. Why is media selectivity of increasing importance today?
2. Why is it important to balance repetition against the irritation factor? How can this balance be achieved?
3. What is the difference between frequency and repetition?
4. In what ways can a major competitor influence an advertising media budget and plan?
5. Why are negative assessments of media often avoided when selecting the general types of advertising media to be used in a campaign?

7

COST ESTIMATING IN MEDIA PLANNING

The cost of media involves two steps in the selection process, one in the formation of the strategy and another later stage where audiences are compared with costs. In this chapter we are concerned with estimation techniques used in shaping media plans. Chapter 9 covers cost techniques concerned with the actual selection procedure.

Cost management is of utmost importance in media planning. Advertisers are continually concerned about advertising costs, and inflation has struck the mass media as it has elsewhere. Gone are those times when a marketer would advise his agency — "Whatever it takes." Today's marketing demands those who can accurately and efficiently forecast the budget needs for desired audience coverage and impact.

PRINCIPAL SKILLS IN ESTIMATION

Cost forecasting is a skill developed from experience. Advertising agencies start many media department beginners in the estimation process, knowing that people must learn to be cost-intelligent before they can handle any other functions. Some of the work is no more than using media rate schedules and laying out schedule costs. There are, however, campaigns or promotions where many alternatives are considered and where decision changes are the rule rather than the exception. Here it takes some special talents and methods to handle estimation under more demanding circumstances. Although experience teaches the estimator many things, there are three principles that anchor the techniques: accuracy, flexibility and speed.

Accuracy. Even though the estimation of cost might be made months before the start, the marketer's tolerance for error in forecasting media costs is low. Neither overestimation or underestimation is acceptable. Underestimating the cost of media means either the audience goals must be lowered or more money found. Overestimating is also bad because it earmarks dollars for media activity when those dollars could be invested or directed to other promotional activities. The degree of accuracy on estimation will vary by firm, but adjustments of more than a few percent are generally unacceptable.

Flexibility. Planning media strategy and tactics means change, alternatives, and shifts of target audiences and geographics. It is a trial-and-error process that must be accommodated. Cost estimation procedures must anticipate any sort of shift or change of emphasis and be capable of producing new projections under highly pressured circumstances. The flexibility to handle demands is borne of estimation procedures well tested and thought through before the planning begins.

Speed. The reciprocal of flexibility is the rate at which forecasting can be made and modified. Speed is, in part, delivery — an ability to give accurate estimates as soon as they are needed. Speed is also individual efficiency. The more effective the forecast process, the more time the estimator can give to analysis and other duties. Estimators capable of swift projection are a valuable asset to a media department.

MEDIA COST REFERENCES

Though all cost information invariably begins with the media, much of the estimation reference originates with sources beyond the media. Similarly, there are alternative sources to the same medium, some more expeditious, others more accurate. The purpose of this description is familiarization, it is not intended to suggest one source as superior to another.

Media Sources

The most basic cost reference is the rate card; all publications, broadcast stations and network, as well as outdoor and transit operations have them. The rate card is a collection of facts that represent needed information for contract, scheduling, and production. The format and style of rate cards varies considerably by medium and by vehicle, but all give essential information on costs, discounts, alternative methods of purchase (print), production/mechanical requirements and deadlines for creative materials. Rate cards are readily available and prospective buyers need only contact media sales department or national representatives to receive a copy. The rate card should be able to answer all cost questions an estimator might have. The following pages show some sample rate cards for both national and local media. Though hardly exhaustive, they will give you some idea how this important cost source is organized and formatted.

The only medium that has low reliance on rate cards is network television. Unlike the formal rate structures of others, network sales is handled much like the commodity or stock markets: costs are quoted on a "bid" and "asked" basis. Certain programming does have rate structure but little of the sale of network time is done strictly by rate card. Prices fluctuate daily according to a number of variables including ratings, audience demographics, advertisers' interest, and potential investment of the prospective buyer. The most common procedure is for negotiators to submit budget levels to network sales representatives and evaluate the packages proposed. The salespeople understand that, whenever possible, the buyer will circulate proposals to competitive networks in order to increase bargaining leverage. Similarly, salespeople will play one client (buyer) against another for the same purpose. For further estimation, media planners must use very general guides based on past experience of network clients and projected inflationary trends.

APARTMENT LIFE™

RATE CARD No. 8

Issued July 15, 1978
Effective February 1979

Published Monthly by
Meredith Corporation
Locust at 17th Street
Des Moines, Iowa 50336

NATIONAL RATES: National Edition Rate Base: 800,000

BLACK & WHITE	1 ad	3 ads	6 ads	9 ads	12 ads
Page	$9,100	$8,645	$8,190	$7,735	$6,825
2/3 page	6,700	6,365	6,030	5,695	5,025
1/2 page*	5,320	5,054	4,788	4,522	3,990
1/3 page	3,660	3,477	3,294	3,111	2,745
1/6 page	2,000	1,900	1,800	1,700	1,500
per line	29.40	27.93	26.46	24.99	22.05
BLACK & 1 COLOR**	1 ad	3 ads	6 ads	9 ads	12 ads
Page	$10,980	$10,431	$9,882	$9,333	$8,235
2/3 page	8,110	7,705	7,299	6,894	6,083
1/2 page*	6,440	6,118	5,796	5,474	4,830
1/3 page	4,440	4,218	3,996	3,774	3,330

** Black & 1 Color Production:
When the second color of a black & 1 color ad is not a process color, the publisher reserves the right to produce it by using a combination of two process colors.

4 COLOR	1 ad	3 ads	6 ads	9 ads	12 ads
Page	$12,850	$12,208	$11,565	$10,923	$9,638
2/3 page	10,530	10,004	9,477	8,951	7,898
1/2 page*	8,280	7,866	7,452	7,038	6,210
1/3 page	6,420	6,099	5,778	5,457	4,815

COVERS Non-Cancellable	1 ad	3 ads	6 ads	9 ads	12 ads
2nd cover (4 color)	$14,130	$13,424	$12,717	$12,011	$10,598
3rd cover (4 color)	13,480	12,806	12,132	11,458	10,110
4th cover (4 color)	16,700	15,865	15,030	14,195	12,525

*Digest units priced at half-page rates.
10% charge for bleed, all units. No charge for gutter bleed only.

WSYR am RATES

TIME CLASSIFICATION

AAA	6-10	Monday - Saturday
AA	3-7	Monday - Saturday
A	10-3 12-7p	Monday - Saturday Sunday
B	7-12Mid 7a-12Nn	Monday - Sunday Sunday

SPOT ANNOUNCEMENTS

		6x	12x	18x	24x
AAA	60s	40	38	36	35
	30s	32	30	29	28
AA	60s	27	25	23	22
	30s	21	20	18	17
A	60s	19	18	17	16
	30s	15	14	13	12
B	60s	14	13	12	11
	30s	11	10	9	8

TOTAL AUDIENCE PLANS

DRIVE

	6x	12x	18x	24x
1/2AAA 1/2AA				
60s	30	28	26	25
30s	24	22	21	20

TAP NO. 1

1/2AAA&AA, 1/2 other

	6x	12x	18x	24x
60s	24	22	21	20
30s	19	18	16	15

TAP NO. 2

1/3 AAA&AA
1/3 A
1/3 B

	6x	12x	18x	24x
60s	18	16	15	14
30s	14	13	12	11

DON DAUER

	1x	3x	6x
5 - 7 am	30	28	26

TOTAL NEWS PLANS

	3x	6x	
AAA	56	50	6am thru 830am
AA	42	37	330p thru 610p
A	24	21	930a thru 235p
B	15	12	730p thru 1135p

DRIVE	3x	6x
1/2AAA1/2AA	44	39

TNP NO. 1	6x	12x
1/2AAA&AA		
1/2 other	33	29

TNP NO. 2	6x	12x
1/3AAA&AA		
1/3 A	26	21
1/3 B		

10 SEC. RATE 60% OF MINUTE RATE ★ REQUEST BULK RATES ★ REQUEST LONGEVITY RATES

Market	GRP's Daily	Allotments Reg.	Allotments Ill.	Cost Monthly
ROCHESTER METRO MKT.	50	40	26	$9,240.00
Population 967,000	25	20	13	$4,620.00
S.P.V. 9.2				
ROCHESTER-MONROE COUNTY MKT.	100	20	40	$9,600.00
Population 707,600	75	15	30	7,200.00
S.P.V. 9.0	50	10	20	4,800.00
	25	5	10	2,400.00

GREATER FINGER LAKES MARKET — $96.00 per month per panel.

DISCOUNT— A 10% Discount will apply for a 12 month uninterrupted schedule of 25 GRPs or larger.

O'Mealia poster allotments provide effective market coverage and the O'Mealia Co. guarantees that the basic unit of sale — 100 gross rating points — will deliver a daily effective circulation equal to, or greater than, the population of the market.

POSTING DATES — Regular posting dates are the 1st, 8th, 15th and 22nd of each month.

REPOSTING OR EXTRA POSTING CHARGE— When an advertiser desires a change of copy other than the normal monthly posting, the charge will be $40.

1980 POSTER INFORMATION

GENERAL TERMS — Our published rates and allotments apply to all showings for posting space on or after 12/25/79. Posters should reach O'Mealia ten (10) days in advance of the posting date. Should late arrival preclude O'Mealia Company using normal operating practices, from meeting scheduled posting dates, advertisers will be billed for the full scheduled period even if the posters cannot ride full period. For replacement due to damage or loss of location, it is recommended advertisers supply at least 10% extra posters. A leeway of five (5) working days from the accepted posting date is required to complete the posting of any showing. Credit for loss of service will be rendered pro-rata on the basis of the average monthly cost per panel for the market if a panel or panels of equal value cannot be substituted.

ROTARY PAINTED BULLETIN RATES

SIZE — 15' x 48' BLEED FACE UNITS — $900. per month. (Add 10% if less than 12 months.)

Rate provides for painting of design 3 times a year, quality high impact illumination from dusk to midnight, and relocation six times a year.

CIRCULATION — Average daily effective circulation is 32,667 per unit based upon current traffic counts certified by the Traffic Audit Bureau.

COPY LEAD TIME — 30 working days.

ADDITIONAL PAINTS — at $2.50 sq. ft. gross.

CUT-OUT EXTENSIONS — at $7.00 sq. ft. gross (one time charge). Painting or Re-Painting of Cut-Out Extensions after Initial Paint at $2.50 per square foot.

PERMANENT PAINT

Permanent paint units are available. Information upon request.

SHIPPING (posters, preprint bulletins, artwork):

O'MEALIA
Outdoor Advertising
745 PARK AVENUE
ROCHESTER, NEW YORK 14607
Phone - (716) 244-6660

Rate Catalogs For market-by-market media and magazines the *Standard Rate and Data Service* (SRDS) provides an excellent rate source. Each month SRDS publishes rates in a systematic format. This means that media buyers or planners seeking information on radio or television spot market stations, newspapers, or business and consumer magazines can subscribe to all available rate cards. SRDS uses a standardized format for each medium that provides an easily referenced access to nearly all cost, discount, production, and market information. Where geography is the key, SRDS is arranged alphabetically by state and by market. In magazines, the organization is by editorial category. The SRDS rate cards are invariably intended for national regional

THE PITTSBURGH PRESS
Evening and Sunday
RETAIL DISPLAY RATES
Effective July 1, 1979

Open Rate	Per Agate line	Daily $2.20	Sundays $3.40

Contract rates are available in Bulk Space Brackets. Daily and Sunday lineage may be combined to earn any contact brackets.

Effective July 1, 1979

Per Agate Line	Daily	Sunday
Amusement	$1.49	2.16
Churches	1.21	2.06
Charity	1.37	2.01
Educational	1.44	2.06

Independent Cinema Directory

	Daily	Sunday
10 agate lines listed proper directory	$10.45	$15.75

Drive-In Theaters

	Daily	Sunday
10 agate lines	$10.45	$15.75

Tie-In Advertising

	Daily	Sunday
Per agate line	$1.4325	$2.185

Available to advertisers without contract or one less than 1000 lines using space in special promotions.

DAILY COMIC STRIP

Only units available 4 col. x 35 or 70 lines.
Minimum schedule 13 times in 13 weeks.
Advertiser's Blackand White rate plus 15%.

POLITICAL ADVERTISING

Local Retail Rate is applicable for Allegheny County offices or Congressional offices. State or Federal where candidate represents only a district located chiefly in Allegheny County.

ZONE RATES

Complete information on Zoned Editions available on reguest or phone 263-1341.

THE PITTSBURGH PRESS
RETAIL DISPLAY RATES
Yearly Bulk Space Contracts

EVENING

OPEN RATE *per agate line*.....$2.20

CONTRACT SIZE		PER LINE
250	LINES	**$1.6025**
500	LINES	**1.5025**
1,000	LINES	**1.4550**
2,500	LINES	**1.4450**
5,000	LINES	**1.4350**
7,500	LINES	**1.4275**
10,000	LINES	**1.4225**
15,000	LINES	**1.40**
25,000	LINES	**1.37**
50,000	LINES	**1.36**
75,000	LINES	**1.3550**
100,000	LINES	**1.3325**
150,000	LINES	**1.33**

R.O.P. COLOR RATES
Minimum Space, 1,000 lines

Black and one color; extra.....$ 837
Black and two or three colors; extra.....$1069
Black and 2 or 3 colors not accepted Wednesday Press.
Advertisers using 20 or more pages during year will receive discount of $40 per page.
PLATE DEADLINE—5 days before publication. Advertiser to furnish complete printing material. Cancellations not accepted after 9 A.M. 4 days before publication.
If paper prepares advertisement, all necessary material is to be received 2 weeks in advance of publication date.

COMBINATION RATE
SAVE 25c per line
POST GAZETTE (Morning) PRESS (Evening)
POST GAZETTE (Morning) PRESS (Sunday)
25c per line off Post Gazette contract rate when ad is repeated within 5 days.

Combination rates applicable for local display contract and educational rates only.

advertisers and pricing includes agency commission. Advertisers eligible for retail (local) rate schedules should contact the station or publication for noncommissionable prices.

Compilations. For plan purposes, media analysts often need reasonable but nonspecific rates for estimating costs. For example, a client may be interested in the combined cost of 50 markets in radio. television or newspaper. The planner wants to know what is available for network television estimates *if* ideas are sought *before* plans are formed. The fact is that many planners need general rate information — not by station, network, or newspapers, but by market or by network daypart (portions of the daily broadcast schedule).

The major or larger advertising agencies use their media research departments to evaluate current client cost experience and forecast costs by market for all major media. Costs for the top U.S. markets arranged usually by size in increments of 10 are provided. For newspaper, costs are developed according to popular sized advertisements (600 line, 1000 line, etc.). Some estimates for newspapers now forecast costs by degree of newspaper penetration (e.g., cost per market and per point of coverage). Here is an excerpt from a typical newspaper compilation. If a planner wanted five 1000-line messages in the top 50 markets, it would cost $92,250 for at least 60% coverage.

Newspaper Market Cost Compilation
based on papers needed for
60% plus household coverage

ADI Markets	# Papers	Total Circulation	Open line Rate	Cost, 1000 Line B/W
Top 10	4	12,700,000	$83.00	$8,250
Top 20	64	17,125,000	125.00	11,875
Top 50	112	25,802,000	190.00	18,450

For broadcast markets, data are arranged by day part and use basic length, and costs are reported *per rating point*. Dollars show the cost of one point (e.g., rating) of exposure (see next section for full discussion). Here is a typical format for spot television. To illustrate, if the goal was 10 rating points per week in prime time, the cost for the top 10 markets would be estimated at $17,500 per week.

Cost Per Rating Point (HH)
(30-Second Announcements)

ADI Markets	Prime Eve	Late News	Daytime
Top 10	$1,750	$1,200	$ 515
Top 30	3,200	2,100	930
Top 60	3,950	2,700	1,350

Outdoor sets up nearly the same with the rating point equalling 1 percent of market coverage.

Paper Poster Costs Per Month
(30 sheet size)

ADI Markets	50 GRP Coverage*	Cost/GRP
Top 10	$368,000	$7,360
Top 20	484,300	9,686
Top 30	587,000	11,740

*Daily coverage for one month

According to the chart above, to achieve coverage of half the adults in the top 20 markets would cost $484,300. Daily coverage is a single day's exposure, so we would assume that during the month's contract many more adults would be exposed beyond the 50 percent daily figure.

The majority of this compiled information is created internally for the advertising agency and its clients. Although the information is not secret, public access is limited. However, a number of agencies produce media cost and audience guides that are available to the public. J. Walter Thompson, Ogilvy and Mather, BBDO, Inc., and Ted Bates Company all produce guides available for estimation use. The costs are only general estimates but usually reflect an accurate assessment of market conditions. In addition, such guides include a wealth of summarized audience research and reach and frequency projections. These guides are strongly recommended and can be secured by contacting the respective media departments.

SPECIALIZED ESTIMATION PROBLEMS AND TECHNIQUES

Much of cost estimation is a routine checking of sources and accurate calculation of a proposed schedule. On certain occasions, estimation can be more challenging.

For purposes of illustration two specialized estimation circumstances are used to demonstrate flexible estimators that allow rapid calculation without sacrifice of accuracy.

Broadcast Estimation on Cost Per Rating Point. Until fifteen or so years ago, television and radio announcements were estimated on a unit cost basis. Budgets were set up on so many announcements per week at a unit price. As research developed, advertisers learned that the audience value of an announcement changed dramatically *when the cost did not.* Television spots could have a 10.0 or 15.0 or even a 20.0 rating, yet all sold for nearly the same price. It was obvious, too, that more schedules were designed on the basis of potential audience exposure (ratings per announcement) and *not* on the announcements scheduled per week. The number of announcements was not important because the audience varied from program to program. The significant dimension was how much it cost to expose a certain level (size) of audience. This audience was expressed most simply as a percentage or a rating. In parallel fashion stations and networks moved from assigning costs by time segment to costs by rating popularity. This use of cost per rating has gained acceptance beyond broadcast and it appears, in time, much of media planning will be done on costs by degrees of coverage or exposure.

The cost per rating point or CPR computation is very simple and follows the same format for all of the media.

$$\text{CPR} = \frac{\text{Average Unit Cost}}{\text{Average Audience Rating (or Percent Coverage)}}$$

To develop a cost per rating point, you begin with the appropriate audience research report, preferably one that shows audience as a percentage. For example, in spot market television, the estimator can check the ratings, or references can come from recent client purchases. To assure a fair cost that will be achievable, the estimator looks for neither the highest or the lowest rating, but values that are normally representative.

Once the average rating values are done for each station, an average is drawn by daypart (prime, early or late fringe, and daytime). This represents the average rating value that the buyer/planner could expect in purchase. Obviously, the rating values can be computed for any measure done by a research service — homes, by adults, by age, or by gender.

The same process is used to find representative costs. Estimators feel that past actual costs are preferable for cost reference but rate cards or media cost estimates are often used. Again, cost values should represent reasonable expectations. In broadcast some estimators insist on calculating costs per calendar quarter, arguing that pricing is a function of seasonal advertiser demands.

Once average rating and cost are determined, the remaining step is to divide. Assume the "average homes using television rating" in daytime for the Philadelphia market is 4.0. This means the estimator determines that the average homes value of an expected daytime announcement is 4 percent of Philadelphia TV homes. Similarly, the expected average cost of a daytime 30-second announcement in Philadelphia is $200. If these are projected, the CPR would be:

$$\frac{\text{Avg. Cost} \quad \$200}{\text{Avg. Rating} \quad 4.0} = \$50 \text{ CPR (TvHH) in Philadelphia}$$

For every percent of daytime TV household exposure in Philadelphia, the cost in spot market TV is $50 (e.g., 50 GRP weekly means $2500). Using CPR figures as a common denominator allows media planners to estimate total rating points from the allocated budget.

Suppose the Philadelphia budget allocation was $10,000 and the planner wanted to estimate how much daytime television could be purchased; he need only divide the allocation by the cost to learn how many points of exposure are affordable.

$$\frac{\text{Mkt Allocation}}{\text{CPR}} = \frac{\$10{,}000}{\$50 \text{ CPR}} = 200 \text{ rating points}$$

To determine the budget required to achieve a specific audience goal, assume the marketer wanted to achieve a 50 percent reach of Philadelphia TV homes for a 3 month period (13 weeks). The planner could consult reach estimates for daytime and spot television and learn it takes 45 daytime GRP to achieve a 50 reach over four weeks. To cost such a scheme the formula would be:

$$\text{Reach } 50\% = 45 \text{ GRP} \times 13 \text{ Weeks} \times \$50 \text{ CPR or } \$29{,}250$$

Media weight planning for market-by-market advertising often involves a list of markets slated for a common level of advertising weight. Each market would receive the same media mix and level of advertising. This form of planning must fit budget constraints and invariably estimation adjustments must be made. The skill to adjust costs for multiple markets depends on how well the estimation by rating or coverage point is organized. The following illustration suggests how multi-market costing and adjustments could be made; again, a television example is used.

A regional soft drink firm is considering a budget of $100,000 for fifteen markets in the Midwest. The client is most interested in prime time, 30-second announcements. The estimator is asked if a level of 55 prime GRP can be afforded for fifteen markets. The estimator is also asked to provide alternatives if the goals cannot be met. The following steps are the logical process to answer these questions.

1. Determine CPR for prime time for each of the fifteen markets. That means determining the average rating and unit cost for all fifteen markets.
2. Add the CPRs for markets to find the total cost for one rating point for prime time. (Let's assume the CPR is $187 for all fifteen markets.)
3. To find the estimated weekly cost, multiply CPR by weight level desired.

   $187 × 55 Prime GRP/WK = $10,285 weekly cost for 15 markets

4. To find how many weeks could be scheduled for fifteen markets, divide weekly cost of 55 GRP ($10,285) into budget ($100M).

$$\frac{\$100{,}000}{10{,}285} = 9.7 \text{ weeks}$$

5. If the 9.7 weeks is satisfactory, the estimate is finished. If, however, the client wants more weeks of advertising, the estimator could recommend a lower GRP level than 55, or a less expensive daypart could be mixed with prime time, or the market list could by trimmed. Estimation means use of several variables to satisfy as many of the campaign goals as possible.

CPR in Nonbroadcast Media. When the audience exposure or coverage for any medium is represented as a percentage, CPR estimation can be used. Outdoor advertising a number of years ago shifted from "showings" to GRPs, thereby making CPR the logical basis for cost comparisons between media.

Magazines, through media research services, receive numerous exposure ratings, any of which could be used for CPR. Similarly, newspaper can be estimated based on circulation as a percentage of ADI homes.

Historically, CPR was created to suit broadcast demands, but it is understandable why many planners and estimators are interested in expanding the cost per point procedure to a common denominator used in many media.

COST PER THOUSAND CIRCULATION ESTIMATIONS FOR MAGAZINES AND NEWSPAPERS

Most estimation for magazines and newspaper supplements is uncomplicated once you understand how each publication's rate card works. Some purchase situations are more complex, however, and demand nontraditional techniques for estimation.

Many consumer magazines offer regional or market purchases. Innovations in data processing and development of postal codes allow advertisers to use a publication's circulation in countless geographic designs. Some publications offer customized purchase of circulation; the advertiser can purchase coverage to match his distribution. This was a problem with rate cards because not every circulation possibility could be described. To guide planning and estimation, publications set up geographic space rates based on the thousands of circulation purchased. Advertisers could then estimate the cost of space by (a) the page size, (b) presence of color, and (c) how many thousands of circulation were used. Some illustration will demonstrate this process of estimating space on a per thousand of circulation desired.

A client wants regional use of a magazine, for special promotional purposes, to cover the eastern and western coasts. The magazine being considered has an Eastern region edition, a Western region edition, and also offers New York City and Los Angeles metropolitan area editions. The magazine's rate card shows this information.

Region	Cost Page B/W	Regional Circulation
Eastern	$2,045	146,000
Midwest	2,590	185,000
Southwest	1,568	112,000
Southeast	1,512	108,000
Western	1,890	135,000
N.Y.C. Metro.	1,930	138,000
Chicago Metro.	1,372	98,000
L.A. Metro.	1,246	89,000

Circulation Level	CPM Black & White		CPM 4-Color	
	Pg.	½ Pg.	Pg.	½ Pg.
200M-34OM*	$8.25	$4.95	$10.25	$6.15
340.1M-480M	7.85	4.70	9.95	6.00
480.1M-620M	7.40	4.45	9.50	5.70

*M = 1,000

The 4-area combination the client desired amounts to a circulation of 508,000, which falls in the 480-620M range. Once the CPM factor has been identified it can be applied to the circulation. The client wants to consider 4-color pages so $9.50 CPM is correct. This means for every thousand circulation used in color pages, the magazine is paid $9.50. Since the client's areas add to 508,000 circulation, there are 508 thousands. The number of thousands of circulation multiplied by the CPM circulation ($9.50) gives a total cost of $4,826 per insertion.

Some magazines offer a CPM variation employing a base cost plus a CPM factor for circulation that exceeds the base level. Here is how these cards are organized.

Circulation Level	Page 4-Color Base Cost	Per Thousand Factors
110,000	$ 965	$11.50
220,000	1,850	8.65
400,000	3,600	8.50

If the client used 508,000 circulation here, the calculation on this basis would be:

For 400,000 = \$3600 (Base Cost)
For excess over 400,000 \$8.50/M
108 excess = 19 thousand × 8.50 or \$918.00
Total Insertion Charge \$3,600.00 Base Cost
918.00 (additional)
\$3,761.00
(Full-Page 4-Color in Eastern, Wester, N.Y.C. regions)

There are a number of other variations but the principle of CPM estimation is the same. Remember, each magazine can design its own rate card scheme. Before estimating regional space *be sure* you know what each magazine requires.

QUESTIONS

1. Estimating the cost of advertising media is a difficult task because marketers will not accept cost projections far from the eventual realized cost. Underestimating media costs is an obvious problem, but why is overestimating media costs also a serious problem for client management?

2. Much of the sale of network television prime time is done like sales in the stock or commodity markets. Explain.

3. Buying regional or metropolitan editions of national magazines involves buying circulation on a CPM basis. Explain how this works and then check your explanation by doing a simulated buy using a magazine listed in SRDS.

8

AUDIENCE FACTORS IN MEDIA SELECTION

Most advertisers express the goal of quantitative media selection in deceptively simple terms — find the media vehicles that provide the largest prospect audiences for the lowest possible cost. While easy to express in practice, "finding the most for the least" is a challenging task for media analysts. Part of the complexity is due to the number of analytical procedures available for vehicle analysis. Another problem is the large amount of media audience data that must be reviewed for best decision making. This section of the chapter discusses the major approaches to media data analysis and illustrates the selection operations.

Quantitative examination of media audience involves two levels: single exposure levels (e.g., one issue of a magazine, one day's traffic for outdoor, or one program in broadcasting) and measures of unduplicated audiences exposed over time (e.g., the total number of different people watching a program in a month's period or the total number of different readers exposed to a group of magazines over a campaign period).

Beginning with single exposure methods, the next two sections illustrate many of the analytical methods used to measure audiences. The nature of how we "consume" media dictates the way in which audiences are measured. As a result, no matter if a single or multiple exposure is considered, the techniques between media differ even though the principle is the same.

Measurement Language

Although obvious to all observers of communications media, it is well to keep in mind that there is a wide variety of terms used to report media audiences. This terminology is not standardized and, in some cases, is confusing and even contradictory. This text provides a glossary (see appendix) and a summary of audience and media analysis formulations (appendix), but it is worthwhile to cover some of the audience basics here.

Single Exposure Measures. In addition to reporting the size of audiences per exposure in raw numbers, there are other ways of recording this information.

PRINT

Circulation. A raw number, but it reflects the number of copies of a magazine or newspaper sold. Thus, a circulation of 100,000 means for an average day (or month) that many copies of the publication were purchased, either at newstands or by subscription.

Coverage. A percentage representing the percentage of households (newspaper) or people (magazines) that may be exposed to the issue. Warning: broadcast and outdoor also use the term but with different meanings.

BROADCAST

Rating. A percentage representing the number of viewers or listeners exposed to a program at a certain time. The percentage is based on the actual number of estimated viewers/listeners *as a proportion of the total estimated viewers/listeners available in the area* (10 rating means 10 percent of the area's sets were tuned to the program).

Share. A percentage representing the proportion of the total viewers/listeners at a given time exposed to a particular program. The percentage is based on the number of viewer/listeners as a proportion of those viewing/listening *at that time*. (50 share means of those viewing or listening, one-half were tuned to one program.)

Note: The confusion between "rating" and "share" is reduced if you remember the "rating" is based on *all* sets available and "share" is based only on sets tuned in at the time of measurement.

Coverage. In broadcast, this generally refers to potential audience as a function of technical facility. A radio station then could have coverage of 1,000,000 homes — *if every home tuned in*. This term refers to possible (not probable) audience size.

Unduplicated Exposure Measures

To differentiate audiences exposed only once within a specified time, certain terms are used to identify these net exposures. We begin with terms that are common to all media before discussing the other, more limited, terms.

Reach. A percentage of the audience exposed at least once. In broadcast and outdoor the measure is done within 4-week units. In magazine measurement, research firms use the "life" of a particular issue. Accumulation only counts new exposures; once an audience member is counted, additional exposure cannot increase the reach.

Frequency of Exposure. This factor of repeated exposure shows the number of times one could see or hear a message within a period of time. Repeated exposure factors are critical to advertising memorability, many believe.

Here are some of the more specific terms used by each medium.

Coverage (Outdoor and Transit). An estimated percentage of people who pass sign locations in a month's period. (Essentially the same as reach).

Coverage (Magazine). A percentage of different people who read within an issue. (Essentially the same meaning as reach).

Cume Rating (Radio). The percentage of listeners who hear a given station during specified programs over a week's period. Shows the percent of an area's listeners who hear each station. Cume is unlike reach in that it references the *potential* for unduplicated exposure.

This list of terms is not exhaustive but it gives you an idea of the major designations while demonstrating the lack of consistency in usage. Readers are reminded to be clearly specific when using measurement language. The definitions, in most cases, are illustrated in the following pages.

SINGLE EXPOSURE MEASURES

The single or average audience measure is the oldest of the research techniques. It is essentially the size of the audience one could expect from a single or average use. In some respects it is the common denominator because the measure assumes no more than a single use — one issue, one program or one day. To illustrate these exposure measurements, print and broadcast and outdoor examples are used. vered.

PRINT MEDIA

NEWSPAPER

Of the major consumer media, daily newspapers offer the least complicated means for ranking and selection.

Research Sources. Newspaper popularity is measured in terms of copies sold. The report of newspaper sales is known as the circulation report. It is an audited and verified report done by the Audit Bureau of

Circulations (ABC). This independent organization of auditors reports average copies sold by newstand and by subscription. In addition, sales (circulation) is reported by geographic areas of the market — most notably *City Zone,* metropolitan area, and *Retail Trading Zone* — covering the area serviced by the market's retailers.

In some larger and more competitive markets, individual newspapers invest in private reader studies that give demographic and product use detail. Though valuable, such research is not produced regularly nor does it always reflect the objectivity desired for conclusive decision making by media planners.

Single Exposure Measures in Newspaper. Circulation is the audited average number of copies sold per day. It is therefore a measure of *potential* readership or audience. Most newspaper selections are made on circulation or upon market coverage (circulation as a percentage of households). Circulation is given in average total copies sold and by various geographic breakouts. Here is a typical circulation summary.

Net Paid as Audited by A.B.C.

	Total Circulation	City Zone	Trading Zone	Other
Morning	89,083	51,781	29,683	7,619
Evening	37,788	28,718	8,400	670
Morning & Evening	126,871	80,499	38,083	8,289
Sunday	123,429	72,855	42,205	8,369

While circulation as a measure of *potential* audience has satisfied retail advertisers, firms less able to learn audience reaction to newspaper advertising have demanded some calculation of what circulation means in terms of adult readers. Some response has come from the Newspaper Advertising Bureau (NAB), which through independent research has arrived at a Readers Per Circulated Copy factor. According to NAB, on a national average one circulated copy of a newspaper is read by 1.04 adult men and 1.09 women (combined 2.13 adults). While these reader factors could vary from newspaper to newspaper, those firms anticipating a large purchase of numerous newspaper markets could estimate average adult readership by multiplying the circulation anticipated by the appropriate reader factor:

Circulation of papers in

Top 10 U.S. Markets	×	Readers/Copy	=	Estimated Adult Readers
15,775,000	×	2.13	=	33,600,075

MAGAZINES (CONSUMER)

The magazine industry, operating as newspapers in copies sold per issue, also saw a need to measure the total number of readers for an average copy. This would mean counting all those who saw an issue whether they bought the issue or not. Advertisers supported attempts to identify all available readers per copy and this research has lead to magazines' popularity with major U.S. advertisers.

Basic circulation study for magazines is done by the Audit Bureau of Circulation. These reports give average circulations for six month periods producing an average issue count. The reports are organized by region, state and county size. Circulation has limited use, but for regional advertising, circulation is the basis for determining space cost.

The estimate of total readers per copy is provided by a number of syndicated firms, most notably *Target Group Index*. This yearly report of more than 100 magazines covers readership by numerous demographic and product usage profiles. The basis of the single exposure measure is a raw number and a percentage showing an advertiser what could be the expected audience from a typical issue of the magazine. Examination of methodology shows that the projection is based on a combination of reader opportunities: readership of the purchaser and family, readership of neighbors or friends who receive the magazine from the issue purchaser (called pass-along readers) and from those who might see the issue out-of-home (in a hair salon or professional offices). These are collected and projected as the "average audience" of the publication. Audiences are reported as total readership and readership by product/service usage by the reader. The following illustration is based on the TGI format and reports a portion of magazine audiences who use a category of product.

Publication	All Users of Product			
	A[1] (000)	B%[2]	C%[3]	D Index[4]
Newsweek	5,281	8.8	91.0	100
Sports Illustrated	2,644	4.4	91.6	100
Time	5,545	9.2	90.6	99
U.S. News and World Report	2,080	3.5	92.0	101

[1] A shows the average number of readers who are users.
[2] B shows average readers as percentage of all users of the product
[3] C shows the percentage of magazines' readers who are also users.
[4] D indicates as an index the chances of exposing a product user with that magazine. 100 = average chance, above 100 means a better than average chance, below 100 is less than average.

Since *Newsweek* shows 5,281,000 readers who are also users of the product, if we used ten issues of *Newsweek* during the year our total reader impression total would be 10 times the typical or (5,281,000 × 10) 52,810,000. The multiplication is used to determine total campaign reader impressions.

To learn how many total readers see a typical copy, find the estimate of total readers and divide by the circulation. For the sake of illustration assume *Newsweek* has a total audience avg. issue) of 15 million-adult readers and a circulation of 2.9 million:

$$15{,}000{,}000 \div 2{,}900{,}000 = 5.1 \text{ RPC (Readers Per Copy)}$$

Some advertisers do not like using whole numbers in magazine readership and use percentages instead. The percentages in TGI's column B from the example are the same as a broadcast rating; they indicate *Time Magazine* has a 9.2 rating of product users or gross percentage of 9.2. If the advertiser used *Time* and *Newsweek* he might project that combined audience as 18.0 GRP (9.2 + 8.8). The significance of gross ratings for magazines will be covered more under the unduplicated measures of audience.

BROADCAST MEDIA

SPOT MARKET RADIO

As an entertainment medium, it is vital that a radio station be able to identify audience size or popularity. As radio becomes more a personalized medium, audience measurement by social and economic characteristics is done more often.

Research Sources. The calculation and projection of station audiences as whole number or as a rating percentage is done by several syndicated research services, most notably the *ARBitron Radio Report*. ARBitron covers most of the top 100 markets with monthly studies collected by a listener diary method. Audiences are reported by gender (male-female) and by age.

The basic station measure is the average number of listeners on an average quarter-hour basis. These quarter hours are usually summarized (averaged) by major parts of the day. Separation is made between Monday-Friday and the weekend and days are also separated. The standard dayparts for metropolitan markets are (with minor variation by market):

Daypart	Time
Morning Drivetime	6 a.m. - 10 a.m.
Midday (Housewife)	10 a.m. - 3 p.m.
Afternoon Drivetime	3 p.m. - 7 p.m.
Evening	7 p.m. - 12 m.

The following table is an exerpt of an average quarter hour summary produced by ARBitron.

Metropolitan Survey Area (MSA)
Average Quarter Hour Listening Estimates
Monday — Friday 6-10 a.m. and 4-7 p.m.

Station	Adults	Adult Rating*	Share
WAAA	5,000	5.0%	47%
WBBB	3,000	3.0%	28%
WCCC	1,800	1.8%	17%
Others	800	.8%	8%
	10,600	10.6%	100%

*Total Adults in Market = 100,000

$$\frac{5000}{100{,}000} = 5.0\%$$

The adults column reports the projected number of people hearing a typical 15-minute segment during the hours indicated. Thus for WAAA, any advertiser running an announcement between 6-10 a.m. or 4-7 p.m. should have 5,000 adult listeners. The 5,000 is also shown as a percentage or a rating (5.0). Typically, advertisers assign the rating value to each announcement run in the daypart. For example, if a buyer brought ten announcements on WAAA per week it would be reported as 50 gross rating points or 50 GRP (10 × 5.0% = 50 GRP). The significance of using ratings to measure schedule values is apparent if the buyer purchased WCCC from the above example. The purchase could be ten announcements but it would only account for 18 gross rating points. The buy summary shows:

Station	Units/Wk.	GRP	Gross Impressions
WAAA	10	50	50,000
WCCC	10	18	18,000

Clearly ten units will not have the same audience size as ten units on another, and in this case less popular, station.

The ARBitron also reports each station's share of listenership. In our example, WAAA adults (5,000) accounts for 47% of all adults listening ( ) during the average quarter hour. Share is a relative measure. It does not reflect the *amount* of listeners (e.g., a 50% share could mean two listeners of four; 2,000 of 4,000; or 2,000,000 listeners of 4,000,000). Because share is comparative, it is a measure of greater concern for station management than it is for advertisers. That is because the advertiser wants the largest audience in absolute terms. The broadcast manager, however, is concerned with having the largest proportion of listeners hearing his station. He makes program decisions on the share of audience listening.

NETWORK RADIO

Due to the comparatively limited investment in network (for every dollar invested in network radio there are five for spot market) there is limited activity in national audiences. Audience estimates are available from *Radio All Dimension Audience Research* (RADAR) but these generally follow the rating and share format of market reports.

NETWORK TELEVISION

The size of advertiser investment in television obigates the medium to a high degree of audience measurement.

The primary source of network television audience research and the only week-to-week service is by the A.C. Nielsen Company. Through a 1,200 household sample hooked electronically and augmented by another diary measured sample, the *National Television Index* (NTI) reports on program-by-program habits. For advertisers desiring a more in depth examination of audiences, Nielson supplements the NTI with the National Audience Demographic reports (NAD).

The format of the Nielsen NTI report offers substantially the same type of average program audience as in our radio illustration. A sample of one program would look like the following:

CBS — Saturday Movie 9-11 p.m.	Rating	# Households
Total Audience[1]	25.2	18,370
Average Audience[2]	21.2	15,454

[1] Percent of U.S. TV homes viewing *at least one* 15-minute segment.
[2] Percent of U.S. TV homes viewing the *average* 15-minute segment (total of eight segments in the film).

The average audience figure or average per quarter hour gives the advertiser the mean average for all the 15-minute segments. Participating advertisers prefer this as a more valid estimate of the potential audience for a single announcement.

Selections made on an average or typical program would base the decision on the highest average homes viewing or the rating. In addition, audience characteristics from the NAD studies could be used to examine the social and economic characteristics of viewers. After the program availabilities had been ranked, the firm would purchase the program with the highest rating or prospect viewers within the budget limitations.

SPOT MARKET TELEVISION

Some of the principles of audience measurement discussed in the network section apply to spot activity but differences are sufficient to justify a separate discussion.

Research Sources. There are somewhat more than 200 local markets in the United States served by commercial television service. Measurement of program audiences is provided by A. C. Nielson and by ARBitron. The reports are issued on a sliding frequency from two to twelve times yearly. Both firms report the categories of information covered in network — ratings, share, age, and gender demographics. A variation on the network service is a multiplicity of geographic breakouts in the spot market reports. Viewers and ratings in each service are represented for (a) SMSA metropolitan areas, (b) the total service area of the station, and (c) for special areas where the home service signal dominates the county television usage. These exclusive television market designations are known as *Dominant Market Area* (DMA) for the Nielsen NSI service and *Area of Dominant Influence* (ADI) for ARBitron. In terms of scope of measurement, the metropolitan is the smallest and the total survey area the largest geographic measures of viewership.

Single Exposure Measures in Spot Market Television. The primary function of Nielson's *National Station Index* (NSI) and ARBitron's *Television Market Reports* is to report the *average* audiences per program for a month. Measurements are done on a quarter-hour and half-hour basis. The audience estimates follow the pattern of disclosure found in radio and network television — ratings and audience estimates for each program.

For an illustration of how this audience information was used, examine this situation.

The producer of an all purpose liquid cleaner is ready to buy 30-second announcements in daytime television in Winesburg. The buyer has contacted each station and requested openings (availabilities). The station's suggestions have been summarized. The buyer's object is to schedule 35 GRP (minimum) per week based on TV homes (that is, select spot positions which will accumulate to at least 35 rating points per week).

Market: Winesburg
Rating Report: February
Target Audience: Women — particular emphasis on 18-34
GRP: 35/Wk.

Station	Program	Rating (HH)	Women	Women 18-34
WAAA	Mike Douglas	9.0	15,200	9,400
WAAA	Dinah Shore	7.0	12,700	8,600
WBBB	Phil Donahue	6.0	13,100	8,800
WCCC	Bewitched	4.0	9,800	5,700
WAAA	Today	3.0	8,900	6,800

According to the budget allowed, the buyer will select those programs giving the most desired audience. Many of these shows are "stripped" (M-F) so the buyer may have to use multiple exposure to reach the GRP goal. He could buy four Douglas ($4 \times 9 = 36$ GRP) or five Shore ($7.0 \times 5 = 35$) or he could mix the programs up to spread the announcements out. The point of the illustration is to show how average program performances are used to make schedule selections.

OUT-OF-HOME MEDIA

OUTDOOR

The measure of outdoor sign exposure is the traffic flow past each available sign or billboard location. Traffic counts are monitored by each outdoor company and audited by an industry association, *Traffic Audit Bureau* (TAB). On the basis of average cards passing and projected passengers per car, estimates of population exposure are developed and incorporated into the showing levels (e.g., 75-100) or coverage.

Each percentage point represents one percent of the population exposed in a day. Thus, if an outdoor firm makes a package of 30-sheet locations and identifies it as a 100 GRP level exposure, theoretically 100 percent of the population will see the message during each day. Understandably, outdoor showing levels are only rough estimates but since contracts run for a month's lease, high exposure levels are possible.

UNDUPLICATED MEASURES OF MEDIA EXPOSURE

THE CONCEPT

Media habits of people are seldom fixed or static. We are not exposed in the same media as our friends do and even if the same, then not at the same intensity. Even our own media habits vary by day. Because people's exposure to mass media changes, audiences change and the process, over time, is quite dynamic. For advertisers, audience shifts mean that advertising messages will be exposed to different people over time. Moreover, some will be exposed to the advertising message much more often than others. Part of the selection process is then to learn which media or media vehicles have greater or lesser audience change (turnover).

The audience turnover has many faces and this has resulted in many different names being given to describe the accumulation. Commonly, the terms "net" or "net coverage" or "different audiences" or "unduplicated audience" are used to describe this condition, but it is simpler to use the more popular concept of an "unduplicated audience" to describe the process generally and the term "reach" to identify those research figures showing the unduplicated measurement.

Similarly, the rate of repeat exposure carries several names. The more popular term used to describe audience repetition or rate of exposure is *frequency*. Thus, we say the number of times a person is exposed (reach) in a period of time is called the frequency.

As was done in single exposure measures, examples of reach and frequency applications in the major media are described here to give you an introduction to measures of unduplicated audiences.

NEWSPAPER

The daily newspaper, because of a short life span, does not have a great ability to accumulate many unduplicated readers from the same copy. However, to ignore reach potential is wrong because there is some multiple reader exposure going on.

Certain advertising agency researchers, working with the NAB reader-per-copy figures and other baseline data, have been able to project the reach and frequency for certain newspaper insertion schedules. The table below estimates the total number of different people exposed based on the number of newspaper issues used in the schedule and the number of newspapers (coverage) used.

% Coverage Metro Area (Duplicated)/	Estimated Reach of Metro Adults by Number of Issues Used			
	1	2	5	10
30	25	32	43	50
60	45	55	64	68
90	64	75	88	91

*Coverage determined by total circulation (metro) of newspapers used as a percentage of metro households.

To demonstrate the projections let us assume an advertiser has decided to purchase enough newspapers in each of his markets to give a 60 percent coverage (that's total circulation of the paper ÷ population = giving a 60 percent level). Many people purchase more than one newspaper; therefore the circulation amounting to 60 percent are, in fact, covering the *same* readers over again (duplicated readership). The question is, if he uses enough newspaper to provide 60 percent coverage and he uses these newspapers to run ads on ten separate occasions, how many unduplicated or different readers might be exposed? To estimate the reach or unduplicated readers we need the gross coverage (60 percent) and the number of issues to be used (10). Mark the 60 percent line on the table and move across until the 10 issues level is found. The estimate is 68 percent. This means, if we begin with a 60 percent coverage in circulation, at the end of 10 issues we could expect 68 percent of the metro adults would have been exposed. This is called the reach of the schedule.

To calculate the average frequency of exposure we add the combined exposures and divide by the percentage of unduplicated audience. The table tells us 68 percent is the unduplicated. Now we must calculate the duplication. Each time the advertisers schedule runs it is 60 percent — that's the gross audience. It runs ten times or a value of 600 percent. Here is how the calculation looks.

Issue	1	2	3	4	5	6	7	8	9	10	Total GRP
Coverage	60	60	60	60	60	60	60	60	60	60	600*

(Gross Coverage)
* = 60 × 10 issues
Average Frequency = GRP ÷ Reach or (600 ÷ 68%)
Average Frequency = 8.8 times

The frequency calculation means the average reader in the city would be exposed or reached in nearly nine of the ten issues used.

CONSUMER MAGAZINES

The longer issue life of a magazine enables it to accumulate different readers. These unduplicated reader characteristics can be measured by estimating the reach from three dimensions: (a) a single magazine over a number of issues, (b) a series of magazines on a single issue basis, or (c) a series of magazines over a number of issues.

a. Multiple issue reach of a single magazine. Will an advertiser increase his audience reach potential if he uses multiple issues of the same magazine? Undoubtly, yes. We know the amount of newsstand sales, and the additional non-purchaser readers indicate such potential. Clearly the more often (issues) an advertiser appears, the more exposure potential available. Accumulation rates are developed by research firms to estimate the potential. The following table shows how magazine reach estimates are given. The significant element is to see how the reach potential of one magazine is improved by increasing the number of issues used for a campaign.

Magazine	Avg. Issue Reach	3 Issues	6 Issues	12 Issues
P	8.7%	13.3%	16.9%	20.5%
R	27.8%	36.5%	40.9%	44.9%
T	28.6%	37.3%	41.7%	45.7%

The reach value of Magazine *P* is worth examination. For any one issue nearly 9 percent might be reached but if we used *P* for 12 issues we might reach 20.5 percent. That means for *P* we can get 2.4 (20.5 ÷ 8.7) times greater unduplicated audience than with a single issue. If you calculate Magazines *R* and *T* in the same manner you will find different rates of accumulation. Some magazines have a greater capacity for new readers than others. To calculate frequency of repetition for a single magazine schedule, we apply the format used in newspapers. Each time Magazine *P* is used, 8.7 percent are exposed, so 8.7 is the GRP delivered gross rating points. The total issues used is twelve, so the total GRP would be (8.7 × 12) 104. Our estimated unduplicated audience for a 12 issue schedule is 20.5 percent. To calculate, divide 104 GRP (gross readers) by the 12 issues reach of 20.5 and the frequency is 5.09 or the average reader of Magazine *P* would see five of the twelve issues.

b. Computing Reach on a Combination of Magazines. People who read magazines regularly are quite likely to read more than one. The result is overlap or duplicated readership. This can be graphically represented by two circles representing Magazines *P* and *R*. If used together for a campaign, the duplicated readership (readers seeing both) would intersect.

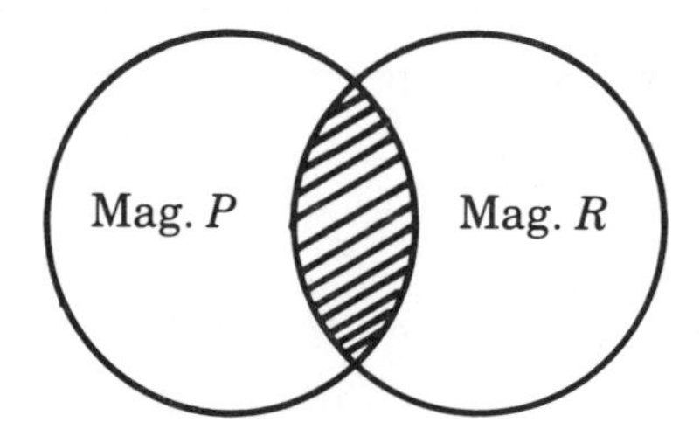

The unshaded area *P* is the exclusive readers of *P*.

The unshaded area *R* is the exclusive readers of *R*.

The shaded area shows a group of readers who see both *P* and *R*.

Here is an illustration of how combined audience reach is calculated.

If an advertiser were interested in a combination of magazines, his examination of media audiences could be done this way (using the Magazines *P*, *R*, *T*):

Assume the firm can buy two of the three magazines shown. The first magazine selected (based on size and cost) becomes the pivot in the combination reach analysis. For this example, the advertiser first selected *P*, not because of size but due to previous successful use. Now it wants to add another. For a combination, the firm must determine which of the other magazines (*R* or *T*) complements *P* by having the largest number of different readers (those *not* reading *P*). In other words, by using the audience of *P* as a base the combination analysis determines whether *R* or *T* gives the most different (unduplicated) readers *when used with magazine P*. The advertiser consults a research service which indicates these estimates:

Combinations	Duplicated* Adult Readers	Unduplicated** Adult Readers	% Reach
P and *R*	53,800,000	48,500,000	33.0
P and *T*	54,800,000	48,160,000	32.7

* Found by adding the average issue audience.
**Tabulated by TGI.

Note that *P* and *T* have more total reader impressions, while *P* and *R* have less duplicated readership. For the largest unduplicated combination, the advertiser would select *P* and *R*. Reach percentages are found by dividing the unduplicated readers of the combined magazines by the audience base. In this example, that is total U.S. adults (147.OMM).

$$\frac{48{,}500{,}000}{147{,}000{,}000} \quad \frac{\text{Unduplicated Readers}}{\text{Total U.S. Adults}} = 32.99\%\ (33.0\%)$$

c. Computing Reach on a Combination of Magazines in Multiple Insertions. Reach and frequency calculations can also involve several magazines combined over multiple issues. Research firms have elaborate formulae based on interviews to predict such conditions, and such tabulations are available to advertisers on a special-order basis. However, if a planner wished to estimate the reach and frequency without professional aid there is a statistical approach that gives a reasonable solution. Here are the steps used to calculate a 3 magazine combination used for six issues (i.e., a total of eighteen insertions.)

Step One: Find the average Issue Readership from Existing Research Sources:

Magazine	% of U.S. Adults Exposed, Average Issue Basis
A	21
B	18
C	11

Step Two: Consult the same research sources to find the 6-issue reach for each publication (unduplicated after six issues)

Magazine	% of U.S. Adults Average Issue	% U.S. Adults 6 Issues
A	21	30
B	18	25
C	11	15

Step Three: Reach of A .30* + Reach of B .25*
less (−)
Reach of A .30* × Reach of B .25*
.30 + .25 = .550
− −
.30 × .25 = .075
.475 or 48% Combined Reach of AB

Step Four: Reach of AB .48 + Reach of C .15
less (−
Reach of AB .48 × Reach of C .15
.48 + .15 = .63
.48 × .15 = −.07
.56 or 56% Combined Reach ABC

Comment: The above procedure is simple statistical probability and bears no direct relation to reader activity with these magazines. It is a formula available for *any* combination of reach levels, no matter what media, and for planning purposes is an adequate estimation procedure.

Step Five: The average frequency is achieved by dividing the total GRP of the schedule by the reach of the combination after six issues.

Magazines	% U.S. Adults Coverage Issue	
A	21	
B	18	} 50 GRP × 6 issues = 300 GRP
C	11	

300 GRP ÷ Combined Reach (ABC) 55.4 =
5.4 times Average Frequency

Therefore, the ABC combination of magazines would reach an estimated 55.4 percent of adults in a 6-issue period. The average reader would see more than five issues of the eighteen scheduled.

RADIO SPOT MARKETS

The rating and share figures as basic single exposure measures do not reflect the patterns of most advertisers' schedules — announcements spread over multiple dayparts of a number of stations. Advertiser interest in unduplicated audiences has prompted ARBitron and others to develop unduplicated audience research. Now advertisers are able to estimate the unduplicated listeners for a single station and the reach and frequency of combinations of stations. Here are illustrations of each application.

a. Unduplicated Listeners for Each Station (Station "Cumes") ARBitron is able to estimate how many different people will hear a program/daypart by the end of a week's exposure. These weekly "cumulative audiences" are reported in each ARBitron. Here is a sample.

Market Service Area
Adult Listeners M-F
6-10 A.M.

Station	Avg. Listeners Per Quarter Hour	Different (Cume) Adult Listeners
WAAA	5,000	7,800
WBBB	3,000	8,100
WCCC	1,800	5,600

Note: While WAAA has the largest audience per quarter hour, WBBB will reach more unduplicated listeners by the weeks' end. The unduplicated audience is not likely achieved by an advertiser *unless* he schedules a message in each quarter hour, Monday through Friday. This is the only way to assure the maximum reach. However, stations are often selected on their potential even if schedules could not cover each quarter hour.

Finally, the high reach of WBBB may not make it a "must buy" but if the buyer is searching for another station to expand the audience, the high "cume" would make WBBB a serious contender.

b. Calculating Reach and Frequency for Combinations of Stations. Buyers of radio time know that major market schedules demand use of multiple stations to achieve high audience exposure levels. Multi-station purchases have directed major advertising agencies to run special tabulations on reach and frequency. The procedure is usually to have the research company compute the data on many schedules and then summarize the findings in a reach table. Assume an advertiser is considering a buy involving the three stations just discussed. The product is adult directed and morning and afternoon "drivetime" schedules are involved. Here is the package as proposed.

Station	Spots Per Week	Avg. Rating	Wkly. GRP
WAAA	10	4.0	40
WBBB	10	3.0	30
WCCC	15	2.0	30
Totals	35		100

To find the estimated reach and frequency a special radio table is consulted:

Reach Estimator (four weeks)
Adult Listeners Monday-Friday
Morning and Afternoon Traffic Periods
(Based on Schedules 6-10 A.M. — 4-7 P.M.)

Adult Rating Points Per Week*	% Adults Exposed Number of Stations Used/Market			
	1	2	3	4
25	20	30	NA**	NA**
50	25	40	45	55
100	30	45	52	60

* percentage based on using on a 4-week basis (i.e., 25/wk × 4 – 100)

** N.A. = Not Applicable; 25 Rating Points is too few to be spread over three or four stations in a market.

This table indicates GRP per week and number of stations. If the advertiser would use a 100 GRP schedule over three stations, the table estimates that at the end of four weeks 52 percent of adults will be exposed to the schedule. Notice, to increase the reach, the table indicates increasing weekly GRP or the number of stations or both. This is no more than a reflection of dispersion: the more announcements, the better the chance of exposure to all available listeners on each station; the more stations used, the more opportunity for "new," unduplicated, listeners. The average frequency follows the formula of total GRP ÷ reach, or in this problem:

$$\frac{\text{GRP: } 400\ (100 \times 4)}{\text{Reach: } 52} = 7.7 \text{ average frequency of exposure in four weeks}$$

NETWORK TELEVISION

A. C. Nielsen Company maintains a constant monitor of its national audimeter sample and it is able to provide advertisers with reach projections for all programs on network television. This data base has been providing accumulation figures for years on literally thousands of schedules.

The magnitude of this research record means network advertisers or those considering such activity have available reach and frequency estimates for any possible schedules. Nielsen clients need only call to get an estimate on a certain selection of programs. Further, advertising agencies, through heavy experience, have been able to project certain reach and frequency levels for composite schedules. The following table of reach projections is developed from a great number of schedules covered by A. C. Neilsen computations over the years. For planning purposes it gives reasonable estimates for schedules that would be designed to gain as large an unduplicated audience as possible.

Adult Women and Men
4-Week Reach Projections

	GRP/WK	Day	Late Fringe	Prime
Women 18+				
	25	35%	36%	60%
	50	45%	48%	78%
	100	50%	53%	88%
Adult Men				
	25	—	37%	58%
	50	—	47%	76%
	100	—	52%	82%

The use of the chart is relatively simple for planning purposes. Assume an advertiser wishes to reach half of the women audience in television (50 percent). By locating that reach level on the chart, the firm learns that it could use less than 25 rating points weekly in prime time, 50 or better in fringe, or 100 GRP in daytime to reach 50 percent. Planning could also be done from affordable GRP. That is, one decides how many GRP could be purchased by daypart and then uses the reach estimate to judge the size of the unduplicated audience.

The average frequency is acheived in the same manner as previous in media:

$$\text{Avg. Frequency} = \frac{\text{GRP four weeks}}{\text{Reach after four weeks.}}$$

If the advertiser, in the example above, used the 50-day GRP to reach 45 percent the calculation would be:

$$\frac{200\ (\text{GRP/Month})}{45}$$ 4.4 times per four weeks or slightly more than one exposure per week.

An average frequency calculation can be misleading if a small proportion of audience does the preponderance of viewing. Advertisers concerned about the distortion can submit a representative schedule to the A. C. Nielsen Company for detailed frequency analysis. With a schedule to work from, Nielsen can show the percentage of women seeing each successive program. Assume that the schedule discussed earlier of a 45 percent reach and a frequency of 4.4 was composed of five programs used per week for four weeks. Therefore, in an average month (four weeks) those exposed would see from one to twenty programs (five programs × four weeks). A Nielsen frequency distribution could look like this:

% Women Reached by
Frequency of Programs Watched

	Programs Viewed					
	1	2	3	4-6*	7-10*	11-20*
* Reached	10.2	8.5	6.5	7.4	6.2	6.2

Notice, of the 45 percent of women reached, 7.4 percent were near the average frequency of four times, but 10.2 percent would see only one! Further, nearly 20 percent of the audience would see two or less programs of the twenty telecast. Such analyses give network advertisers a better picture of the distribution of exposure and helps them seek ways to even out exposure.

SPOT MARKET TELEVISION

As in network tables, the spot reach estimates are arranged by daypart. The following example is based on evening opportunities, i.e., "Fringe Evening" usually represents the hours surrounding the Prime Evening (5:30-8:00 and 11:00 p.m.-1:00 a.m. EST) and "Prime" represents 8:00-11:00 p.m. (with some variation on Sunday).

4-Week Spot Market
Adult Reach Projections

Adult Monthly GRP	Fringe Evening	Prime Evening
60	27	34
100	42	49
200	57	66
300	70	87

Combining Reach for Different Dayparts. The table above gives us an opportunity to examine procedures used when a combined reach is sought for different dayparts used. Assume the following circumstances.

We are using 15 GRP/Wk in Fringe Evening (60 GRP/Month)
25 GRP/WK in Prime Evening (100 GRP/Month)

The table above tells us projected reach for these schedules would be:

60/Month (Fringe) = 27% Reach (4 Wks.)
100/Month (Prime) = 49% Reach (4 Wks.)

Now we want to know the unduplicated audience from *both* schedules. That is, what proportion of the fringe viewers would *not* see the prime programs, and vice versa.

Using the same formula we used in combining magazines, here is the result.

100 − 49 (Prime) × 100 − 27 (Fringe) = (100 − 51 × 73)
or 37.2 (duplicated adult viewers)
100 37.2 = 62.8% Reach (unduplicated)

If more than two dayparts are involved, rank order (highest first) and begin calculation with the first pair. Then, once the pair is combined, recalculate with the third daypart and so on. Again, see the magazine example earlier in this chapter.

The average frequency poses little difficulty since once the total GRP for the schedule is identified and the reach is known, the division of the two gives the figure:

$$\frac{160\text{ GRP}}{62.8\text{ R}} = 2.5 \text{ times in four weeks.}$$

REACH AND FREQUENCY PRINCIPLES

The chapter has given numerous methods analysts use to estimate unduplicated media audiences. Beginners in analysis tend to see these procedures as mutually exclusive or independent of each other. In fact, there are underlying aspects common to all the media. Before we conclude quantitative measures we should deal with some of these principles.

a. How is single exposure related to reach? Reach is the measure of unduplicated "new" audiences. People only have to be exposed once to be included in the audience.

   To illustrate, suppose the TV rating book says the average adult rating for program A is 10.0 percent. Each time that program runs, 10.0 percent of adults are viewers. Many, however, are repeat viewers while some are viewing for the first time. Here is how the program would be examined over time, separating new from repeat viewing.

Week	Avg. Rating	New Viewers Rating
1	10.0	10.0
2	10.0	4.0
3	10.0	2.0
4	10.0	1.0
Monthly GRP	40.0	Reach 17.0

The first week every viewer is new, but in successive weeks a smaller proportion of each audience is new (four of ten; two of ten; one of ten). The reach is the sum of the new or 17.0 percent in this example. This is what the accumulation projections try to determine: What portion of each successive audience has not been exposed before.?

b. Which audience dimension is more important in media planning — reach or frequency? It depends. First, most planners realize that by stressing reach, the frequency or repetition could be limited. Similarly, when frequency is sought, the duplicated audiences tend to limit reach. Many advertisers, understanding the integral relation between reach and frequency, seek some sort of balance rather than forcing serious trade-offs.

Sometimes, however, the balance should be tipped. Companies with new products or repositioned products, tend to emphasize high reach in media planning. Not sure where their prospects are they wish to expose as many prospects as possible. On the other hand, firms with a well-identified market may wish to seek frequency opportunities in order to reinforce message delivery. Similarly, products purchased on a frequent basis need more repetition than those purchased infrequently. Look at your product situation carefully before deciding to stress one media value over another.

c. Are there minimum levels for reach and frequency? Unduplicated audience estimates are like college examinations — the higher the better. Clearly, a 100 percent reach of a target audience is ideal but hardly achievable within budget restraints. Instead of maximums, many analysts work on minimums or the lowest effective level of exposure.

There are some media planners who believe that qualifying a person "reached" on one exposure is wrong. Recall that unduplicated audience means a prospect only has to be exposed on a single occasion to be counted. Those wishing to qualify reach by the number or frequency of exposures would *subtract* those with one contact. The earlier example from network television will illustrate.

This was a schedule of five programs in day delivery 50 GRP each week projected to a 45 percent reach of women. In that example we saw how Nielsen would report the reach for each exposure (twenty shows maximum and one show exposure the minimum). Note that 10.2 percent of reach was for women projected to see only one program; if this exposure was thought ineffective, that reach should be removed.

Thus, instead of a reach of 45 percent it would be slightly less than 35 percent after qualification. If should be stressed that qualifying reach in this way is not universally done, although discounting reach when only one exposure is involved does seem to be a reasonable treatment. Similarly, many advertisers learn that they need a certain level of reach to "break through" audience awareness. You may assume most of these situations concern reach levels beyond 50 percent.

d. How does a planner increase reach or increase frequency? First, planners realize there are certain techniques to emphasize one audience dimension over another. Whether the manipulations are correct is another question and must be considered only in a product-by-product context. Further, the budget available also dictates the degree to which a schedule can be "tuned" to increase reach or frequency. Here are some methods (though not necessarily recommended) to heighten exposure or repetition.

REACH EMPHASIS

Magazines. To increase unduplicated audience, the largest publications would be used. The greater the circulation base, the better the opportunity. Also, magazines of greatest editorial diversity mean a better chance for unduplication. If the target audience is broad enough, two entirely different editorial formats might offer the most new readers.

Television. The same principle is applied to programming and dayparts. Prime evening time offers the best chance for unduplication while daytime offers the least. Similarly, a combination of dayparts may offer higher reach. If adult women are involved as prospects, the media planner may purposely use daytime and late evening periods to expose both working and nonworking women.

Outdoor. By nature, poster schedules account for high exposure. Out-of-home media might be included in a media mix to raise the level of unduplicated reach.

FREQUENCY EMPHASIS

Radio. Because of a *relatively low* per unit cost, radio is thought to be a medium well suited to developing large GRP levels (higher than average frequency).

All Media. Some planners are willing to trade off impact (potential awareness) for repetition. This means using *smaller* or *shorter* message units for the same dollars. Theoretically, the cost of a page in print could buy four ¼ page ads, and two 30-second TV units for every 60 seconds. The danger in such a manipulation (though it literally increases exposure opportunities) is that a shorter length or smaller size might *not* be as well seen, heard, or remembered. Unless message research suggest a favorable trade-off, this procedure is risky. While reach or frequency can be augmented, it is recommended that beginners avoid such tuning in favor of balance.

QUESTIONS

1. Although rating and share are both used in evaluating broadcast audiences, advertisers are more interested in ratings and broadcasters in share. Explain.

2. Discuss this statement regarding magazine coverage — "Strong pass-a-long readership produces a high readers-per-copy ratio (RPC)."

3. When counting an audience for a media vehicle, the person needs only to be exposed *once* to be counted as part of the reach or unduplicated audience. What does this mean?

4. What marketing situations might indicate the need for emphasizing reach over the frequency of exposure? What circumstances would dictate the reverse?

9

COST FACTORS IN MEDIA SELECTION

There are few, if any, companies that can afford to plan media strategies with no regard to cost. The cost of mass media in the United States simply forces even the largest firms to be very careful of media expenditures. In fact, a major problem with cost considerations is that many firms tend to overemphasize efficiency to the detriment of all other communication values. Cost, then, is a primary factor in the selection and use of media.

COST PER THOUSAND EVALUATIONS

HOW COST IS UTILIZED

It is the experience of most media professionals that vehicles with the largest and/or most desirable audiences also demand the highest prices. If the unit price is too high, the message value is limited because the company is paying a premium for the audience. To help guide pricing and negotiation, the CPM concept or cost-per-thousand analysis is used in nearly all media analyses. The basis of CPM as explained in Chapter 2 is simple. It compares the anticipated audience figure with the cost of the unit.

$$\text{Cost Per Thousand Audience Exposures} = \frac{\text{Unit Cost (page, 30-second)} \times 1000}{\text{Audience}}$$

Remember, the CPM is a comparative analysis. The actual values are determined primarily to allow the planner to choose between options rather than to make absolute judgments on the message effectiveness of a medium. It isn't that vehicle X has a $4.95 CPM readers; it is how the $4.95 compares with others. The analysis was developed to make intramedium selections instead of making pronouncements on how inexpensively advertising exposes prospect audiences.

Again, the principle of the cost per thousand is to find the lowest cost for exposing a desired audience; the lower the CPM the better. Further, the CPM can be based on any audience segment. Any demographic unit (age, income) any type of audience (viewers, listeners, readers), or any level of a product usage (heavy users, light users) is fully acceptable for comparison.

CPM APPLICATIONS

The CPM formula shown earlier is basic to all media and all audience categories, yet there are changes in application. Better appreciation of CPM comes from examining a number of applications or typical analyses done for the major media.

NEWSPAPER

Because newspaper selection is dominated by circulation, analysts have determined that it is the best common denominator, even though readership measures audience. To compare newspapers of widely varying size, it is the practice to relate the cost of one line (one column wide and one-fourteenth of an inch deep) *per million* copies. The CPM examination is called determining the *milline rate.* The use of per million is done practically. First, "millions" encompasses all U.S. newspapers. It also means the calculation *will not* end up in fractions of a cent.

$$\frac{\text{Cost of a single line} \times 1{,}000{,}000}{\text{Total Single Issue Circulation}}$$

Illustration. There is a competitive newspaper situation in Emerald City. Here is the summary of basic data from which the buyer will make a single paper selection.

Newspaper	Daily Circulation	Open Line Rate
Daily Planet	204,000	$ .60
Green Times	190,000	$ .57

Select only on size of circulation and choose the *Daily Planet* (204M is greater than 190M). Select on lowest cost and it is the *Green Times ($.57 vs. $.60). The milline analysis will help us learn which is more efficient.*

Daily Planet

$$\frac{.60 \times 1{,}000{,}000}{204{,}000} = \frac{\$600{,}000}{204{,}000} = \$2.94 \text{ Milline Rate}$$

Green Times

$$\frac{.57 \times 1{,}000{,}000}{190{,}000} = \frac{\$570{,}000}{190{,}000} = \$3.00 \text{ Milline Rate}$$

The most efficient purchase would be the *Planet.* Although it has a higher open rate, its circulation more than compensates.

MAGAZINES

Magazines, although circulation analysis is available, prefer to check efficiency on the readership figures provided by *Target Group Index* and others. The formula adaptation is as follows:

$$\frac{\text{Cost of Desired Unit (Page or Fraction)} \times 1{,}000}{\text{Audience of the Magazine (Either by Usership or Demographics)}}$$

Illustration. A womens' clothing firm (mail order) is selecting home service magazines for a schedule of half-page 4-color (4C) advertisements. The cost and audience data appear as follows.

Magazine	Adult Women Readers Using Mail Order	Cost ½-Pg., 4C
FC	3,800,000	$24,000
BH & G	3,500,000	23,425
GH	3,450,000	18,500

On audience size, FC would be the choice. To learn which magazine gives the largest audience for the lowest cost, the CPM calculation is used.

FC ($24,000 × 1,000) ÷ 3,800,000 = $6.32 CPM Women Readers Using Mail Order

BH&G ($23,425 × 1,000) ÷ 3,500,000 = $6.69 CPM Women Readers Using Mail Order

GH ($18,500 × 1,000) ÷ 3,450,000 = $5.36 CPM Women Readers Using Mail Order

On a CPM basis GH is the choice since for each 1,000 readers it charges less. Does this mean GH is the best to select? Not necessarily. Media analysts may wish to balance efficiency along with reach and other dimensions. CPM, although important, should only be part of the selection process.

RADIO AND TELEVISION

Since both media operate from basic audience information contained in rating reports, we can look at CPM studies interchangeably. Whether the audience is a demographic segment from a television program's viewership or the number of listeners to a radio station's morning program, the process is this.
ram, the process is this.

$$\frac{\text{Cost of Announcement}^{*} \times 1000}{\text{Homes or Viewers Exposed by Program or Time Period}}$$

*If a program sponsorship is involved you may wish to divide the program CPM by the number of commercials.

Television Illustration. A buyer representing a producer of automobile accessories (aftermarket) has these availabilities from the Salem stations. The target audience is men 18-34 years of age.

Availability	TV HH Rating	Total Viewers	Men 18-34	30-Sec. Cost
CBS Early Evening News	16.0	19,000	5,700	$50.00
NBC Tonight Show	8.0	8,000	5,400	35.00
ABC Wide World Sports	5.0	5,500	5,200	40.00

On the basis of rating data alone, the selection is difficult, but observe the separation when CPM analysis is used.

CBS $\frac{\$50.00 \times 1000}{5700} = \$8.77$ CPM Men 18-34

NBC $\frac{\$35.00 \times 1000}{5400} = \$6.48$ CPM Men 18-34

ABC $\frac{\$40.00 = 1000}{5200} = \$7.69$ CPM Men 18-34

Even though the *Tonight Show* offered the second largest audience, favorable pricing made it by far the most efficient purchase. The CPM analysis also highlights the wasted audience impressions. Not every viewer was of value to the automotive client, yet the television stations price time on the basis of general audience. Therefore, although the CBS evening news delivered 138 percent greater viewership than the *Tonight Show*, it lead in young men only by a little more than 5 percent. CPM analysis can uncover and identify such unneeded waste viewership.

SPECIAL CPM APPLICATIONS

The use of efficiency analysis is usually considered, along with other factors, as shown in the preceding examples. But certain marketing situations need more creative use of the CPM. This section illustrates some of these special ways of using the analysis and demonstrates, at the same time, the value of cost examinations.

MULTIPLE SELECTION FACTORS

As media audience research has improved the description of consumers, advertisers have found the need to use more complex consumer profiles. It is not unusual for an advertiser to have more than one audience or multiple characteristics to consider. The movement to more detailed profiles has complicated the CPM analysis, but there is a procedure of weighting that makes the process less difficult.

If all audience segments are not of equal value to an advertiser, there is a method of setting value priorities. To balance the relative contributions of each segment, a weighting process is used. For an illustration, consider the producer of a scented hair shampoo. The product is marketed to women but it is used by them in varying degrees. The client's research suggests assigning these audience weights to women by age.

Age	Weight
18 — 24	1.00
25—39	1.20
40—49	.40
601	.20

This indicates that primary emphasis should be given to women under 40 years with lowered emphasis for older women. What this demonstrates statistically is that while women of all ages use the product, women of certain ages are more likely users.

The audience weights can now be used to shape the media priorities. A magazine may appeal to all women, but in this case those readers under age 40 are given higher (disproportionate) value. The CPM screening process is designed to recognize the advertiser's priorities.

Here are three magazine candidates for women readers.

Magazine	Total Women Readers (In Millions)	Millions of Women Readers By Age			
		18-24	25-39	40-59	601
A	18.5	4.5	5.7	6.2	2.1
B	10.2	8.0	1.4	.7	.1
C	14.7	5.0	8.3	1.0	.4

With priorities given to younger readers, the total women reader rank is not as important. To balance advertiser needs with magazine delivery, the advertiser value weights are assigned to the media audience figures.

Weighted Readers By Age (Millions)

Magazine	Cost Pg 4C* (000)	1.00 18-24	1.20 25-39**	.40 40-59	.20 601	Weighted Readers
A	$46.1	4.50	6.80	2.48	.42	14.20
B	18.6	8.00	1.70	.30	.02	10.02
C	30.0	5.00	10.00	.40	.08	15.48

*Page — 4-Color

* * 5.7 (25-39 yrs) × 1.20 Weight = 6.80

The new weighted audiences are then used for the standard CPM analysis.

UNDUPLICATED AUDIENCE AND CPM

To this point we have applied the efficiency process to single measure audiences, but it is equally valuable to look at unduplicated audience exposures on a CPM basis. This is particularly true where the size of the unduplicated audience is a primary consideration in the plan. We use a radio illustration to demonstrate how the analysis is done. The following is the rating book summary on Homeville.

Average Quarter Hour Listeners

Station	Cost/60-second	M-F 7-9 A.M.	CPM
WAAA	$18.50	16,000	$1.16
WBBB	20.00	18,000	1.11
WCCC	15.00	12,000	1.25

On the average audience (single measure) the clear choice is WBBB; it has the largest *average* audience at the best CPM.

The client is interested in a weekly schedule that runs for several weeks. He wishes to know how many *different* (unduplicated) listeners will be exposed in a week's time. The research firm has cumulative audiences for each station. The analyst goes a step further and calculates a CPM on the different potential listeners that could be exposed to the advertising message.

Station	Cost/60-Second	Aug. Audience M-F 7-9 A.M.	Cume Audience (1 Wk) M-F 7-9 A.M.	CPM	Cume CPM
WAAA	$18.50	16,000	21,000	$1.16	$ .88
WBBB	20.00	18,000	30,000	1.11	.67
WCCC	75.00	12,000	20,000	1.25	.75

Remember, the cume identifies the greatest number of *different* listeners who would hear at least one 15-minute segment in a 5-day (M-F) period. Notice that on a cume basis WBBB improved its position as the top audience station (on average audience basis WBBB was 4.3 percent lower in CPM than WAAA but on the CUME, WBBB was 24 percent lower).

The buyer selects WBBB but learns additional dollars are available for another station. WAAA has the next largest unduplicated audience (21M) but WCCC has a lower cume CPM ($.75). The standard procedure in such cases is to determine which station complements WBBB by offering listeners who will not hear announcements on WBBB but will listen to another station. The analytical question becomes, "Which station delivers the largest unduplicated audience *when used with WBBB*?" The audience data on exclusive listeners are provided by the radio research firm. Once the exclusive audience measures are in hand, the CPM analysis can be done.

Station	Cost/60	Aug. Audience	Exclusive Cume* M-F 7-9 A.M.	Exclusive** CPM
WAAA	$18.50	16,000	11,000	$1.68
WCCC	15.00	12,000	18,000	.83

**Example: This column for WAAA would include all listeners who hear WAAA during the week *except* those WAAA listeners who also listen to WBBB between 7-9 A.M.
**Example WCCC: $15.00 ÷ 18,000

Obviously, if the goal is to find two stations that can offer the largest unduplicated audience potential, WBBB and WCCC are the best combination. Their programming is of such a contrast that few of WCCC listeners are interested in what WBBB is programming and vice versa.

A final note of caution: When you discuss cume audiences in radio, it is *not* the same as reach. A cume is the *potential* audience. To use cume as reach an advertiser would have to schedule an announcement during each quarter hour period throughout the week. Only this way could we presume to expose all of the station's different listeners.

CPM PRINCIPLES

As with any instrument used to evaluate, the cost per thousand analysis is subject to limitations in reliance and application. In fact, it is not the flaws in the process that are in question but the *way* the information is used. The CPM is a significant means of evaluating media opportunities when the following guides are followed.

INTERMEDIA APPLICATION

You are advised not to compare different media directly on audience efficiency. To equate broadcast with print or outdoor with direct mail in exposure value is a risky task. The exposure value of one medium is substantially different than another's; the perceptive process is different; the length of exposure is different; and the audience's relation with each medium is different. Since the conditions of exposure are different, then it is illogical to use a common measure to force an artificial comparison. Restrict CPM analysis to intramedium evaluation and avoid embarassing reminders of "apples and oranges."

COMPARABLE MESSAGE UNITS

The lower the CPM for an advertising schedule is, the more the client is likely to be interested. With pressure for better and better efficiency some planners are tempted to mix the CPMs of "larger" message units with CPMs of smaller space or shorter lengths. If the quarter-hour audience is available for a one-minute announcement, the same audience is available for a 10-second announcement. The audience size is the same but the price for a 10-second may be half that for the minute. The effect on the CPM is obvious: it would *drop* one-half. As a result, the overall CPM is lowered. The same situation occurs if you mix the CPM for magazine full pages with the CPM for ⅜-page units. Is this reasonable and fair? Ask yourself if the exposure impact of a 10-second announcement is equal to the minute. What are the odds that the ⅜-page will attract as many readers as the full-page? If the impact is different, how can we justify equal audience values? It is less troublesome to limit CPM analysis to message units of comparable size or length.

CPM AS SOLE CRITERION

The costs of marketing and media have made efficiency or CPM analysis very important in selection. Yet it is a serious mistake to choose on CPM alone — it must be balanced with other dimensions of audience value. Vehicles commanding large audiences are not likely to have the best audience efficiency. If you ignore reach opportunities for CPM you could end up with a number of smaller audience vehicles that have little intrusive impact upon consumers. Penetration must be maintained as well. The best advice is to use the CPM analysis diagnostically to select the most efficient of the high- and moderate-reach candidates.

This does not mean ignoring the lesser audience vehicle. CPM analyses are capable of identifying excellent audience values in the most modest vehicles. Think of using CPM to select the most efficient smaller audience vehicles to be added to schedules of higher reach potentials. The combination of high impact and audience efficiency is a valuable balanced contribution.

CPM WHAT?

CPM analysis is not reserved for any one audience measure. As long as you use comparables, the examination can be based on homes, viewers, readers, listeners, by demographic groups or by levels of product usage. Use it as often as you like. Similarly, there is no one special point in the media planning process at which the CPM study is exclusively employed. Many use it continuously, as a preliminary screening device for vehicle candidates through the final evaluation of the unduplicated audience of the proposed plan.

QUESTIONS

1. What is a weighted audience CPM and why is it used?

2. *Inter*media cost-per-thousand comparisons are very risky for media selection. Why?

3. Cost efficiency, though important, is felt by many to be insufficient as the sole criterion for media selection. Why?

10

QUALITATIVE FACTORS IN MEDIA SELECTION

Media planning is primarily based upon audience performance measured as size, unduplicated reach, or cost efficiency. Companies demand verification that media dollars are spent on options exposing the most prospects for the least cost. This is a function of quantity, of numbers. But these quantities are not the sole criteria for planning or for selection.

Experienced planners realize there are other dimensions of performance less tangible but equally important for advertising success. These are the qualities of media environment that enhance or detract from performance. Although subjective and often incapable of specific value, they are nonetheless important. This chapter discusses some of the major qualities with the thought that message environment is a critical aspect of media planning.

FACTORS ENHANCING MEDIA EFFECTIVENESS

Enhancement means any part of the vehicle's make-up that will improve audience awareness or acceptance of the advertising message. What is it that might assist the message? What is there in the medium-audience relationship that will improve the message's ability to communicate? Of the many aspects that fall within a qualitative environment, two — content and perceptual involvement — deserve particular attention.

CONTENT AUTHORITY AND APPROPRIATENESS

People attend to media sources for different reasons. Some media inform and "educate," providing the information necessary for us to function as participants in society. Other media provide the leisure, recreation, or entertainment desired for a pleasant life. To the degree that each medium satisfies these needs we reward them with our time and investment. However, we are not as discriminating as we could be. We read more magazines or hear more radio stations or view more TV programs than needed or desired. True, we have priorities among our media habits — we enjoy some vehicles (newspapers, programs) more than others. The problem is that this qualitative value is lost in the quantitative measure of size. While we may enjoy one magazine over others, we subscribe to several; although we have favorite television programs we do not limit viewing exclusively to favorites. Circulation, readership, or ratings do not give quality insight — for this, planners have to look elsewhere. Here are some approaches used in major media.

Content in Magazines. Much of a consumer magazine's success today is dependent upon editorial matter that is tightly focused on reader interests. The closer the editorial content to the advertiser's product, the better chances are for audience exposure and processing. In some cases, the advertiser's message is the equivalent of editorial material — skiing equipment in a skiing magazine, cosmetics in fashion and women's service publications, seeds and fertilizers in gardening magazines. There must be an extra value when readers of certain magazines spend as much reading time on advertisements as they do features.

Beyond editorial interest is authority. Does the publication have a strong and loyal reputation with readers? Advertisers know from research that advertisements appearing in certain magazines gain prestige merely from association. Influence is difficult to verify but a number of years ago, a home service magazine ran a supermarket experiment to test the influence of its reader authority. Brands on store shelves were randomly given a small sticker with the publication's guarantee on it. Results indicated a significant number of shoppers chose those brands apparently on the credibility of the magazine alone. Perhaps there is no way for a planner to incorporate such findings into the selection process but it would be foolish to ignore such a relationship.

Content in Newspapers. Newspapers do not have specialized content as do magazines, but there are still editorial values to consider. What is the reputation of the newspaper in the community? Does it have public trust? Does the editorial page reflect genuine concern for community welfare? What about page make-up? Is it clean, well-designed and easy-to-read? Are advertisements handled in a careful manner? How well is the paper produced day after day and issue after issue? Advertisers have been known to limit allocations with newspapers of largest circulation in favor of those with fewer readers but better make-up and reproduction.

Newspaper sections do have reader loyalty and the media planner can check out reader preferences if available. In the same way magazines serve, newspaper section editors and/or columnists develop reputations for interest and fairness. Isn't it logical to assume a section earning solid reader loyalty means more potential believability for the company advertising?

CONTENT IN TELEVISION

Except for some sponsorship decisions, television selections are "number based". Decisions, though, do occasionally reflect quality of content. Quality can be a matter of the topic or it can be simply the value of performance regardless of topic. There are special interest programs of specific appeal to certain advertisers, i.e., sports and outdoor recreation shows, or home service and cooking, or business programs. These programs attract audiences with above-average concern for products associated with the activity. In the same way that magazines operate, certain TV shows give an ideal atmosphere for the advertiser's message.

Authority is also found in the entertainment values of television programming. Many advertisers appreciate the respectability of news programming. Both network and local news and news magazines (e.g., CBS' "60 Minutes") carry premium prices because advertisers like the editorial environment. Authority of a sort also accrues to situation comedies or drama programs. Family products benefit from the special values of "Walt Disney Presents," "The Waltons," or "Little House on the Prairie," and other shows with outstanding reputations for quality and wholesome entertainment. Corporations check ratings but they also seek measures of viewer appreciation with a presumption of good will "spillover."

CONTENT IN RADIO

Content in radio means the format or style of programming done by stations. The very personal nature of radio listenership has encouraged radio programmers in larger cities to design programming narrowly. Planners generally leave station selection to the time buyers but it is worthwhile for those designing the campaign to decide how the intrinsic relations between format and listeners could be utilized. Many extremely successful campaigns have used radio, not on the reach of the station nor the rating points delivered but based on the mood or environment of a program or personality. Such things have been measures of advertising success for years in radio.

AUDIENCE ATTENTION

Many media researchers agree that the "tests" used in media research to qualify an audience member are not rigorous. To be a reader of a magazine you need not read very story or see every page. To be a viewer of television or listener of radio, one must see or hear only a minor portion of the broadcast quarter hour. Standard audience research does not show the *degree* of attention or readership. But as surely as people have favorites, there are differences in the ways we attend to certain media vehicles. Here are two examples of how attention is measured.

Television. From observational research we learn that a substantial portion of television viewing is done in conjunction with other activity — meals, household duties, hobbies, even reading and conversation. Competition is such that many programs, while they gather enough attention to be counted for ratings, have anything but the complete attention of the viewer.

The following table, based on a number of research studies, indicates the average full attention given to various program types.

Percentage of Credited Viewers at Full Attention

Program Category	Men 18-49	Women 18-49
Early Morning News	42	28
Daytime Serials	70	70
Primetime Movies	85	80
Situation Comedy	80	75
Late Evening Variety	70	68

It is unknown if some advertisers avoid the weaker programs, but, at the least, such research could justify heavier GRP levels to compensate for more casual viewing.

Magazines. In similar fashion to TV attention, planners also consider the number of days a reader spends with a magazine and the actual time spent reading. If one magazine is read an average of three days during issue life and that of a competitor one and one-half days, the magazine with a 3-day exposure offers better potential for initial or even additional contact with the advertisement. Similarly, reading time suggests to some analysts the care and interest by readers. It is also a measure of potential for exposure since the more time spent in reading means a better opportunity for advertising exposure.

Another dimension of the magazine reading direction is the *pace* that a magazine has in accumulating readers. How quickly do subscribers and newstand purchasers read each issue. In a number of situations advertisers favor magazines that are able to expose the advertisement more quickly. Here is a table showing some sample rates of accumulation. The data come from advertising agency compilations from numerous research studies.

	Type of Magazine		
Issue Age	News	Newspaper Supplements	Women's Service
Within 1 Week	51%	95%	35%
Within 2 Weeks	79%	—	51%
Within 4 Weeks	87%	—	70%

According to the findings above, an advertiser running in an issue of *Time* or *Newsweek* could expect a majority of each magazine's readership would see the issue the first week and nearly 90 percent by month's end.

Outdoor and Transit Exposure. Neither of these transportation media is particularly intrusive upon travelers. Therefore, although many analysts design outdoor and transit schedules around quantitative figures of coverage and reach, there is discounting of the figures because attention is suspect. Though there have been numerous studies to demonstrate the eye to sign contact, there is no satisfactory measure of how much eye contact indicates perception.

DETRACTIONS FROM MEDIA EFFECTIVENESS

Anyone who follows mass media performance understands there is sizable criticism of performance by the public. Questions of taste and authenticity have been continually a part of print and broadcast operation. Some advertisers are concerned about the quality of editorial and entertainment performance but *all* advertisers are worried about another qualitative problem — over-commercialization. This problem, popularly characterized as "clutter," reaches the heart of advertising effectiveness. To date, the advertising industry has done little more than talk about over-commercialization. Yet the problem grows each year and each year it is more difficult for a single message to penetrate the jungle of competing messages. It may not be long before media analysts will generally discount audience projections because of clutter problems. The problem is serious enough for some detailed discussion of this major influence upon message effectiveness.

REASONS FOR OVER-COMMERCIALIZATION

Both the advertiser and the media are guilty of the serious inflation of advertising messages. The advertisers in resisting price increases have encouraged one medium to compete with another over prices. At the same time, the media are experiencing a great demand for time and space. The media, seeking higher profit levels without setting unconscionable prices, have allowed more and more advertising units to be scheduled. The one-minute commercial died on television because advertisers refused to pay higher and higher rates. The 30-second commercial was the alternative, but television did not reduce the limits for commercial time, so we now have twice as many messages competing for viewer attention. The greater the number of competing messages, the less likely that a particular message is recalled. Marketing's initial reaction to lower awareness was to increase the frequency of exposure. This only led to increased demand and more messages — the snake swallowing its tail.

All media have difficulty in overexposure, but some have more than others. The question for media planning is whether a medium should be discounted or graded lower if there is likelihood of overexposure. This seems a delicate question because if followed too rigorously it could force avoidance of most major advertising media. On the other hand, ignoring saturation is impossible. We must acknowledge that year to year some advertising schedules become less influential because the message is unable to break through the clutter barrier. The following discussion identifies some of the more serious conditions in media. At the same time it should be clear that all mass media forms are affected by some degree of message inflation.

Television. This is the medium that seems most affected by "clutter." As an expensive selling medium, television faces a "damned-if-you-do-and-damned-if-you-don't" attitude. Currently, stations and networks are guided by a self-regulatory code for limiting the amount of nonprogram time. The code is developed and maintained by the *National Association of Broadcasters Code Authority*. Here is a summary of current limits.

Daypart	Nonprogram Limits Per Hour (in Minutes)
Daytime	12.0* — 16.0
Fringe Evening	16.0
Prime Evening	7.0* — 9.5

* Self-Imposed Network Limits occasionally exceeded.
0Source: NATBC

With commercials reduced to 30-seconds and shorter lengths, there is reason for concern about how well the public can discriminate one brand or one network's program plug from another.

Another dimension in television's crowding is the number of program interruptions allowed. Viewers universally dislike continued interruptions in most shows and the public lobbies for fewer commercial breaks. Since neither station or network is inclined to reduce the amount of nonprogram time, fewer interruptions mean longer periods of nonprogram materials. This *clustering* is not a pleasant prospect for television advertisers. Here is the current recommendation from NAB.

NAB Program Interruption Limits (Per Hour Basis)

Daypart	Interruptions
Day (7 A.M. — 6 P.M.)	8
Prime (6 P.M. — 12 M)	4

If broadcasting continues its pressure to reduce interruptions, advertisers could soon be watching their prime time 30-second commercial compete with five to seven others consecutively! The prospect of higher viewer awareness in such conditions is extremely limited.

Radio. Radio offers the identical problem in overcrowding. Current NAB requirements state no more than eighteen minutes per hour (roughly one-third of a program hour) is allowed for nonprogram materials. As in the television situation, there are reports of many radio stations exceeding the guidelines — some running as high as 40 percent commercials in peak advertiser periods.

Clustering commercials has become a popular programming device with radio stations. Program managers, attempting to reduce channel switching among music listeners, have found the more records back-to-back, the less the station loses listenership. The inevitable result is a series of records followed by commercial clusters that send listeners on to other interests. It is a vicious circle with advertising the loser.

Newspapers and Magazines. The print media are hardly fault-free. The news "hole" (proportion of editorial space to advertising space) gets smaller each year in newspapers and small space advertisements are difficult to fit. Magazines suffer editorially, too. The "heavier" issues of magazines allow anywhere from twenty to fifty pages of nearly pure advertising before the first editorial section is found. What's more, competitors abound. It is not unusual to find a large issue of a magazine filled with handfuls of product competitors — page after page. This hardly assists recognition and product awareness.

FACTORING QUALITATIVE DECISIONS

Is there a way to introduce these "intangible" considerations into the selection process? There is, if a planner is willing to assign a numerical value (plus or minus) to subjective judgments. Once the planner is resolved to apply numerical values, designing a system of application is simple. As illustration, observe how one planner might want to work with attention levels in television.

A manufacturer of kitchen appliances is interested in a prospect audience of younger adult women. The planner begins with a standard CPM analysis of daytime and late evening fringe:

Daypart	CPM Women 18—34
Day (9 A.M. — 4 P.M.)	$ 5.30
Fringe (11:20 — 1A.M.)	$10.50

On credited audience, day is clearly superior but the planner wants to utilize attention research findings as follows.

Daypart	Viewers at Full TV Attention
Day	60%
Fringe	80%

The planner, on the assumption the commercial is best exposed to those at full attention, decides to discount or factor the CPMs. If only 60 percent and 80 percent are fully attentive, it is decided to increase the CPMs for day and fringe by 40 and 20 percent respectively.

Daypart	CPM	Attention Factor	Adjusted CPM
Day	$ 5.30	(x) 140	$ 7.42
Fringe	10.50	(x) 120	12.60

The adjustments in this case were not enough to change the ranking of dayparts, but the planner received a more sensitive picture of value. Such weighting values can be assigned for clutter, editorial quality, program atmosphere and for any other quality the planner wishes to introduce into the media calculus. There are no given formulas to assign factor values or weights because it is a subjective process to begin with. Assign values with purpose and reason and you incorporate dimensions of media vehicles that are essential in the selection process.

QUESTIONS

1. Media analysis dealing with qualitative audience values concerns factors that enhance measures and those that detract from quantitative audience measures. Explain.

2. A magazine's editorial content that complements advertised products is considered beneficial. What does editorial compatibility have to do with attention to the message of the advertiser?

3. What is clutter and how does it influence TV viewer awareness?

4. Is it possible to give qualitative factors a finite weight in media selection? If yes, how?

SECTION IV: REPORT PREPARATION

INTRODUCTION TO SECTION IV

Once the selection strategy is finished and a representative schedule is worked out, the media plan must be written and presented. The quality of organization and writing this challenging document are the subjects of Chapter 11. It covers the sequential outline and style needed to produce a compelling rationale for a media plan.

The better the presentation of the media plan, the more likely that the plan will be accepted and used, and the less likely that important aspects will be challenged or even eliminated because of poor rationale or justification. The media plan itself, whether written or oral, is essential to the success of the process.

11

REPORT FORMAT AND ORGANIZATION

Once the advertising media plan has been prepared, the task is still not complete. The plan must be written in a solid business report format and presented to the advertiser. In most cases, the media plan will be a part of the overall advertising campaign plan. The highlights of the proposed campaign are often presented orally, in person, by the advertising agency to the advertiser. Because this presentation may be as short as thirty minutes and seldom longer than two hours, it is not possible to include all the details of the campaign — just the most important points and the most pertinent or interesting information. The plans are included in the presentation, but the supporting facts must be found in the written campaign plan. This written report is often called a "planbook" or, because it contains the supporting facts, a "factbook."

On some occasions, the media plan is written up separately. Certainly, in its first draft the media plan is written for review by the rest of the advertising agency or by a special group known as a "plans board" that must approve all work prepared by the agency. So even though the media plan may eventually become part of the overall campaign factbook, it is still appropriate to examine the written media plan report more closely.

It is not possible to state absolutely that "all media reports should start with the analysis of the competition," nor is it possible to present any other hard and fast rules about media plans. Not every advertising campaign problem or situation will lend itself to the same treatment, so the organization of the report may need to be altered to meet the particular needs at hand. Likewise, some media planners may have very good reasons for following a slightly different organization. Most often, the same topics will be included, although there may be some variation in the order and even in the special terminology that is used. There is no single "right way" to prepare a media plan report, although the suggestions in this chapter will be suitable for most situations and are a good guide for the beginner to follow.

SAMPLE OUTLINE OF A MEDIA PLAN

Overview of the Total Plan (Summary)

Research Analysis
- Product Analysis
- Market Analysis
- Consumer Analysis

Competitive Analysis

Objectives
- Marketing
- Advertising
- Media

Budget Determination

Targets
- Market Profiles
- Consumer Profiles

Media Selection
- Media Types
- Vehicles
- Units

Budget Allocation

Schedule or Calendar

Contingency Plans

OVERVIEW

At the beginning of any good business report there is a table of contents. Ideally, this table should present an outline of the report, so that the reader may peruse the table and gain a clear understanding of the organization of the report before actually reading it. The appropriate page numbers should be included so that the reader can refer to certain sections in a hurry, if necessary. It is a poor practice to prepare any business report without numbered pages; the page numbers help keep the pages in order, help guide the reader to the appropriate section or topic, and help in collating multiple copies of the report.

The next item is the report is also of use to the reader, to help speed up the reading and understanding and improve comprehension on the reader's part. It is called an "executive summary" or an "overview," and it contains only a couple of pages that summarize the main points of the report. In a media plan, the overview outlines the basic objectives and strategies of the proposed plan. The specific plans and the justification and rationale that support those proposals can be held back until the main body of the report. This overview is only to give the reader some advance idea of the context and direction of the report, so that the actual reading can be faster without the need for repeated reading of certain items to gain better understanding. Do not overlook the importance of this section; a very busy executive may just read the overview and then skim the rest of the report and read only portions with great care, allowing others to read the entire report or having each manager concentrate on those sections and topics that have greatest relevance to his or her particular responsibility.

Obviously, because the overview is a summary of the rest of the report, it must be written last, even though it is placed in the front of the report.

COMPETITION

Some media planners prefer to start the report with the various objectives and goals that will be the achievement of the plan. However, it is often helpful to establish some general research findings before setting the objectives, because these results will have an impact on the objectives. So it is difficult to justify talking about objectives until they can be based on some secondary, and perhaps primary, research.

In the same vein, it is probably necessary to analyze the competition's marketing and advertising efforts and take them into account when establishing the objectives. For these reasons, it may be most sensible to begin the media plan report with an analysis of the competition and with any other pertinent research information that has been gathered.

The competitive analysis should be, as is true with most sections of the media plan, as complete as possible. All the major competitors should be considered, and even firms that do not manufacture or market items identical to those you are advertising may still be important, because they may sell items that could be substituted for yours. For example, manufacturers of what is called "hard roll" candy must be concerned with competitors who make the same kind of candy, of course. But they may also be concerned with manufacturers of candy bars, and perhaps chewing gum should also be considered a possible substitute product. All possible competitors should be analyzed.

General marketing programs of competitors would be important. For the media planner, the more specific advertising plans and media patterns might be even more relevant. However, there is often a problem when presenting this kind of information. The facts about competitive marketing and advertising efforts may simply be discussed, without any particular emphasis or perspective. It is better to talk about the competition in the ways that it relates to your own product or service, to your own marketing and advertising, to your media plans and proposals. Just repeating data from some of the sources of competitive advertising records is not as helpful as seeking out the specific information that is important to your situation and then presenting that information as it relates to your own media plan.

OBJECTIVES

As was stated earlier, some media planners prefer to start the report with the objectives, but it may make more sense to state these objectives after the proper groundwork has been laid with general and competition research findings. The objectives are what the plan is intended to accomplish. Some planners differentiate between objectives as longer than a one-year time and goals as those things which should be accomplished within the next year.

Many persons have difficulty in establishing sound objectives, most often because they do not really understand exactly what an objective is. If an objective is something that the advertising expected to accomplish, then it makes sense that the objective should be able to be stated as a verb; a simple infinitive "to do" form of a verb is an easy test of a good objective. Thus, one sample marketing objective might be phrased "to sell the product" or "to grow at a rate double that of the industry in general."

Too many times, the objectives are not specific enough. The advertising agency that prepares an advertising plan may wish to keep the objectives somewhat vague because it is difficult to achieve specific objectives. On the other hand, the advertiser may prefer more specific objectives, such as "to increase sales volume by 11 percent during the next year," because it is easier to judge when the objectives actually have been accomplished.

The marketing objectives may already be established before the media planner becomes involved; the same may be true of the general advertising objectives. If the marketing and advertising objectives are not established in advance, then they should be proposed and approved before the media objectives can be started. In this way, the media objectives will work in conjunction with the marketing objectives and the advertising objectives. A good media plan is impossible if the media objectives do not mesh with the marketing and advertising objectives, just as the advertising objectives must themselves be harmonious with the more general marketing objectives.

Keep in mind, too, that the use of the media themselves are not media objectives. Using radio or newspapers or transit advertising would be a strategy, a part of the plan. Media are strategies, not objectives. Media are ways of accomplishing objectives, but the use of advertising media is not an objective to be accomplished and not an end in itself. Determine objectives of what is to be accomplished, and then perhaps the use of advertising and media will be one means of pursuing the objectives. Keep in mind, too, that justifying the objectives is of great importance.

TARGET MARKETS AND TARGET GROUPS

The profiles of consumers and markets to which the advertising effort should be directed may be covered as part of the objectives, but these kinds of targets are not really goals or objectives; they are directions to be utilized in the accomplishment of the objectives.

Whether target markets or target groups should be treated first is an individual decision. What is important is that both consumers and markets must be detailed and justified, and that each topic probably deserves a separate section in the report.

How to go about selecting target markets and target groups has already been discussed in earlier chapters. It may be useful to outline the most important (primary) targets and plan on directing the bulk of the advertising effort toward them. Then there can be secondary targets that will receive lesser emphasis, and perhaps tertiary targets, third in importance, could also be included if necessary.

It is not enough to justify these kinds of consumer and market profiles simply by referring to data from a standard advertising source such as Target Group Index. In fact, such sources do not indicate what the proper targets should be; they indicate only a lot of detailed data about consumer and geographic factors. The decisions that are eventually based on these information sources are made by the individual planner, not by the sources. Two different media planners can vary on their selection of targets even when they use the same source of information. So the decisions must be fully justified, including demonstrating clearly which items of information led to which conclusions and what interpretations intervened.

Each stage of the process must be explained and justified — the selection of the targets themselves and then the rank or order of which targets have first priority, which are next in importance, and so on.

MEDIA TYPES

After the research and competitive information, the objectives, and the target markets and target groups are presented, it is time to determine which media will be used for the advertising effort. It would not be appropriate to select individual media vehicles or units at this time. Instead, concentrate on which media best fulfill the objectives.

The information given in Chapter 6 would be helpful in this kind of determination. The characteristics of the media can be matched with the objectives and the targets for this campaign plan. The kind of table shown in Table 6-1 would be helpful, too, as would the media usage data from a source such as Target Group Index.

The media planner may be able to prepare a list of all the types of media that could be used, and then put them in order from the one most likely to be selected down to the medium that is least likely to be used (perhaps to be used only if the budget is adequate). Then, depending upon the level of the advertising budget, the media toward the bottom of the list might have to be eliminated.

It is not enough simply to tell which media will be used. Also needed is an explanation of why the media selected fit into the overall scheme, and how all the major objectives can be achieved with the use of these particular media. One common problem is forgetting to mention the media that have *not* been selected for the plan; all the media that have been considered would be discussed. It is almost as important to talk about why certain media were not selected as it is to justify those that were chosen. Media planners are careful to analyze rejected media positively, explaining why those chosen are superior; this positive criticism underscores the objectivity in the plan, while overzealous criticism might preempt the use of that medium by the advertiser at some later time.

VEHICLES AND UNITS

It may be possible now to begin listing which specific media vehicles will be used in the advertising campaign. In broadcast, this kind of selection is tentative. In network television, for example, there may be one or two programs that best meet the demands of this particular plan, but it may be that the commercial time on those programs has already been reserved. In general, the broadcast media are less predictable because there is only a certain amount of time available for advertising, so the first choices may not always be achievable. In print media, on the other hand, the space for advertising is not quite so limited because the amount of advertising often determines the size of the particular issue of a magazine or newspaper. Therefore, the selection of certain print media vehicles can be more definite, while the selection of broadcast (and maybe outdoor and transit) media vehicles cannot be as firm, because it is based on characteristics rather than on specific programs.

The determination of the units of advertising, such as the advertisement size, the use of color or bleed in print media, or the length of the commercial message in broadcast media, can be decided upon with a great degree of certainty. This is because the broadcast media may be used even if the first-choice broadcast vehicle is not available. Keep in mind, however, that many of the decisions about advertising units may be influenced by the creative portion of the advertising campaign; the size of an advertisement, the length of a commercial, or the use of color may be critical to the success of the copy that has been written or the layout that has been drawn, so the so-called "creative" departments may have a great deal of influence in these decisions about advertising units. These decisions are more arbitrary, but the rationale behind them still should be explained.

BUDGET ALLOCATION

The advertising media planner may not determine the size of the advertising budget. That is often done by, or at least approved by, the advertiser. The media planner often receives a budget amount that has previously been discussed and decided upon, and then that amount is to be used for the media selected for the campaign.

However, the amount of the advertising budget must be explained and justified and the rationale and method for that amount must be included in the advertising campaign plan. It may also be most appropriate to include it with the rest of the budgetary information that is necessarily a part of the media plan. The media effort requires a large monetary investment and it must be detailed and explained, so other budgetary information may fit in well here.

The allocation of the funds to the various advertising media certainly must be explained. How and why these allocation decisions were made is an essential ingredient of a solid media report. It is simply not adequate to demonstrate what percentages of the budget are to be allocated to each medium and to figure the actual dollar amounts that will be spent on each medium. That information is necessary, but it comes in the middle of the budget portion of the report. First must come an explanation of what factors were considered, how they were evaluated and ranked, the processes that were followed in determining the various needs and allocations, and similar rationale. Then can come the actual decisions, percentages, and amounts of money, followed by a full discussion, justification, and explanation of how the budget level and allocations fit into the overall media and advertising plans.

SCHEDULE OR CALENDAR

An effective plan should include a visual representation of the schedule of advertising activity. Scheduling the advertising is an art, because it is being done before the actual buying contacts are being made with the media vehicles. However, general temporal patterns of advertising can be established, even though specific days and times of day may not be pinned down yet.

That is one reason for using a flow chart. It can show the general timing patterns and weights of advertising impact during the various weeks or months of the year without the necessity of selecting certain days, as might be required if a calendar actually were used.

Some people may prefer to take an actual calendar that has large spaces for each day and fill in what media events will be occurring for any given day. However, this results in much repetition and it also implies that specific dates are feasible, when, indeed, part of the schedule may need to remain flexible in case certain space or time availabilities are no longer for sale.

Another approach is to type in the various months as headings and then list certain weeks or days within each month when certain portions of the media plan will occur. However, this format does not lend itself to easy and quick understanding, something that is possible with the combination of visual movement and printed information in a flow chart.

CONTINGENCY PLANS

Every media plan should have a standby plan or contingency paln, to spell out what will change in the media plan if the desired expectations do not occur. Too often, these contingency plans are too brief and oversimplified. They should be detailed enough so that they could actually be put into use if they are needed. If events do not turn out as they were planned, the contingency plans will be put into action on short notice; there will not be enough time to go back through them and fill in any gaps that may exist. A media planner hopes that the original plan will be accepted, approved, and that it will work, but a solid contingency plan in some detail is still a necessity.

As has been mentioned before, there really need to be at least three contingency plans: one for each kind of unexpected occurrence that might come up. What will be done if the expectations are not being met, what will be done if the expectations are exceeded, and what will be done if some competitor takes some action that throws off the plan — all should be considered with specific contingency plans. In addition, there may be special circumstances that apply to your individual situation and that might require separate contingency plans of their own.

OTHER CONSIDERATIONS

There are several other factors that must be considered throughout the media plan report. These items do not fit into any certain part or topic of the report. Rather, they apply to all aspects and parts, because they comprise some general standards and rules that must be considered in almost every sound business report, and especially advertising plan reports.

Every decision must be explained in detail: how it was approached, how it was arrived at, and perhaps most important, how it was justified. The "hows" and "whys" must be covered. Every decision must be fully justified and supporting rationale should accompany the explanation. Telling how and why is vital.

The quality of writing, too, is important. Good grammar, correct spelling and punctuation, in short, following the precepts of proper expression, are all essential. There are rules that apply to the English language because they aid in expression and reading and understanding; if you do not follow these rules, you will have more difficulty presenting your ideas and your reader will have more difficulty comprehending what you are trying to say. Proper writing also implies that you know what you are talking about; improper writing will cause the readers to infer that there may be problems in the plan, too, that are reflected in the sloppy writing.

It is safest to avoid slang expressions, such as "ad" instead of "advertisement," "avail" instead of "availability," and "metro area" instead of "metropolitan area." If you find that you must use such slang terms, be sure that you spell them out in their entirety the first time you use them, and then always place them inside quotation marks so the reader will realize that you knew the words were slang.

The same rule applies to abbreviations. It would be cumbersome to spell out "Standard Rate and Data Service" thoughout a report, but you can spell it out in first reference, giving the abbreviation "SRDS" in parentheses, and then using the abbreviation in the rest of the report. Other abbreviations that can be treated the same way include

"ADI" for Area of Dominant Influence, "DMA" for Designated Market Area, and "TGI" for Target Group Index. However, there are some common abbreviations that border on slang, such as "TV" for "television," and in those cases the best policy is to spell out the correct word in its entirety.

Another important rule is to proofread what you have written, and then proofread the report after it has been typed, and then proofread again before anything is forwarded to a superior or to a client. The best job of proofreading is often done by someone other than the person who wrote the report, because it is easy to overlook errors if you were the writer. However, the writer should do a thorough proofreading first, before asking anyone else to read through the report again. While you are proofreading, be sure to look for grammatical errors and awkward word and sentence construction, as well as typographical errors. You can also read the material at the same time, being certain that the recommendations and supporting facts are specific enough and relate well to one another.

When you write a report, be sure to remember that not everyone who reads it will have the same background as you; in fact, some of the chief executives will not have much knowledge or experience in advertising. For that reason, as well as common courtesy, it is best to define any specialized terms that are used, such as "availabilities," "spots," "waves," "preemptions," "hiatus," and similar words that are common in advertising but not in other businesses.

Be sure, too, to give the sources of the information you use. You can footnote source citations or place a brief citation in parentheses following any particular item of information. A full bibliography is also desirable, in case someone wants to double-check any of your figures or find additional information from one of the sources you have used.

Do not simply present data or tables of detailed information from the reference sources. If it is easier to include a Xerox copy of a page from Target Group Index, for example, then use colored ink to highlight the relevant data. Be certain that you explain how the data relate to what you are using them for, and tell how you have interpreted and applied the data. Just giving pages of data or tables of numbers may be meaningless, and could lead to interpretations that are contradictory to your own.

If you would like to see a complete media plan report, a good example of one may be found in the appendix to this book.

QUESTIONS

1. What is the purpose of an executive summary? Why is it at the beginning of a report?
2. What are the advantages of stating objectives as specifically as possible? The disadvantages?
3. Why is the selection of broadcast media vehicles a more tentative process than is true in print media?
4. What are the advantages of a flow chart for showing an advertising media schedule?

SECTION V
PURCHASING TECHNIQUES

INTRODUCTION TO SECTION V

None of the previous media strategy texts has attempted to discuss the buying process, even though this tactical stage is critical to the success of the plan. The reason for this avoidance is that buying is a practical process rather than a theoretical one. It is difficult to explain and discuss a process as variable as the personalities of the people who do it.

Still, the years of compiled experience can be distilled into certain basic principles of negotiation, scheduling, and monitoring. Chapter 12 isolates some of the most challenging aspects of media buying and illustrates them.

12

MEDIA BUYING TACTICS AND PROCESSES

Although media planning is vitally important, the strategy used is only as good as the execution (how it is purchased). Advertising and media strategy are fully dependent upon how close the actual schedules are to the planned objectives. We call this tactical phase the implementation or media buying, but it is more than just purchase orders. Buying involves cost estimation, negotiation and skillful monitoring of schedules.

In many organizations the separation of function between the planning and the buying is very small. Often the media dictate the difference. In the planning of a consumer magazine schedule, once the publications are chosen according to audiencee values, the costing of a specific schedule usually exhausts the media process. The planning covers nearly all of the buying function. In spot market broadcast schedules, however, the planning reflects broad reach and frequency goals and the needed GRP to achieve them. No program or unit cost specifications are made until the buying begins; those are the buyer's duties. The rating point goals must be translated into station availabilities, the negotiation for price, and the scheduling of each participation. These are duties primarily done by media buyers when the company has both planning and buying personnel.

In larger firms, the volume of media activity demands a separation of planning and buying. But even though the rules of planner and buyer shift, there is a clear recognition of the duties and skills that are desired in media buying. In this chapter, those skills and techniques are discussed with a particular focus upon how a media buyer can offer the best service to the firm and the media representatives he or she deals with.

MEDIA BUYING TECHNIQUES

Certain skills shape the significance of media buying regardless of the style or size of the company involved. These techniques must be mastered whether the buying duty is an executive or a clerical function. The reader may note that certain duties require mechanical or procedural skills while others also demand social or interpersonal ability. The selection is purposely done. We want you to understand that media buying, when practiced expertly, uses a broad range of talents and skills.

MEDIA RESEARCH SKILL

A primary tool of media analysis is audience research and the media buyer must learn to use a multitude of sources.

Earlier chapters have explained that there are a number of research reports produced for the major media on regular and systematic schedules. Each report has an individual format and data organization that the buyer must learn. No two are alike and the buyer must learn the differences between an *ARBitron* and *Nielsen* or another syndicated audience research service. Some companies also demand that buyers learn the standard survey methodology, to be able to evaluate discrepencies between competing reports. It takes repeated use of an audit statement or a broadcast rating book to handle the information accurately. To gain facility there is little substitute for daily exposure and use.

Beyond regularly scheduled syndicated research there are numerous special audience studies subsidized by stations or publications. These *ad hoc* reports are used by media representatives to fill gaps in knowledge or to counter research reports done by competitors. Typical illustrations would include when a smaller radio market station purchases a telephone coincidental survey to measure popularity, or a magazine underwrites a reader study to show editorial authority and influence. The problem for the buyer is how to utilize such information.

Dismissing all media-sponsored research is not the answer and neither is a blind acceptance of every research study passed across the desk. Partisan research may be valid and reliable but the buyer must know the methodology well enough to judge whether the study is objective and if it is helpful in making a decision.

MEDIA COST ESTIMATION

Many advertising agencies begin media trainees in cost estimation. In part this is done because estimation is relatively uncomplicated, but firms also use estimation because no individual can contribute in media analysis until he or she has a good understanding of media cost policies and discount applications. Unfortunately, the learning process is complicated.

For a number of years the advertising industry has pleaded with the media for standardized rate cards and discounts but with only modest success. Each station or publication sets rate schedules and discount policies to suit its particular needs. Situations dictate many alternatives and buyers have had to accustom themselves with many different ways of calculating time or space. The next section illustrates examples of more popular rate schedules and discounts.

"STATE OF THE ART" MEDIA KNOWLEDGE

Media buyers pride themselves on being the intelligence arm of advertising. They should be primary sources for all current information on media operations.

Knowledge of editorial shifts or broadcast program changes, changes in inventory in broadcast or revisions in costs and discount policies are all areas of information vital to media planning. Because the media buyers operate close to the salespeople, the buyers have an excellent opportunity to be current on changes.

As buyers gain experience from outside information sources, they can provide the long-term advice on costs and projected availability of media features. Although the acquisition of such knowledge is primarily informal (i.e., the "grapevine") the buyers' specialized expertise is highly valued in media planning and even account managment.

NEGOTIATION

Some of the major media are, by tradition and nature, flexible in pricing. This means that one buyer may purchase the same space or time at different rates than another even when all contract aspects are equal. In part this is circumstances, but it is also due to the skills of the buyer who was able to extract the best (lowest) price.

Nothing disturbs an advertiser more than learning he paid more for a media schedule than necessary. This is especially true when media rates are caught in inflationary increases. In tight money periods, negotiation abilities are essential for professional buying performance. The skill is in balancing the medium's anxiety to sell with the advertiser's need for the given spot or participation. As in any negotiation, the buyer must practice patience, frankness, and even-handed relations with salespersons. It is an ability that can contribute generously to a campaign's success.

MONITORING

Advertising schedules bought in advance and scheduled for longer periods of time are highly susceptible to change. Audience flow, rate increases, and editorial and programming shifts all affect the performance of a schedule in exposing an audience. Media buyers must monitor schedules to assure advertisers that the audience values originally planned are still in force.

Forms of oversight include review of broadcast schedules with current rating reports, checking in copies or "tearsheets" the location of advertisements in magazines or newspapers, reviewing broadcast affidavits to verify schedule times, and "riding" an outdoor showing to monitor traffic and board condition. If deficiencies are found from these investigations, the buyer is then expected to begin negotiation for adjustment.

In the opening of this section, we noted the more intangible skills needed by successful media buyers. Clearly, acquiring media expertise, negotiation, and some monitoring functions demand interpersonal talents. There are no rules, codes, or specifications on how the buyer can capitalize on media contacts. Similarly, the discussion avoided a "how-to" attitude because there are many different ways to negotiate or learn the media business and the buyer's personality may dictate the best approach. Thus, beyond practicing a fair and consistant manner in professional relations, the buyer's technique is dependent upon personal perspectives.

COMMON RATE AND DISCOUNT POLICIES

In the discussion of media cost estimation we explained that the major media use a bewildering number of rate schedules and discount structures. There is no easy way to learn them. Mastery comes from daily exposure and use. However, there is still an opportunity to shorten the mastery process by learning some of the basic approaches to discounting used by the media. The following discussions do not exhaust all the possible policies used but do identify most of the cost techniques employed.

PRINT MEDIA (MAGAZINES AND NEWSPAPERS)

Print historically has been more stable than broadcast in discount policies. Published rates for newspapers and magazines have traditionally been the only prices most publishers would accept for space. While rate stability has made space costs easier to estimate, publications are far from simple in rate card design and function. Since the basic unit of sale in a newspaper and in a magazine differ, each print medium is covered separately.

Newspapers. For national and regional advertisers the primary source for newspaper cost data is the monthly *Standard Rate and Data Service* (SRDS). Almost all daily newspapers (and weeklies in a separate volume) present rate cards in the generalized SRDS format. These are national rates, and if there is any possibility that the firm is eligible for the local (or retail) rate, the newspaper should be contacted for a retail rate schedule. The difference in costs and discounts is usually substantial.

The unit of sale is the *line* (one-fourteenth of an inch deep by a column wide) or the *column-inch* (column wide by one inch deep). Pages and fractional pages are listed as specific costs in the larger city publications. Similarly, color charges are shown separately and are added to the black-and-white space costs.

Newspaper discounts are primarily based upon bulk lineage (per contract year) but some newspapers give percentage discounts for page units, while still others discount on the number of insertions run within a specified period. Here are illustrations of each.

Bulk Lineage:	Black and White Line Rates	
Lines/Contract Year	Daily	Sunday
5,000	$.65	$.68
10,000	.62	.66
30,000	.60	.63

Note: If your schedule falls between two rates you must use the rate level *earned*. Thus, in example above a 9,000 line schedule would use $.65 as a daily line rate even though it is closer to the 10,000 rate. The extent of discounts is strictly up to the publishers but few list discounts beyond 150,000 lines per year.

Page Discounts:

R.O.P. Full Page Discounts

Pages/Contract Year	Per Page (BW)
10 Pages	$1,780.00
20 Pages	1,720.00
50 Pages	980.00

Note here that the cost has already been calculated. Thus, an estimator can figure that ten pages would cost the client $17,800, while twenty pages would cost $34,400.

Frequency Discounts:

Minimum Contract Period Cycles (% Discount Off Open Rate)

Minimum Lines/Week	12 Weeks of 13 Weeks	24 Weeks of 26 Weeks	48 Weeks of 52 Weeks
300	3%	4%	6%
600	6%	9%	12%
1,500	11%	13%	17%

To use this discount you must know the open rate for the newspaper, the number of weeks consecutively you will run and the amount of weekly lineage used.

To illustrate suppose the newspaper had an open line rate of $2.00 and the client wishes to run at least twenty-four weeks at 1,000 lines per week.

Open line rate	$2.00
Less 9% discount*	– .18
Cost per line	$1.82
Total lines	× 24,000
Total cost	$43,680.00

* Your discount period is 24/26 and 1000 lines/week earns the 600-line discount of 9 percent.

Rates are quoted for ROP (Run of Press), which means the newspaper controls the location of the advertisement. Advertisers desiring a section or a page will be accommodated whenever possible but if the position must be guaranteed it may be necessary to pay an extra *special position charge*.

Color charges for newspaper are listed in SRDS as extra costs *above the space rates*. Calculate the space cost per unit and then add the color charge. This charge is applied each time you run the advertisement (i.e., each insertion). Discounts are seldom applied to color charges.

Magazines. The primary reference for magazine costs is SRDS. Due to the bulk of publications and the length of rate cards, the service is obliged to publish separate editions for consumer magazines and for trade and industrial magazines. While the style of rate schedules varies considerably between consumer and trade, the formats are similar and the discussion of discounts in consumer areas is similar to industrial and trade.

Magazines sell display space (other than classified) in page and fractional page units, so most discounting is arranged in this fashion. Black-and-white rates are shown separately from color rates. Estimators are cautioned that some publications show color rates *inclusive* of space charges while others show color charges as a special cost to be *added to* space rates. Another magazine rate phenomenon is the charge (or absence of) for *bleed advertisements*. A bleed is a process where the illustration or graphic in the message is extended to the outside edge of the magazine page (no border). Some publications set a standard premium for such production. This charge can be as much as 15 percent of the space charge so it deserves serious consideration.

Magazine discounts for national editions are based on the frequency of insertion (issues used or units used), the volume (pages or page equivalents) in space, or the volume in dollars. Some illustrations will identify the variations.

a. Frequency Discounts: Based on the more issues appeared in the lower the unit cost.

Black and White	**1 ti***	**3 ti**	**5 ti**	**7 ti**
1 Page	2160	2010	1945	1900
2/3 Page	1730	1610	1555	1520
1/2 Page	1405	1305	1265	1235

* = times (issues)

Discounts for frequency may be achieved only by insertions of like units, i.e., all pages or all 1/2-pages. Be alert, however, to publications that will allow smaller space units to combine with larger units for a more favorable discount on smaller units:

Five full pages are scheduled along with two ½-page units.

If allowed, the publication will combine space (5 + 2) to let advertiser receive the 7 time rate.

b. Column (Page Equivalent). Certain publications understand that advertisers run mixed size advertisements in their schedules. Rather than limit discounts to the same size unit, magazines allow all space to be combined for its equivalent in pages. Suppose an advertiser planned this schedule for the year:

9 — pages
6 — ½-pages
4 — ⅓ pages

On a straight frequency, only units of the same size could earn discounts but on equivalent pages here is the result:

Space	Page Equivalents
9 Pgs (9 × 1) =	9
6 ½ (6 × .5) =	3
4½ (4 × .33) =	1 (1.32)
Total	13

If the publication has a discount for ten or more pages per year, this schedule would qualify.

A variation of page-equivalent discounts may be offered on dollars spent. A straight percentage discount is given (usually beyond) to advertisers once a given number of dollars is contracted for.

The following excerpt of dollar volume schedule is from a leading consumer publication in the home service area. Note that the advertiser may combine all sizes, national and regional space, black-and-white with color to identify the dollar volume.

Dollar Volume Range	Discount
\$149,985 to \$299,969	3%
\$299,970 to \$449,954	5%
\$449,955 to \$599,939	8%

Thus, if an advertiser's total space contract amounted to \$150,000, he would earn a 3 percent discount or \$4,500 reduction.

c. Purchase of regional space (i.e., a section of the U.S. or a state or a metropolitan market) is becoming quite common even for national advertisers. Geographic flexibility allows these firms to customize the amount of magazine advertising pressure for each sales area. However, the arrangement of estimating regional space can be bewildering to a beginner. Naturally it is possible for a magazine to compute a rate discount schedule for every geographic possibility but that would make for a long rate card. The favored alternative is to list the circulations for each area and allow them to be combined in any manner for discounts. The method is purchasing space with a cost factor based on the number of thousands of circulation used.

Assume an advertiser has selected ten separate markets (often called metro editions) and wants to know the total cost for a schedule of *page* units in *black-and-white*. Here are the steps used to calculate the rate:

1) Add the individual circulations of each area (magazine will provide the circulation figures for each). For this example the ten metros totaled 280,000.
2) If the publication does not show separate cost schedules for each market it will use a cost-per-thousand circulation schedule in a format much like this:

		CPM		
Circulation Range	**B/W**	**1 Pg**	**½ Pg**	3/8 Pg
to 125,000		14.60	10.60	5.60
125,000-299,999		10.20	5.80	4.00
300,000-499,999		8.80	5.00	3.50

The correct factor for the ten markets (280,000 Circ.) is $10.20 per thousand of circulation.

3) Compute cost per insertion.

280	Thousands of Circulation (280 × 1,000)
× $10.20	Cost for each Thousand
$2,856.00	Cost for a black-and-white page (ten markets)

4) Some publications, instead of a range of calculation, have a fixed charge for so much circulation and follow with a cost per thousand factor for the remaining surplus circulation. The process ends in the same way; the calculator can accurately estimate the space cost of a fully customized market pattern.

A final caution on magazines estimation is the *closing date*. These are production deadlines. If the cost estimate is made shortly before (i.e., several months) the intended start date, it is vital to check with the magazine on how late the production materials can arrive. It is senseless to propose and estimate a schedule only to learn that the publication's *closing* has passed.

BROADCAST MEDIA (NETWORK RADIO, AND TELEVISION, SPOT MARKET RADIO AND TELEVISION)

Buying broadcast time is the most lively purchase activity encountered. Broadcast buying can also be anxious and frustrating. It is difficult to determine why this is true but the changes in programming and commodity pricing traditions have had substantial impact on buying procedures.

The chemistry of broadcast buying will be clearer if the process of making a purchase is discussed. Unlike media planning in print, broadcast plans and estimates seldom include specific stations and networks or programs. The reason generally is that someone planning months in advance cannot know which stations or networks will have the best commercial time available.

The process begins with the media plan that has specific audience targets, GRP levels and/or CPM limits and schedule periods. The buyer informs the broadcasters of these needs and the stations offer plans or, in the case of network television, program availabilities. The buyer reviews the competitive submission and begins to negotiate for better programs (higher ratings) and lower prices.

Negotiation is a transaction process where the buyer contacts competitive stations or networks and informs them of what the others have offered. It is a form of auction. Depending on supply and demand the process may reduce prices or improve availabilities or it may be a waste of the buyer's day. Once the buyer is satisfied that the spot or participation schedule is as close to the plan specifications as possible, the orders (followed by contracts) will be made. The amount of time involved in the broadcast negotiation is ultimately dependent on the buyer's resourcefulness and the station or network's willingness to negotiate.

While the above process fits both television and radio, and network and spot activity, there remain substantial differences in other aspects of the purchase process. The following individual discussions highlight some of the most distinguished characteristics of each.

Network Television. In some ways the network negotiation is the easiest to buy, while in other ways it is the most difficult. The process of scheduling, ordering, and shipping commercials is much simpler than spot activity because it is one of each for a network purchase. On the other hand, the dollars at stake and the unstable nature of audience preference and pricing make network television buying a risk-filled activity.

The pricing for network programming is based upon the 30-second length, although 60-second units are also available. If sponsorship is involved the advertiser can arrange the length of commercials to his own use as long as the network's guides of total commercial time and number of interruptions are met. The costs are assigned on a program-by-program basis by the networks. At the same time numerous areas of network programming operate like a commodity market with prices fluctuating according to demand.

The only source of costs is the network directly. There is no SRDS for network costs because pricing is too fluid. One can learn the general ranges from reading trade journals but the only accurate source is the network.

Currently there are two methods of network purchase — selected program participation or by scatter plan.

In the *selected program procedure* the buyer has studied the audience histories of shows and learns which offer the best target prospect groups. Program candidates are located at each network and the negotiation begins. This method will guarantee the desired audience characteristics and will usually involve the higher rated programs. It is a more expensive means to buy television. Why? The best prospect programs are in demand by a number of buyers and this supports higher network pricing.

The *scatter plan* works on a different theory. Here the buyer tells the network the audience specifications and indicates the amount of dollars available. The network develops a package of programs of various popularity and scheduling and offers a package. The buyer has done the same with other networks and once the initial proposals are in, competitive negotiation begins. The network wants the budget and the buyer wants the best programs for the lowest possible price. The sacrifices on such sales are that program quality is usually uneven (one excellent show is packaged with average and even mediocre ones) and there is little continuity in the schedule. As a general rule, advertisers seeking more broadly defined audience prospects favor the scatter plan, while firms with narrower profiles are compelled to seek more selective programming.

Spot Market Television. The trade-off in spot buying is an advantage of geographic flexibility against the logistics of dealing on a multi-station basis with a variety of sales plans and discount arrangements. Buyers learn the necessary shortcuts to make spot buying more time efficient but it is a demanding aspect of media buying.

Television stations, because they can sell announcements between programs as well as within, offer more variations in length than networks do. The 30-second unit is the standard; however, 60-, 20-, or 10-seconds are offered where and when available. Stations with a 60-second long break can sell it as two 30s or a single 60 so buyers can expect reasonable opportunities in these lengths. Stations seeking to achieve high sales will substitute shorter length positions for 30s or 60s so advertisers seeking 10- or 20-second lengths have learned to monitor station inventories.

Standard Rate and Data Service publishes the rate cards of nearly all stations. Investigation of the rate schedules will assist buyers in two ways: as a general price guide and as a resource for the type of discounts used. SRDS also usually lists the sorts of programs offered by daypart to give buyers some idea of what programming *might* be available. The final word on availabilities and prices comes from each station. Buyers of spot television, for example, should never form expectations from SRDS alone.

Spot television discounts are not standardized and they present numerous options to broadcast buyers. The philosophy of television spot rates is two-fold: the station wishes to gain as much revenue as it can from each spot placement within constraints of competitive offers, and discounts are designed to provide incentive for advertisers to spend more dollars with the station in return for lower unit costs. Stations use a number of different schemes to achieve these objectives.

a. **Fixed position.** A unique condition in broadcast spot selling is pricing by permanence. Advertisers wanting to be guaranteed certain placements or positions can pay the so-called "fixed" rate (the highest available for that placement) and be assured of the placement throughout the schedule.

b. **Preemptible positions.** For many advertisers the trade-off between the higher fixed rate and the risk of losing the position is worthwhile. They gamble that the station will not find another advertiser willing to pay the higher fixed rate. The savings (up to 50 percent) are attractive. Preemptible conditions are offered in various *degrees of notice*. The conditions of notice are tied to the price. Here are the conditions an advertiser is considering in using a preemptible schedule. If he pays the next lowest rate under "fixed" he would receive two weeks notice if a fixed advertiser is found. This means the announcement will run for two weeks before being "bumped." For an even lower rate he may receive only a weeks notice (or even less), or no notice at all (immediate removal).

   All these preemptible conditions are predicated upon how high the advertiser demand for time is at the time of scheduling. If the market is in heavy demand by advertisers, preemptible scheduling could be dangerous — the station cannot guarantee it will have a supply of alternative positions. Conversely, in times of lessened activity, fixed position prices might be unnecessary for all but very popular programs. Here is an illustration of a station rate card offering several degrees of preemptibility.

Daypart	**30-Second Spots (Per Spot)**			
	F1	**P1**	**P2**	**P3**
8-11 p.m. Mon-Sun	$320	$280	$260	$240
9 a.m.-4 p.m. Mon-Fri	50	45	40	35
6-7 p.m. Mon-Sat	120	110	110	90

F1 = Fixed position
P1 = Preemptible with 2-weeks notice
P2 = Preemptible with 1-week notice
P3 = Preemptible (no notice)

c. **Rotation Packages.** Some stations, especially in more active spot markets, forego advertiser selection of specific availabilities in favor of *prepackaged availabilities*. These packages are a series of different shows that each participating advertiser *must* take on a rotation, with no substitutions. By packaging these rotations or *"orbit plans,"* stations can assure more equitable scheduling for all clients. Stations fear a few opportunistic advertisers would skim off all the best locations and leave the station to compete with only lower rated adjacencies. As advertisers become accustomed to these fixed rotations, the rotation method of selling spot television is accepted as a consequence of the market. Besides, it could be argued that rotations among different programs and different days can expose a greater number of different viewers. You might expect an "orbit" to be shown as follows:

Prime Orbit Plan (30-second)
$900 per 30

Position will rotate through the following programs:

Monday	10:00 pm	"Lou Grant"
Tuesday	9-11 pm	"CBS Movie"
Wednesday	10-11 pm	Specials
Sunday	7-8 p.m.	"60 Minutes"

Each announcement purchased would appear in all four positions in a month's time.

d. **ROS (Run of Station).** The lowest priced announcements are scheduled at station discretion. The advertiser, beyond requesting a maximum number of announcements per week, has little or no control over the program segments or even the dayparts scheduled for him. In periods of lower client activity, the ROS advertiser may find excellent scheduling at very favorable prices. In other times, ROS schedules may *not even be run*. Companies interested in broadly defined prospect groups and companies seeking a high number of announcements to run in a compressed period of time would be those most likely to seek ROS rates.

e. **GRID Rates.** This is the ultimate in rate card flexibility. No time periods are noted on the rate card, but rather a series of classes (grids) and prices for each class according to fixed or preemptible status. In this way the station gives only the *range* of prices, committing a price only when the buyer requires availabilities. The fluctuations in audience levels and advertiser demand are accommodated without change to the card. Here is an excerpt of a popular GRID format.

Class	F	P2	P1	P
1	25	20	15	10
2	45	40	35	30
3	65	60	55	50
4	85	80	75	70
5	105	100	95	90

F = Fixed
P2 = 2-weeks notice
P1 = 1-week notice
P = immediately preemtible

GRID cards are generally disliked by planners and estimators. Buyers experienced in the market can provide estimates based on recent availabilities.

Network Radio. National radio is making a serious resurgence through the development of evening drama shows and expanded coverage of national sports. The networks in radio are plentiful including NBC, CBS, and four separate network divisions for ABC (contemporary, information, entertainment, and FM). In addition there is the nonconnected Mutual system along with a number of other nonprogram networks. The latter cooperate on sales and billing rather than programming. Information on network radio rates is limited and buyers tend to depend on sales representatives for costs.

Spot Market Radio. Market-by-market radio pricing is very much like spot television in style of discounts and nonstandardized rate cards. There are some modifications that are worthy of note.

Rates are based on the length of the announcement and when the spot is scheduled. Beyond this there are several types of discounts offered.

a. **Yearly frequency.** Many smaller stations do *not* discriminate between time periods but base discounts on spots used per year.

Such a discount schedule would appear as follows:

Times/Year	Cost/60 Second
26X*	$15.00
130X	12.50
260X	11.00
520X	9.50

(*X = times)

If an advertiser wished a 40-week schedule and wanted fifteen spots per week, the buyer would use the 520-times rate since 600 (40 × 15) is sufficient to earn the 520 × discount.

b. **Weekly Package Plan.** A more popular discount sets the incentive on a weekly basis for number of announcements ordered per week. On a weekly package it is not necessary to use a long campaign to earn significant discounts. Here is a typical format:

Spots Per Week	Cost/Spot Announcement
12	$12.00
18	11.00
24	10.00
36	9.50

The weekly basis recognizes a large proportion of radio spot advertising is concentrated in short periods.

c. **Fixed/Preemptible Rates.** Following the lead of spot market television stations, popular stations in the more active radio markets offer discounts for advertiser schedules that may be moved by higher rates. The procedure operates identically with television by offering lower rates to advertisers who are willing to risk being displaced from a more popular program segment.

In radio the discounting is called "high range-low range," the high being the fixed position. A standard format might look like the following:

	Per Spot Cost					
	High Range			Low Range		
#/Week	AAA	AA	A	AAA	AA	A
6 Plan	150	90	60	125	75	45
12 Plan	145	85	55	120	70	40
18 Plan	140	80	50	115	65	35

AAA: 6-9 am; AA: 3-7 pm; A: 9-3 pm

Notice that this station, in effect, has three separate ways to discount announcements: by dayparts, by announcements per week, and by fixed or preemptible status.

d. **ROS.** Radio has made more use of the run of station discounts. As in television, the trade off is between price and the loss of guarantee on schedule position. The station has complete discretion on where announcements will run.

Out-of-Home Media. What was once thought of as outdoor billboards now includes painted bulletins, transit signs, and even aerial banners. However, outdoor schedules (paper and paint locations) are still dominant.

The basis for outdoor rental is the traffic (primarily auto and some on foot) passing the location. From this count, outdoor companies project the percentage of the market covered by a given list and number of location. Since such arrangements are made on a market-by-market basis, this is how outdoor is sold — city-by-city.

The cost factors for outdoor are: traffic count (the higher the more expensive), the size of the board, presence of illuminations (lighted by evening use), and whether the sign accepts paper or painted messages.

There are a number of sign variations, but most outdoor contracts involve these types:

a. **Poster panels.** The standardized unit adopted by the Outdoor Advertising Association of America is the 24- or 30-sheet poster. This unit approximately twelve feet high by twenty-four feet long and accepts preprinted message panels that are glued to the board.

b. **Painted bulletins.** This is the largest outdoor display averaging fourteen by forty-eight feet. Large displays are usually painted but recent developments in special inks have provided paper with the gloss and reflective quality of paint.

   Bulletins can be rented individually or in clusters which are physically moved from one preselected location to another at a 30- or 60-day interval.

Outdoor poster panels are sold in packages known as *showings*. Showings of various traffic intensity are offered, with the gross rating point as the yardstick. One GRP in outdoor (as it is in broadcast and magazine) is equal to 1 percent of a population. A standard outdoor purchase of a 100 GRP then means to deliver, in one day, exposure opportunities equal to 100 percent of the market's population. Showings are also offered in 75 percent and 50 percent levels. The standard contract period for outdoor is in *monthly increments*.

Cost for outdoor rental are made by the local companies. Buyers desiring quotations on a large number of markets contact the Institute of Outdoor Advertising or other association groups for reference.

The monitoring of outdoor advertising is an important dimension of outdoor evaluation. Checks must be made to assure expected visability levels. Weather, traffic detours and route changes, and obstructions all affect the motorists' ability to see the message. Firms with substantial advertising investments in outdoor use company representatives to "ride the showing" and report any problems. Considering the investment in outdoor advertising, this is a reasonable policy.

QUESTIONS

1. What are the primary skills associated with media buying?
2. Why are media buyers and planners anxious to have standardized rate card formats?
3. Explain the difference between newspaper discounts based on *bulk lineage* and those based on frequency of insertion.
4. How does a page-equivalent discount operate in magazine buying?
5. What are the trade-offs (benefits-risks) in using preemptible rates for broadcast spot buying?

APPENDICES

APPENDIX A FORMULAS FOR MEDIA CALCULATIONS

PRIMER FOR SOME MAJOR MEDIA PLANNING CALCULATIONS

The following pages outline in a simplified form how to calculate the most significant quantitative functions found in marketing/media planning. These are abridged from the text discussions and it is recommended that the text be read before using this primer.

CONTENTS

MARKETING

Market Development Indices (BDI/CDI)

BROADCAST MEDIA

Rating
Share of Audience
Cumulative Rating

PRINT MEDIA

Milline Rate (Newspaper)
Readers Per Copy (Magazines)

ALL MEDIA

Gross Rating Points
Cost Per Thousand
Reach
Frequency

BRAND DEVELOPMENT INDEX

Description: A comparative, market-by-market measure of a brand's sales performance.

Purpose: Used to decide the relative sales value of one market over another.

Figures Needed:*
a) The brand's sales per market (as percentage of total).
b) Population per market (as percentage of U.S.).

Formula:

$$\frac{\text{Market's brand sales} \times 100}{\text{Market's population in \%}} = \text{Brand development}$$

Steps:
1. Multiply markets sales percentage by 100
2. Divide the sales figure by market's percentage of population.
3. Repeat for all markets.
4. Rank order markets from highest BDI to lowest.

Illustration: Market A has 2.4 percent of brand sales and 3.8 percent of U.S. population. Market B has 2.9 percent sales and 3.0 percent U.S. population. Which market has the higher BDI?

$$\frac{2.4 \times 100}{3.8} = 63 \text{ Market A's BDI}$$

$$\frac{2.9 \times 100}{3.0} = 96.6 \text{ or } 97 \text{ Market B's BDI}$$

*BDI figures are not standardize. Firms use brand distribution, CSI, retail sales, and media coverage populations to compute BDI. Shown is the most basic style used.

CATEGORY DEVELOPMENT INDEX

Description: A comparative, market-by-market measure of a market's total sales (all brands).

Purpose: Used to evaluate the sales potential of a market for a single brand.

Figures Needed*:
a) Total sales of all brands in a market as a percentage of total U.S. sales.
b) Population of market as percentage of U.S.

Formula:

$$\frac{\text{Market's U.S. sales share in percent} \times 100}{\text{Market's population in percent}} = \text{CDI}$$

Steps:
1. Multiply market's total sales percentage by 100.
2. Divide the sales figure by the market's percentage of U.S. population.
3. Repeat calculation for all markets.
4. Rank order CDIs from highest to lowest.

Illustration: Market A's total sales accounts for 5.6 percent of U.S. sales from a population that is 2.6 percent of U.S. Market B is 3.1 percent sales and 1.2% population. Which has the higher CDI?

$$\frac{5.6 \times 100}{2.6} = 215 \text{ Market A's CDI}$$

$$\frac{2.6 \times 100}{1.2} = 216 \text{ Market B's CDI}$$

Note that the smaller market ranks better on CDI for potential. These indices reward effectiveness not size. CDI most valuable when used in conjunction with BDI.

*CDI not standardized. Firms use various marketing statistics for computation. Version shown here is the most basic but some include as many as five elements such as retail sales, percent category penetration (distribution) and some manipulate brand sales against total sales.

BROADCAST RATING

Description: Percentage of a market's population (e.g., homes, adults, men, women, etc.) tuned to a specific program at a given time.

Purpose: This measure indicates the *size* of the program audience.

Figures Needed:

a) Population tuned to program.
b) Total population of the audience group.

Formula:

$$\frac{\text{Audience tuned to program} \times 100}{\text{Total audience population}} = \text{Rating percentage}$$

Steps:

1. From research find estimated viewers/listener audience.
2. Multiply audience by 100.
3. Divide audience figure by the total possible population of that audience.

Illustration: Toonerville has 45,000 adults in its survey area. An audience report shows that during the first Tuesday in October this program had an average audience of 9,200. What is the adult rating for the program?

$$\frac{9{,}200 \times 100}{45{,}000} = 20.4\% \text{ Adult Rating}$$

Ratings can be done on any audience segment as long as there is a total measure of the audience and a program survey has measured the audience segment as a total population.

BROADCAST SHARE OF AUDIENCE

Description: Percentage of viewers/listeners tuned to a particular program at a given time.

Purpose: Indicates the popularity of one program over another at a given time.

Figures Needed:

a) Number of sets of people tuned to a particular program.
b) Total number of sets or people tuned in *at the time.*

Formula:

$$\frac{\text{Program's audience} \times 100}{\text{Total audience tuned at the time}} = \text{Share of audience}$$

Steps:

1. From research find estimated viewers/listeners.
2. Multiply audience figure by 100.
3. From research find total estimated viewers/listeners tuned that are the combined audiences from all programs on at the time.
4. Divide the program audience by the total tune-in.

Illustration: Here is an excerpt from the Toonerville radio audience survey:

Monday 11 — 11:30 A.M.

Station	Listeners
X	200
Y	300
Z	500
	1000

What is the share of audience for station "Z"?

0500 1200

$$\frac{500 \times 100}{1000} = 50.0\% \quad \text{Share of Audience}$$

RADIO CUMULATIVE RATING (Cume)

Description: Percentage of different people or homes hearing a daypart segment during the week.

Purpose: Indicates the potential size of a station's audience during a week. In another way it is used to measure the reach (unduplicated listenership).

Figures Needed:

a) Total different listeners hearing a daypart segment on a Monday-Friday or Monday-Sunday basis.
b) Total possible listeners in station's survey area.

Note: Audience figures must be perfectly compatible, i.e., the same demographic category.

Formula:

$$\frac{\text{Unduplicated listenership by daypart} \times 100}{\text{Total population of listenership}} = \text{Cume Ratio}$$

Steps:

1. Find daypart cume audience in rating report.
2. Multiply cume audience by 100

3. Divide audience figure by the total population of the particular audience segment chosen.

Illustration: Station X has a cumulative audience of 4,100 unduplicated adult listeners tuning in at least once between Monday and Sunday 6 to 10 A.M. If there are 11,500 adults in the survey area, what is the cume rating for that period?

$$\frac{4{,}100 \times 100}{11{,}500} = 35.65\% \text{ Cume rating}$$

Comment: Cume is a *potential* measure only. To expect to expose all of the 35.65 percent adults in the example, the advertiser would have to schedule an announcement each quarter hour throughout the week. That would be sixteen quarter hours each day and seven days or 112 announcements each week to "guarantee" reaching the cume potential.

NEWSPAPER MILLINE RATE

Description: Comparative (efficiency) relationship between the size of the newspaper's circulation and the cost of one line (one-fourteenth inch deep by a column wide).

Purpose: Used to compare the price efficiency of one newspaper with another.

Figures Needed:

a) Average circulation.
b) Cost of one line of advertising. Note the rate can be open or discount rates as long as all papers are measured the same way.

Formula:

$$\frac{\text{Line rate} \times 1{,}000{,}000}{\text{Circulation}} = \text{Milline rate}$$

Steps:

1. Select appropriate line rate. Usually the open rate or a discount rate that is reasonable to earn.
2. Multiply the line rate by a million. This is done to avoid nasty decimals and to make newspapers of various sizes easier to compare.
3. Divide the adjusted line cost by the circulation.
4. Repeat with all candidate newspapers.

Illustration: The Toonerville Trolley News has an open line rate of $1.98 on an average daily paid circulation of 146,000. What is its milline rate?

$$\frac{\$1.98 \times 1{,}000{,}000}{146{,}000} = \$13.56$$

MAGAZINE READERS PER COPY

Description: The average number of different readers who will come in contact with the average issue of a publication.

Purpose: Indicates the relation between circulation and the size of the reading audience. Many advertisers are suspicious of magazines with high RPC believing the primary reader (purchaser) is the best prospect. Further, some feel that all other readers do *not* read with the same interest or dedication that the purchaser does. On the other hand some advertisers value a high RPC because it suggests to them a high reach potential.

Figuref needed:

a) Average readers of a typical issue of the magazine.
b) Average paid circulation.

Formula:

$$\frac{\text{Total readers of an average issue}}{\text{Circulation of an average issue}} = \text{Readers per copy (RPC)}$$

Step:

1. Once you have the readership and the circulation, divide the readers by the circulation.

Illustration: Magazine has an average paid circulation of 895,000 and an average issue readership of 3,675,000. How many readers does it have per copy sold?

$$\frac{3{,}675{,}000}{895{,}000} = 4.10 \text{ Readers per copy (RPC)}$$

GROSS RATING POINTS

Description: Means of expressing the cumulative (duplicated) audience impressions developed by using a series of vehicles. Typical examples include the combined audiences from: a series of magazine insertions, a package of television announcements, and an outdoor posting schedule.

Purpose: GRP calculations have several uses. Used to represent the gross percentage of audience rating. Also used to calculate the average frequency of exposure (see that discussion further on). Most importantly, GRP concept has been adapted to media planning as a shorthand measure of advertising impact.

Figures Needed:

a) Audience value of each vehicle expressed as a percentage. Remember, all ratings must be of the same audience category. You cannot mix women rating points with adults or homes, etc.
b) The number times each vehicle is used within the specified time period (usually four weeks).

Formula: Audience value (Percent) × Schedule = GRPs.

Steps:

1. Find the rating values of each vehicle. If data are raw numbers, convert to percentages using the steps shown in broadcast ratings.
2. Multiply the rating values of each vehicle by the number of times it appears in the schedule.
3. Add the multiplied rating values for a total GRP figure for the period.

Illustrations:

Radio Example:

Daypart	Rating	× Spots per Week	GRP
M-F 6—10 A.M.	2.0	10	20.0
Sat. 3—8 P.M.	1.5	5	7.5
		Total GRP per Week	27.5

Magazine Examples:

Publication	Average Issue Adult Women Readers	×	# Insertions	GRP
X	15.0		6	90.0
Y	19.0		4	76.0
Z	24.0		12	288.0
			Yearly Gross Ratings	454.0

COST PER THOUSAND

Description: Calculation to represent the relationship between the size of a media vehicle's audience and its cost in time or space.

Purpose: Used to measure the efficiency of a media opportunity or the standard of gaining the largest audience of prospects for the lowest cost.

Figures Needed:

a) Gross impressions of the media vehicle. This is the estimated count of homes or people exposed. If vehicle figures are in GRPs you can convert to impressions by multiplying the GRP by the base population. That is, if you had a market TV schedule in GRPs to find impressions just multiply the GRP figure times the representative group (e.g., homes or adults) in the survey area.
b) Cost of the space or time unit. Production costs are not included unless they are a cost imposed by the media company.

Formula:

$$\frac{\text{Cost of media vehicle} \times 1000}{\text{Gross audience impressions}} = \text{CPM}$$

Steps:

1. Determine gross impressions and multiply by 1000.
2. Divide unit cost by gross impressions.

Illustration: A 30-second participation in a prime time movie (TV) costs $250. The Toonerville rating book shows 28,000 adult women viewers. What is the CPM adult female viewers?

$$\frac{\$250 \times 1000}{28{,}000} = \$8.928 \text{ or } \$8.93 \text{ CPM women viewers}$$

The advertiser will pay $8.93 for each 1000 female viewers that view the prime time movie.

UNDUPLICATED REACH

Description: Represents through statistics the probabilities of exposing a percentage of the homes or people with a media vehicle. Reach is calculated within a specified period of time, usually four weeks.

Purpose: Used to estimate how many different prospects might be exposed to an advertising schedule. Advertisers believe the "size" of a vehicle's audience is dependent upon the vehicle's ability to attract "new" audiences over time.

Figures Needed:

a) Audience research must provide the estimated unduplicated audience figures. Such figures or formulas to calculate them are generally available . . . see text.
b) Base audience population. Since reach is a percentage the net audience must be compared to the highest possible which is the universe or base figure.

Formula:

Single Vehicle Reach.

$$\frac{\text{Unduplicated audience impressions}}{\text{Base population}} = \text{Vehicle reach}$$

Multiple Vehicle Reach. Combining various reaches for a schedule estimate.

Reach % of Vehicle A − Reach % of Vehicle B

(−) minus

Reach % of Vehicle A × Reach % of Vehicle B

Combined Reach of Vehicles A and B

Note: If three or more reaches are to be combined, begin with the combined figure for AB and work it with Vehicle C as the formula shows. SEE ILLUSTRATION BELOW.

Illustration:

Advertiser has three magazines on his schedule; A has reach of 21, B has reach of 15 and C is 11. What is the combined audience of the three?

(A) .21 + (B) .15 = .36
minus
(A) .21 × (B) .15 = .03
AB Reach .33 or 33%

and to combine AB with C —
(AB) .33 + (C) .11 = .44
minus
(AB) .33 × (C) .11 = .04
ABC .40 or 40%

THIS MULTIPLE VEHICLE CALCULATION IS FOR ROUGH ESTIMATE ONLY. IT IS NOT SENSITIVE FOR KNOWN VEHICLES BECAUSE IT DOES NOT RECOGNIZE VARYING DEGREES OF OVERLAP OF AUDIENCE.

AVERAGE FREQUENCY OF EXPOSURE

Description: This calculation reports the repetition of exposure to a vehicle or a schedule of vehicles. It is the number of times the average audience exposed will likely see/hear the message within a specified period of time, usually four weeks.

Purpose: Frequency is the twin of reach. That is, frequency is learned to assure that a satisfactory proportion of the audience reached will have sufficient repeat exposure to remember or react to the message.

Figures Needed:

a) Gross impressions of a vehicle(s). The impressions can be in raw form or in the GRP state.
b) Net impressions of a vehicle(s). This is the unduplicated audience over the same period. Again, figures can be raw or expressed as reach (percentage).

Formula:

Single Vehicle

$$\frac{\text{Gross impressions}}{\text{Net impressions}}$$

or

$$\frac{\text{GRP}}{\text{Reach}}$$

Multiple Vehicles (for combined frequency)

$$\frac{\text{Reach of vehicle A} \times \text{Frequency of vehicle A} + \text{(plus)} \text{ Reach of vehicle B} \times \text{Frequency of vehicle B}}{\text{Combined reach of AB}}$$

Illustrations: Single Vehicle. A magazine has an average single issue audience of 20 percent (reach). But over four issues the reach of men will be 30 percent. If the advertiser uses four issues what is the average frequency?

$$\text{GRP Reach} = 20 \times 4 = \frac{80}{30} = 2.2 \text{ Avg. frequency}$$

Multiple Vehicles (combined frequency) Radio station WXXX will reach 15 percent of Toonerville homes with a 6.5 frequency according to the advertiser's schedule. If station WZZZ is added with a schedule equal to a 20 percent reach and a 7.0 average frequency what will the combined frequency be?

$$\frac{\text{(WXXX) } 15.0 \times 6.5 + \text{(WZZZ) } 20.0 \times 7.0}{\text{(WXXX/WZZZ) } 32.0}$$

$$\frac{97.5 + 140.0}{32.0} = \frac{237.5}{32.0} = 7.42 \text{ Combined avg. frequency}$$

*The combined reach of 20 percent and 15 percent is 32 percent according to our reach formula. See if your calculation agrees.

APPENDIX B

GLOSSARY OF ADVERTISING MEDIA TERMS

Across the board — a program broadcast at the same time period every day (see "Strip").

Adjacency — program or commercial announcement adjacent to another on the same station, either preceding or following the other.

Affiliate — broadcast station which grants a network an option on specific times for broadcasting network programming.

Agate line — newspaper advertising space one column wide by one-fourteenth of an inch deep.

Agency commission — usually 15 percent allowed to advertising agencies by media on the agencies' purchase of space or time.

Agency recognition — acknowledgement by media owners that certain agencies are good credit risks and/or fulfill certain requirements, and therefore qualify for a commission.

Allotment — number and type of outdoor posters in a showing (see "Showing").

Alternate sponsorship — two advertisers sponsoring a single program; one advertiser sponsors one week and the other sponsors the alternate weeks (see "Crossplugs").

Announcement — an advertising message broadcast between programs (see "station break," "participation," "ID," "billboard") or an advertisement within syndicated programs of feature films; any broadcast commercial, regardless of time length, within or between programs which presents an advertiser's message or a public service message.

ARB (American Research Bureau) — one of several national firms engaged in radio and television research; the ARB ratings service is called ARBitron.

Area of Dominant Influence (ADI) — ARB measurement area comprising those counties in which stations of the originating market account for a greater share of the viewing households than those from any other market; similar in concept to Nielsen's Designated Market Area.

Audience — persons who receive an advertisement; individuals who read a newspaper or magazine, listen to a radio broadcast, view a television broadcast, etc.

Audience accumulation — the total number of different persons or households exposed to a single media vehicle over a period of time.

Audience composition — audience analysis in demographic or other characteristics.

Audience duplication — those persons or households who see an advertisement more than once in a single media vehicle or in a combination of vehicles.

Audience flow — the movement of a broadcast audience from one program to another when the program change, measured against the audience that stays tuned to the same station or network to view the new program.

Audience profile — the minute-by-minute viewing pattern for a program; a description of the characteristics of the people exposed to a medium (see "Profile").

Audience turnover — that part of a broadcast audience that changes over time.

Audimeter — A. C. Nielsen Company's automatic device attached to radio or television receivers that records usage and station information.

Availability — a broadcast time period available for purchase by an advertiser (slang "avail").

Average audience — number of broadcast homes tuned for an average minute of a broadcast.

Average frequency of exposure — average number of times that an audience has been exposed to an advertisement, usually during a 4-week period.

Average net paid circulation — mean number of copies that a publication sells per issue.

Back-to-back — two programs or commercials in succession.

BAR (Broadcast Advertisers Report) — a commercial broadcast monitoring service available on a network and market-by-market basis.

Barter — an advertising medium selling time or space in return for merchandise or other nonmonetary returns.

Billboard —outdoor poster; cast and production information following a broadcast program; 6-second radio commercial; short commercial announcement, usually eight or ten seconds, at the start and close of a program announcing the name of the sponsor.

Billing — the value of advertising handled by an advertising agency for its clients.

Bleed — printing to the edge of the page, with no margin.

Block — consecutive broadcast time periods.

Booking — scheduling a broadcast program or commercial.

Brand Development Index (BDI) — A comparative measurement of a brand's sales in one market compared to other markets, used to decide the relative sales value of one market versus another.

Break — time available for purchase between two programs or between segments of a show.

Broadcast rating — see "Rating."

Bulk discount — discount offered by media for quantity buys.

Business paper — publication intended for business or professional interests.

Buyer — see "Media buyer" and "Media planner."

Buying service — a company primarily engaged in the purchase of media for advertising purposes; supplants part of the advertising agency media function; also called "media-buying specialist."

Call letters — the letters that identify a station; e.g., WBZ-TV.

Campaign — specific advertising effort on behalf of a particular product or service that extends for a specified period of time.

Car card — transit advertisement in or on a bus or subway car.

Card rate — cost of time or space on a rate card.

Cash discount — discount of 2 percent by media to advertisers who pay promptly.

Category Development Index (CDI) — a comparative market-by-market measure of market's total sales of all brands of a product category, used to evaluate the sales potential of a market for a single brand.

Center spread — advertisement appearing on two facing pages printed on a single sheet in the center of a publication.

Chain — a broadcast network; also, a newspaper or magazine "chain" of single ownership or control.

Chain break (CB) — time during which the network allows a station to identify itself; usually a 20-second spot (slang "twenty").

Checking — process of confirming if an advertisement actually ran.

Checking copy — copy of a publication supplied by the medium to show that an advertisement appeared as specified.

Circulation — in print, the number of copies distributed; in broadcast, the number of households within a signal area that have receiving sets; in outdoor, the number of people who have a reasonable opportunity to see a billboard.

City zone circulation — number of newspapers distributed in a city, rather than in suburban or outlying areas.

Class magazines — special-interest magazines with desirable audiences.

Classified advertising — advertising set in small type arranged according to categories.

Clear time — process of reserving time or time periods with a station or network; checking on available time.

Closing date — final deadline set by print media for advertising material to appear in a certain issue; in broadcast, the term "closing hour" may be used.

Column-inch — publication space one column wide by one inch high, used as a measure of advertising space.

Combination rate — special rate for advertising in two or more publications owned by the same interests.

Commercial impressions — total audience, including duplication, for all commercial announcements in an advertiser's schedule.

Confirmation — broadcast media stating that a specific time is still open to an advertiser.

Contiguity rates — reduced broadcast rates for sponsoring two or more programs in succession; e.g., an advertiser participating in two programs running from 7:00—7:30 and from 7:30—8:00 may earn a contiguity rate.

Controlled circulation — nonpaid circulation that is limited to persons who qualify to receive a publication.

Cooperative advertising — retail advertising paid partly or fully by a manufacturer; two or more manufacturers cooperating in a single advertisement; slang "co-op."

Cooperative announcement — commercial time made available in network programs to stations for sale to local or national advertisers.

Cooperative program — network broadcast sold on a local basis and sponsored by national and local advertisers; e.g., "The Tonight Show."

Cost per thousand (CPM) — a dollar comparison showing the relative cost of various media or vehicles; relationship.

CPM/PCM — cost per thousand per commerical minute.

Cover positions — advertisements on covers of publications, often at a premium cost; 1st cover = outside front dover; 2nd cover = inside front cover; 3rd cover = inside back cover; 4th cover = outside back cover.

Coverage — number or percent of individuals or households exposed to a medium or to a campaign.

Cowcatcher — brief announcement at the beginning of a broadcast program.

Crossplugs — in alternating sponsorship, permitting each advertiser to insert one announcement into the program during the weeks when the other advertiser is the sponsor, maintaining weekly exposure.

Cumulative audience (cume) — cumulative broadcast rating; the net unduplicated audience of a station or network during two or more time periods; also used to describe how many different households or people an advertiser's schedule reaches (also called "accumulative audience," "net audience," and "unduplicated audience"); technically, a cumulative audience is those persons who saw any insertion of an advertisement in multiple editions of a single vehicle, whereas unduplicated audience is those persons who saw any insertion of an advertisement in a combination of vehicles or media, counting each person only once.

Cumulative rating (slang "cume") — percentage of different people or homes hearing a daypart segment during a 1-week period.

Cumulative reach — number of different households reached by a medium or campaign during a specific time.

Dayparts — specific segments of a broadcast day; e.g., morning, afternoon, early evening, mid-evening, late night.

Dealer imprint — inserting local dealer's identification into nationally prepared advertising.

Dealer tie-in — manufacturer's advertisement which lists local dealers; not the same as "co-op."

Demographic characteristics — population characteristics of a group or audience.

Designated Market Area (DMA) — term used by A. C. Nielsen Company: an area based on those counties in which stations of the originating market account for a greater share of the viewing households than those form any other area (see "ADI"); e.g., Lake County, Illinois, belongs to the Chicago DMA because a majority of household viewing is or can be ascribed to Chicago stations rather than to Milwaukee stations.

Direct advertising — advertising under complete control of the advertiser, rather than through some established medium; e.g., direct mail, free sampling, etc.

Direct mail advertising — advertising sent by mail.

Directory advertising — advertising in a buying guide or directory; advertisements in a store directory.

Display advertising — print advertising which is intended to attract attention and communicate easily through the use of space, illustrations, layout, headlines, etc., as opposed to classified advertising.

Display classified advertising — classified advertising of larger size than most classified advertising, possibly with headlines, illustrations, etc.

Double spotting — two broadcast commercials within one commercial time segment; usually, two 30-second commercials (or one 40-second and one 20-second commercial) within a 1-minute time slot (also called "piggybacking").

Drive time — high radio listenership times during local drivers' and commuters' "rush hours."

Due bill — see "Barter."

Effective circulation — those persons with reasonable opportunity to see an outdoor display.

End rate — lowest rate an advertiser pays after all discounts have been applied.

Estimating — process of determining approximate cost of a proposed advertising media schedule.

Facing text matter — in print, a position opposite reading or editorial matter; may have a premium price.

Farm publication — publication edited for farmers or farm families.

Field intensity map — broadcast coverage map indicating the possible quality of reception of the signal; also called a "contour map."

15 and 2 — discounts allowed by media; 15 percent commission to advertising agencies on time and space charges, and 2 percent discount to the advertiser for prompt payment (usually within ten says).

Fixed location — same print advertisement position in every issue.

Fixed rate — maximum rate paid by an advertiser for a broadcast spot to insure that it runs in that position without preemption by higher-rate advertisers; for stations which use sectional rate designations, Section I is the fixed rate, Section II is preemptible time with a 2-week notice, and Section III is immediately preemtible time.

Flat rate — print advertising rate not subject to discount.

Flight (flight saturation) — concentrating advertising within a short time period; an advertising campaign which runs for a specified number of weeks, followed by a period of inactivity (called a "hiatus") after which the campaign resumes.

Floating time — see "ROS."

Fractional page space — advertising space of less than a full page.

Fractional showing — an outdoor showing of less than #25.

Free circulation — publication sent without charge; often controlled circulation.

Frequency — number of times an individual or household is exposed to an advertisement or campaign; the number of times a message is run.

Frequency discount — reduced rate offered by media to advertisers who run a certain number of advertisements within a given time.

Fringe time — broadcast time periods preceding or following prime time; television time between daytime and nighttime is called "early fringe," and television time following prime time is called "late fringe."

Full showing (full run) — number of outdoor posters required to reach all of the mobile population in a market at least once within a 30-day period (see "Gross Rating Points"); one transit car card in every transit bus or car; also called a #100 showing in outdoor.

General magazine — consumer magazine not aiming at a special-interest audience.

Grid card — spot broadcast rates set in matrix format to allow station to set rates based on current audience ratings and buying demand; example,

	60-sec.	30-/20-sec.	10-sec.
A	$250	$175	$125
B	245	172	123
C	240	170	121
Etc.	...	...	...

Gross audience — total number of households or people delivered by an advertising schedule without regard to any possible duplication that may occur; also called "total audience."

Gross billing — cost of advertising at the highest card rate; total value of an advertising agency's space and time dealings (see "billing").

Gross rate — highest possible rate for advertising time or space.

Gross rating points (GRP) — total number of broadcast rating points delivered by an advertiser's broadcast schedule, usually in a 1-week period; a means of expressing the cumulative (unduplicated) audience impressions developed by using a series of vehicles; in outdoor, a standard audience level of 1 percent of the market's population, upon which some market rates are based.

Half run — transit car cards in half the buses or transit cars.

Half showing — a #50 outdoor showing.

Hiatus — a period during a campaign when an advertiser's schedule is suspended for a period of time, after which it resumes.

Holdover audience — those persons tuned to a program who stayed tuned to that station or network after watching or listening to the preceding program.

Horizontal cume — total number of different people who were tuned in to broadcast programs at the same time on different days of the week.

Horizontal publication — business or trade publication of interest at one level or to one job function in a variety of businesses.

House agency — advertising agency owned or controlled by an advertiser.

HUR — households using radio; see "sets in use."

HUT — households using television; see "sets in use."

ID — spot television commercial eight to ten seconds long during a station break; the last two seconds on the visual time may be reserved for showing the station call letters; a 10-second commercial announcement, sometimes referred to as a "ten."

Impact — the degree to which an advertisement or campaign affects its audience intrusively; the amount of space (full-page, half-page) or of time (60-second, 30-second) which is purchased, as opposed to reach and frequency; see "Unit."

Independent station — broadcast station that is not affiliated with a network.

Index — numerical value assigned to quantitative data for easy comparison; usually, 100 = the average, or 0 = a baseline measurement.

Insert — advertisement enclosed with bills or letters; advertisement (often multi-page) bound as a unit into a publication.

Insertion order — statement from advertising agency to medium which accompanies copy and indicates specifications of the advertisement.

Island position — print advertisement surrounded by editorial matter; print advertisement not adjacent to any other advertising; placing a broadcast commercial away from any other commercial, with program content before and after.

Junior unit — permitting an advertiser to use a print advertisement prepared for a smaller page size to run in a publication with a larger page size, with editorial matter around it in the extra space; using a *Reader's Digest*-sized page in a larger magazine is often called a "Digest unit."

Key — a code in an advertisement to facilitate tracing which advertisement produced an inquiry or order.

Kinescope — a film of a television broadcast.

Life — length of time during which an advertisement is used; length of time a publication is retained by its audience.

Linage — in print, the number of agate lines to be used for an advertisement or for a series of advertisements.

Line — see "Agate line."

List broker — agent who rents the use of mailing lists.

Local rate — advertising rate offered by media to local advertisers that is lower than the rate offered to national advertisers.

LOH (Ladies of the House) — term used by A. C. Nielsen Company in its reports, referring to the female heads of households.

Magazine concept — buying a certain number of broadcast announcements from a station with a certain guaranteed audience level, without selecting specific times or programs.

Magazine readers per copy — see "Readers per copy."

Mail-order advertising — advertisements intended to induce direct ordering of merchandise through the mail; the advertisements themselves are not necessarily direct-mail advertisements.

Make-good — a repeat of an advertisement to compensate for an error, omission, or technical difficulty in the original.

Market — see "Target market" and "Target group;" a city or area in which a product or service is to be sold.

Market potential — the reasonable maximum market share that a product can be expected to achieve.

Market profile — demographic description of the people or households that are prospects for a product or service.

Market share — a company's or brand's portion of the sales of a generic product.

Maximil rate — cost of a line of advertising space at the highest milline rate.

Media buyer — person responsible for purchasing advertising space or time.

Media planner — person responsible for determining the proper use of an advertising medium or combination of media to fulfill the marketing and promotional objectives for a specific product or advertiser.

Merchandising — promotion of an advertiser's products, services, and the like to the sales force, wholesalers, and dealers; promotion other than advertising to consumers through in-store displays, guarantees, services, point-of-purchase materials, etc.; display and promotion of retail goods.

Metro rating — broadcast rating figure for a Standard Metropolitan Statistical Area (see "SMSA").

Milline rate — comparing line rates of newspapers with uneven circulation by figuring the line rate per million circulation; determined by multiplying the line rate by 1,000,000 and dividing by the circulation.

Minimil rate — cost of a line of advertising at the lowest possible milline rate.

Net — money paid to a medium by an advertising agency after deducting the agency's commission; slang for "network."

Net unduplicated audience — the number of different persons reached by single issues of two or more publications.

Network cooperative program — network program with provisions for inserting local commercials.

Network option time — broadcast time on a station for which the network has the option of selling advertising.

Newspaper milline rate — see "Milline rate."

Next to reading matter — print advertising position adjacent to editorial material; may be at premium rates.

Nielsen — the A. C. Nielsen Company; a firm engaged in local and national television ratings and other marketing research.

NSI — abbreviation for Nielsen Station Index rating service for individual television stations.

NTI — abbreviation for Nielsen Television Index national television rating service.

O&O station — a broadcasting station that is "owned and operated" by a network.

One-time rate — see "Open rate."

Open-end transcription — a transcribed broadcast with time for the insertion of local commercials.

Open rate — the highest advertising rate before discounts are earned; also called "basic rate" and "one-time rate."

OTO — abbreviation for "one time only;" a commercial announcement that runs only once.

Overrun — additional copies of an advertisement beyond the number actually ordered or needed, to replace damaged posters or car cards.

Package — series of broadcast programs that an advertiser may sponsor as a group.

Package plan discount — spot television discount plans for buying a certain number of spots.

Participation — announcement within a program as compared with one scheduled between programs.

Participation program — broadcast program with each segment sponsored by a different advertiser.

Pass-along readers — readers of a publication who acquire a copy other than by purchase or subscription; see "Secondary audience."

Penetration — the percentage of households which have a broadcast receiving set; degree of advertising effectiveness.

Piggyback — see "Double spotting."

Pilot — sample production of a proposed broadcast program series.

Plans board — advertising agency committee which approves campaign plans for clients.

Plug — free mention of a product or service.

Point-of-purchase advertising (POP) — advertising (usually displays) in retail stores.

Position — the location of an advertisement on a page; the time when a program or commercial will run in a broadcast; special position may cost premium prices.

Potential audience — the maximum possible audience.

Preemptible rate — rate subject to cancellation by another advertiser paying a higher rate; the protection period varies by station, and ranges from no notice to 2-weeks notice; see "Fixed rate."

Preemption — cancellation of a broadcast program for special material or news; the right of a station or network to cancel a regular program in order to run a special program; a commercial spot that may be replaced by another spot if another advertiser pays a higher or "fixed" rate.

Premium — item offered to help promote a product or service.

Premium price — special advertising rate for special positions or other considerations.

Preprint — advertising material printed ahead of the regular press run, perhaps on another press with greater capability for color, etc.

Primary audience — individuals in print audience who purchase or subscribe to the publication; see "Secondary audience."

Primary households — households in which a publication has been purchased or subscribed to.

Primary listening area — area to which broadcast transmission is static-free and easily received.

Primary readers — those persons who purchase or subscribe to a publication; readers in primary households.

Prime time — the hours when viewing is at its peak on television; usually the evening hours.

Production protection — time separation between the airing of broadcast commercials for competitive products.

Profile — used interchangeably with "audience composition" to describe demographic characteristics of audiences.

Program compatibility — programming or editorial content that is suitable for the product or service being promoted.

Projected audience size — the number of viewers, either in total or per receiving set, based on the sample for the rating.

Publisher's statement — the certified circulation of a publication, attested by the publisher.

Qualified circulation — distribution of a publication that is restricted to individuals who meet certain requirements.

Qualified reader — a person who can prove that he read a publication.

Quantity discount — lower advertising rate for buying a certain amount of space or time.

Quarter-run — one-fourth of the car cards required for a full run in transit.

Quintile — one-fifth of a group; usage in broadcast often refers to viewers divided into five equal groups (quintiles), ranging from the heaviest to the lightest viewers.

Radio cumulative rating — see "Cumulative rating."

Rate — charge for media space or time.

Rate book — a book designed to provide advertising rates; e.g., Standard Rate & Data Service.

Rate card — a printed listing of media rates for a vehicle.

Rate differential — the difference between local and national advertising rates.

Rate holder — small print advertisement taken by an advertiser to meet contract requirements for earning a discounted rate.

Rate protection — length of time an advertiser is guaranteed an advertising rate without an increase.

Rating — percentage of broadcast potential audience tuned to a particular station, network, or program.

Reach — total audience which a medium covers; total number of people in the audience (see also "unduplicated reach").

Reader interest — expression of interest through inquiries, coupons, etc.; level of interest in various products.

Readers per copy — the average number of different readers who will come into contact with the average issue of a publication.

Readership — percent or number of persons who read a publication or advertisement.

Reading notice — print advertisement intended to resemble editorial matter.

Rebate — payment by the medium to an advertiser who has earned a lower rate than originally contracted.

Reminder advertising — brief advertisements, often to supplement other advertising, intended to keep the product name before the public.

Rep — a media representative; slang for national sales representative.

Retail trading zone — geographic area in which most of the population makes the majority of their retail purchases.

ROP — abbreviation for "run of paper;" advertising positioned anywhere in a publication.

ROP color — color printed during the regular press run.

Run-of-schedule (ROS) — commercial announcements which can be scheduled at the station's discretion anytime during the period specified by the advertiser; e.g., ROS 10:00 A.M.—4:30 P.M. Monday through Friday.

Satellite station — a station in a fringe reception area to boost the effective range of the main station's signal.

Saturation — media schedule of wide reach and high frequency concentrated during a time period to achieve maximum coverage and impact.

Scatter plan — announcements scheduled at a variety of times in broadcast media.

Schedule — list of advertisements or media to be used in a campaign.

Schedule and estimate — a data form submitted by the advertising agency to the client prior to a firm media purchase; contains price and audience data, and proposed schedule.

Secondary audience — members of a print audience who do not subscribe to or purchase the publication; see "Pass-along readers."

Secondary listening area — outlying area to which broadcast transmission is subject to fading or static; in television, the Grade 3 signal contour.

Self-liquidating point-of-purchase — display for which the retailer pays part or all of the costs.

Self-liquidating premium — item for which the cost is paid by the consumer; the price the consumer pays covers the manufacturing cost of the premium.

Self-mailer — a direct mail piece that is mailed without an envelope.

Sets in use — percentage of households with broadcast receiving sets operating at one time in a market; because many households have more than one receiving set, "HUR" and "HUT" are often used.

Share of audience ("share") — percentage of sets-in-use that are tuned to a particular station, network, or program.

Shopping newspaper — newspaper devoted mainly to advertising, often distributed free to all shoppers or to all households; also called "shoppers."

Short rate — money owed to a medium by an advertiser to offset the rate differential between the earned rate and the higher contracted rate.

Showing — number of outdoor posters necessary to reach a certain percentage of the mobile population within a specified time; many outdoor markets are now purchased by Gross Rating Points; see "Full showing" and "Gross rating points."

Sixty — slang for a 1-minute commercial.

SNR — abbreviation for "subject to nonrenewal;" commercial time that is available if the current advertiser does not renew.

Soap opera — slang for a broadcast dramatic series, usually a daytime program.

Space buyer — person responsible for purchasing advertising in newspapers, magazines, business publications, and sometimes outdoor and transit.

Space position value — effectiveness of an outdoor poster location.

Spectacular — large outdoor lighted sign.

Split run — testing two or more advertisements by running each only to a portion of the audience in a single issue.

Sponsor — advertiser who buys the exclusive right to the time available for commercials in a given program or segment.

Spot — the purchase of broadcast slots by geographical or station breakdowns; purchase of slots at certain times, usually during station breaks; "spot" can refer to the time used for the commercial announcement, or it can refer to the announcement itself.

Standard Metropolitan Statistical Area (SMSA) — an area consisting of a central city of 50,000 population or more, plus the economically and socially integrated surrounding area, as set by the federal government; usually limited by county boundaries.

Station break — time between broadcast programs to permit station identification and spot announcements; slang for a 20-second broadcast commercial.

Station clearance — see "Clear time."

Station identification — announcement of station call letters, usually with broadcast frequency or channel and station location.

Station option time — broadcast time for which the station has the option of selling advertising.

Station posters — advertisements consisting of posters in transit stations.

Strip — a program or commercial scheduled at the same time of day on successive days of the week, either Monday through Friday or Monday through Sunday; see "Across the board."

Sunday supplement — newspaper section in magazine format; also called "magazine supplement" or "magazine section."

Sustaining period — period of time during an advertising campaign when advertisements are used to remind the audience of the product or of the campaign; usually a time of reduced advertising expenditures following the introductory flight.

Sweep — the period of the year when a rating service measures the broadcast audience in the majority of markets throughout the country; e.g., surveys scheduled for November 2 — November 24 would be referred to as the "November sweep."

Tabloid — a newspaper of the approximate size of a standard newspaper folded in half.

Tag — dealer identification usually added to the end of a broadcast commercial to advise viewers where the product being advertised can be purchased in that market.

Target group — those persons at whom a campaign is directed; individuals with similar characteristics who are prospects for a product or service.

Target market — the geographic area or areas to which a campaign is directed; the areas where a product is being sold or introduced.

Tearsheet — a page with an advertiser's message, sent to the advertiser for approval or for checking.

Teaser — advertisements preceding the major part of a campaign intended to build curiosity.

Ten — slang for a 10-second commercial.

Thirty — slang for a 30-second commercial.

Tie-in — see "Cooperative advertising" and "Dealer tie-in."

Time buyer — person responsible for purchasing advertising on radio and television.

Time sheet — used by a time buyer to keep track of the data on a buy; also called a "buy sheet."

Total audience — the number of homes or individuals tuned to a program for six minutes or longer.

Trade paper — specialized publication for a specific profession, trade, or industry.

Traffic count — the number of persons who pass an outdoor panel location.

Trim size — final magazine page size after trimming.

Turnover — the frequency with which the audience for a broadcast program changes over a period of time; see "Audience turnover."

Twenty — slang for a 20-second commerical; also see a "Chain break" or "Station break."

Two-page spread — single print advertisement crossing two facing pages; also called "double "Double spread" or "Double truck."

Unduplicated audience — see "Cumulative audience."

Unduplicated reach — a statistical representation of the probability of exposing a percentage of the homes or the people with a media vehicle. Reach is calculated for a specific period of time, usually four weeks.

Unit (advertising unit) — the form and context in which an advertisement appears in a vehicle; e.g., full-page, half-page vertical, center spread, back cover, 20-second commercial, 10-second ID.

Vehicle — advertising media outlet, such as a certain magazine or a specific station.

Vertical cume — total number of different people who were tuned to successive broadcast programs.

Vertical publication — business or trade publication of interest to all levels or job functions within a single business or profession.

Vertical saturation — many commercial announcements scheduled throughout the course of the same day, generally designed to reach many different people.

Wait order — instruction or request to delay publication of a print advertisement.

Waste circulation — readers of a publication who are not prospects for the product or service being advertised; circulation in a geographical area in which a product is not distributed.

APPENDIX C

A SAMPLE MEDIA PLAN

MARKETING OVERVIEW

The objective of this marketing strategy is to aid Skytrain in reaching goals of efficiency. This will be done by concentrating advertising dollars in newspapers, magazines and spot radio. These media have been chosen because in combination they will best meet these objectives.

The target group will be males 18-24. This target will be reached by using vehicles within the chosen mediums which have a high concentration of these males.

College newspapers will be used to reach these males. *Playboy, Penthouse* and *T.V. Guide* magazines also have a large pull with this target market.

Timing for the advertisements will be in flights with peak times occurring in the spring, summer and fall months.

Advertising must gain awareness of Skytrain since large scale distribution has not been used in the past. The advertising must also give credibility to the product. It must create an image for Skytrain. This image will be achieved successfully by the use of the mediums and vehicles chosen. They do have a credible image.

SERVICE ANALYSIS

Skytrain was started in the fall of 1977 by Freddy Laker. Skytrain is a standby trans-Atlantic flight service.

From the fall of 1977 to the fall of 1978, Skytrain offered only one flight per day. That flight was from New York to London. On September 26, 1978, Skytrain started another flight service from Los Angeles to London. Skytrain uses two Douglas DC-10 jumbo airplanes for both flights.

Skytrain offers a low cost flight. The New York to London trip cost $135 one-way. The one-way flight from Los Angeles to London is $190 in the spring, summer, and fall months and $166 in the winter months. Skytrain is a no-frills flight which stresses equality of all passengers.

The Civil Aeronautics Board has barred Laker from using a U.S. sales force or from making advance reservations prior to the day of the flight.[1]

During its first year the flight service achieved 65 percent occupancy. 55 percent was needed for the flight service to be economically successful. With the added expense of the Los Angeles flight, occupancy levels must be above 55 percent to show a profit.

To compensate for the inability to make advance reservations Skytrain does offer some other advantages. Passenger now may stop by the airport the morning of the flight to buy tickets with no waiting, pay by credit card, and check in their bags. There is also a telephone recording they can dial to see how many seats have been sold each day.[2]

The Skytrain from Los Angeles cannot make as many roundtrips to London as the New York flight because of the greater distance. Skytrain's main drawing card is the low price of the tickets. During the first year passengers on the New York to London flight have sometimes had to wait until the next day to get a seat on the plane.

The following media strategy for Skytrain in 1979 has been designed to meet objectives which will be of economic benefit to the owners of Skytrain.

"Media planners for brands in the introductory stage of the life cycle must pay extra special attention to the competitive approach . . . often a new entry will seek to capture a small segment of the market that has been somewhat neglected by the market leader."[3] Skytrain is doing this by meeting the need of the small group to which price is of prime importance.

MARKETING OBJECTIVES

1. **To achieve sales of $77,240,976.** This is based on 65% occupancy of both the New York to London and Los Angeles to London flights. 65 percent occupancy of the New York flight is 250,000 passengers. At $135 per passenger, annual sales for the New York flight will be $33,750,000. 65 percent occupancy of the Los Angeles flight is 236,364 passengers annually. Three fourths of these passengers will fly for $190, the other one fourth will fly at the $166 price. 177,273 will fly for $190 or $33,681,870. 59,091 will fly for $166 and pay $9,809,106. The advertising budget of $3,150,000 is 4.2 percent of expected revenues.

ANNUAL SALES

New York	
(250,000 × 135)	$33,750,000
Los Angeles	
Spring Summer & Fall Months	
(236,364 × ¾ × 190)	33,681,870
Winter Months	
(236,364 × ¼ × 166)	9,809,106
	$77,240,976

ADVERTISING BUDGET

Annual Sales $77,240,976
Percentage of Sales for Advertising × 4.07 percent
Total Ad Budget $3,105,000

2. **To achieve 65 percent occupancy level.** Skytrain will be a success if 55 percent occupancy is achieved — but, very little profit will be made. The New York to London Skytrain flight achieved 65 percent occupancy during its first year. The Los Angeles flight should be able to do equally as well; particularly with a well-planned media strategy. 65 percent is a realistic occupancy level. Demand for foreign air travel has its peak periods in the

spring, summer and fall months. At these times close to 100 percent occupancy levels can be achieved. During the first year of Skytrain's operation, the demand for Skytrain exceeded the number of flights available during these peak periods. The demand for foreign travel falls off drastically during the winter months. During these months Skytrain cannot expect to achieve 65 percent occupancy. However, an average occupancy level of 65 percent will be a realistic goal for Skytrain. If this occupancy level is achieved, $6.47 per passenger will be spent on advertising.

3. **To market foreign air travel just prior to the time peaks.** This period is during the spring, summer, and fall months and also is high around holidays. It is unlikely that foreign air travelers would change the season of their traveling simply because of an intense marketing of foreign air travel. Foreign air travel is a major purchase which is planned in advance by the consumer. If Skytrain is chosen by the consumer as the best means of travel, he should be willing to wait a day if he cannot get a seat on the day he had planned. Deciding to fly Skytrain can not be a spur of the moment decision. It is important to reach him when he is planning his trip, so he will be aware of and choose Skytrain.

4. **Position Skytrain as an economy flight.** All Skytrain passengers are treated equally in service and price. The price is low, $135 for New York trip and $190 for the Los Angeles spring, summer and fall trip ($166 for the winter trip). This price will allow Skytrain to break even if 55 percent occupancy is achieved and will be insured when 65 percent occupancy is achieved.

5. **Avoid open confrontation with the competition whenever possible.** "If may not be desirable to advertise this product (service) in the same media used by the market leader, since the "underdog" advertiser would run the risk of consumers attributing sponsorship of the message to the market leader."[4] It may not be possible to avoid the media used by the competitors, but it is important to try and avoid the particular advertising message and format which competition has chosen.

6. **Timing should be in flights.** It will be important to have the strongest marketing during the time when trans-Atlantic flights are being planned (prior to the actual peak times of foreign travel). The advertising budget will also go farther and have more impact if flighting strategy is used. Continuity is not viewed as of prime importance. Reach and frequency within the given time periods will be important.

7. **Establish awareness of the service.** The message should be "delivered to the largest possible percentage of the target market in a certain time period." Awareness will be of particular importance because Skytrain is a relatively new service and awareness is important to create confidence of the service. Confidence is important in a service that has as much control over the consumer's safety as a flight service does.

8. **Must be able to reach the target audience with information.** A coupon is needed so that interested people can send in and find out more about Skytrain.

There is too much information to include on the advertisement. But, the information is important for the potential consumer to have.

9. **Have contingency plan in case of unexpected occurences.** Flight services will be affected by the weather and by the activities of competitors, as well as consumer response. It is important to have a back-up plan in case something does not proceed as planned. There will be no contingency fund allotted from the advertising budget. The contingency funds will be taken from flexible areas within the budget if the need arises.

ADVERTISING OBJECTIVES

1. **To create the most effective advertising possible with the alloted budget.** ($3,150.000 for one year's budget beginning January 1, 1979.) This will be done by selecting the media which will most effectively reach the target market.

2. **Advertising must precede the service usage.** The advertising must be timed so that it will create awareness within the target market during the time the purchase of the service is being planned, which is prior to the actual time of purchase in a shopping good such as a foreign air trip.

3. **Printed advertising must include a coupon.** Information about Skytrain must reach the target market. It will not be possible to supply this information effectively without a coupon.

4. **Advertising should be in flights to gain awareness and to best coincide with usage.** A high degree of reach and frequency can be achieved during these specific time periods by using flights. Advertising dollars will be alloted by months according to usage. The summer months will receive the largest percentage of the budget, next will be the spring and fall months.

5. **Advertising must be relatively flexible to react to acts of nature and competition.** In the airline business it is necessary to be able to change advertising on short notice because air accidents or weather can change the market situation. These happen very quickly and advertising must respond very quickly.

6. **Be aware of competition and do not confront them head-on.** Skytrain will create a niche for itself as it continues to have the lowest price for a trans-Atlantic flight. Skytrain will be differentiated from the competition in this respect. The same media will have to be used because airlines are currently using all possible media.

7. **Economy is the big selling point of Skytrain.** Economy should be stressed in the advertising.

MEDIA OBJECTIVES

1. **To achieve reach and frequency which will best achieve the marketing goals.** This can be done by choosing media which will most economically and

efficiently reach the target audience and then timing the use of these media in flights. The reach will be 12,712,000; frequency will be sixty-four times a year. With these reach and frequency goals there will be 812,500,000 total audience impressions (TAI). With the budget of $3,150,000 the cost per thousand will be 4.00.

Budget = $3,150,000
CPM = $4.00
Budget/CPM = 787,000
TAI/Target Group = 787,500,000
Target Group = 12,712,000 (Reach)
TAI/Target Group = 62 (Frequency)

2. **CPM must be better than average.** A CPM of $4.00 or less will be very satisfactory for Skytrain. This can be achieved by using smaller units of advertising in the print media and choosing all-around economical mediums. (For media selection guide see Table 1). Mediums will be selected on the following criteria: (a) economy; (b) flexibility; (c) little advertising outside the target group (does not reach a large percentage of people who are not included in the target group); (d) can have high frequency; (e) can contain a coupon. Of these, economy is viewed as of prime importance. This will be judged by a low CPM of the target group.

3. **Open confrontation with competition must be minimized.** This can be done by differentiating the product on price and allowing it to create its own spot.

4. **Media should be scheduled in wave patters.** Skytrains message will achieve high reach and frequency prior to the peak periods of purchase of foreign air travel. A sustaining period of advertising will be used between these peak periods in the spring, summer, and fall months.

5. **A variety of media will be used.** Reach can best be gained by adding media (rather than increasing frequency of one particular medium. "With an assortment of mediums, reach against the target group is usually extended beyond what can normally be achieved within the practical limits of one medium . . . The different mediums chosen should reach the target market in different psychological contexts. If the message is presented in a variety of media environments, it may maintain the prospects interest over a longer time span than if it were allowed to wear out in a single medium."[5]

COMPETITION

Skytrain has many competitors in the foreign air travel to London from New York and San Francisco. The main competition comes from those airlines who offer a discount flight, though. These airlines are TWA, American, United, and Northwest. These airlines have not felt the need to advertise these economy fares heavily because they have been so successful. These airlines have concentrated their budget on flights which have not done as well.

"Just as TWA is refraining from advertising its proposed Super Coach Fare, other carriers tend to hold back on ads for the routes where prices have been slashed. TWA, American, United and Northwest all have Super Saver fares which now have Civil Aeronautics Board approval."[6]

Charter flights also offer discount fares and they must be considered as competition for Skytrain.

According to the 1978 Standard Directory of Advertisers the major airlines (and some large charter services) use every medium available to advertise, the largest part of their budgets going to newspapers in most instances. The newspapers often receive as much as 50 percent of the total ad budget or more.

Airline advertisement spending last year varied from 1.2 percent of revenues for Northwest Orient to 2.5 percent for Continental.[7]

The government has been gradually deregulating the airlines which will change the competitive market for the airlines. The changes will favor small airlines such as Skytrain. "The Carter administration has said it favors deregulation of airlines, much to the consternation of many airlines."[8]

Skytrain was the first discount air travel to enter the competitive market. At the present Skytrain can hold only about 3 percent of all foreign travelers.[9] But, Skytrain's small capabilities did not force competition to overlook it. "British Airways, Pan American, and Trans World Airlines promptly offered sharply-discounted round trip plans" after Skytrain was introduced.[10]

Freddie Laker, with his Skytrain, has in effect forced the Airlines to compete to some extent on price.

TARGET GROUPS

Primary Target Group: Male, 18-24 years old
Secondary Target Group: Female, 18-24 years old
Tertiary Target Group: Male-Female, 25-34

Primary: Males were chosen for the primary group because they are a cohesive group which will be easy targets for marketing. 19.6 percent of all males have taken a foreign trip. This is opposed to only 17.9 percent of all females who have taken a foreign trip. These percentages are relatively close but a male is somewhat more likely to take a foreign trip than a female. The male is viewed as more likely to take the Skytrain trip than the female.

18-24 years olds were selected because 21.6 percent of all people in this age group are foreign travelers. This is the highest percentage of any age group. 20.8 percent of all foreign travelers who travel for vacations are in this age group. The foreign vacationer is the largest user of Skytrain. The business traveler is not concerned with price. He is concerned about times and schedules, he often passes the price of his fare on to his company. The personal traveler is often in a hurry to get to his destination for personal reasons. Time, instead of price, is of prime importance to him, also.

Secondary: Females are a slightly larger group than males, making up 50.4 percent of the total U.S. population. The key factor in choosing females 18-24 are the characteristics of the age group 18-24 — which contain the highest percentage of foreign travelers. The 18-24 would have more of the daring spirit to take the unplanned traip. Flight time is not as important to this group. They have fewer ties on them. They are also more aware of the pocketbook. But, tight budgets don't necessarily deter them from flying. They do search for the best buy. And, they find Skytrain.

Tertiary: This group is composed of all adults 25-34. 22.2 percent of all foreign travelers in the past three years are from this group. 21.1 percent of all foreign vacationers are from this group. This group will receive much of the advertising directed to the primary audience because they do have similar media usage patterns.

Target Group Size: 49.6 percent of all adults 18-24 are males. This is 12,712,000 males.

Characteristics of Target Group: 91.6 percent of all foreign travelers are white. 81.7 percent of all foreign travelers have at least a high school education.

Psychological Characteristics: The people who fly Skytrain must have some sense of adventure; a willingness to try something new. The reason 18-24 was selected as the age group is that they would have more of the adventuresome spirit. They are not tied down to families and other responsibilities. TGI for males reported the 18-24 year old male have the highest percentage of this characteristic than any other age group.

21.5 percent of men 18-24 are brand loyal, so they shouldn't be as opposed to flying an airline which isn't well known. These men have the largest brand loyalty percentage of all the age groups of males. These men also have the lowest amount of caution, 23.9 percent. They are not as worried about the tried and true ways. They should be willing to take Skytrain. 25.6 percent are experimenters. Average of all men is 21.5 percent.

TARGET MARKET

The target markets will be counties which are designated as size A. These are all counties belonging to the largest 26 metropolitan areas. 57,782,000 of a total 145,434,000 U.S. citizens live in these counties. The twenty-six areas (listed by their major cities) are:

1. New York
2. Los Angeles
3. Chicago
4. Boston
5. Philadelphia
6. San Francisco
7. Detroit
8. Washington D.C.
9. Cleveland
10. Pittsburgh
11. Dallas-Ft. Worth
12. St. Louis
13. Houston
14. Minneapolis
15. Miami
16. Atlanta
17. Tampa-St. Petersburg
18. Seattle-Tacoma
19. Baltimore
20. Indianapolis
21. Hartford-New Haven
22. Denver
23. Portland
24. Sacramento
25. Cincinnati
26. Milwaukee

MEDIA SELECTION

Media were selected on five criteria. (See Table 1) Newspapers received the highest ranking with 6. Magazines and spot radio were second with 5 each. The other major media had 3 or less.

Newspapers have a very economical CPM. They can contain a coupon, which is a marketing objective. The timing for newspapers is relatively short. The closing time for an ad is rarely ever more than one week prior to publication. Newspapers also have the ability to have high frequency. An advertisement can run every day (this high frequency is necessary to create awareness). 71.2 percent of all foreign travelers who are vacationing read daily newspapers. It will be least expensive to reach the majority of the target audience with this medium.

Magazines have a low CPM compared to television and other mediums. The CPM of magazines drastically drops when the consideration of how well the target group is being reached is taken into account. Magazines have the least amount of advertising which reaches people who are not within the target group (when vehicles are chosen on the basis of target markets). Magazines can also contain the important coupon.

Spot radio has very flexible timing. An advertisement can be added up to air time as long as there are time spots available. The advertisements can be removed just as swiftly. Spot radio will have little wasted advertising in the 18-24 male market when radio stations are selected which effectively reach this market. This age group listens to a specialized type of format. 48.2 percent listen to "Top Hits" radio stations, with the majority of these listeners (36.1 percent listening between 7:30 - 11:00 p.m.) There can be a practically unlimited amount of frequency on spot radio.

The college newspapers will effectively reach 12.1 percent of the total target group at a low CPM (9.07 CPM of the target group). This low CPM is because there is very little wasted circulation. Most of what does not reach the primary target group does reach the secondary target group.

TABLE 1

Media	Criteria Total	Economical CPM	Coupon	Flexible Timing	Little Advertising Waste	High Frequency
Newspaper	6	**	**	*		*
Magazine	5	*	**		**	
Spot T.V.	3			**		*
Network T.V.	2			*		*
Spot Radio	2			*		*
Outdoor Advertising	1	*				
College Newspaper	5	**	**		*	

(A double * is given to the medium that best fulfills the criterion)

MEDIA RANKINGS

Newspapers are the primary medium to be used. This is because they have the highest ranking in meeting the specific objectives. College newspapers, a section of all newspapers, are very efficient in reaching a high percentage of the target market. Newspaper advertisements will be distributed in the geographical areas where the majority of foreign air travelers have come from in the past. This will be in the largest twenty-six counties.

College enrollment drops during the summer also, so during the times when colleges are in summer session, the reach of the audience would be very small. Timing is not very flexible for the same reasons, an advertisement can only run during certain times of the year.

The media that will not be used are network TV, Spot TV, network radio and outdoor advertising.

There are two main reasons why Spot TV and Network TV were not chosen: (1) they could not contain a coupon, and (2) the high CPM Network TV and Spot TV would also have a great deal of wasted advertising which would reach people other than those in the primary, secondary, or tertiary target groups.

Network radio was not selected because it will not be as efficient in meeting the objectives as the media which have been chosen. Network radio cannot contain a coupon, would conceivably have a great deal of wasted advertising because specific vehicles (stations) could not be selected. The CPM of network radio is not inexpensive.

The media objectives of economical CPM, a coupon, flexible timing, little advertising waste and high frequency are being met with the selected media.

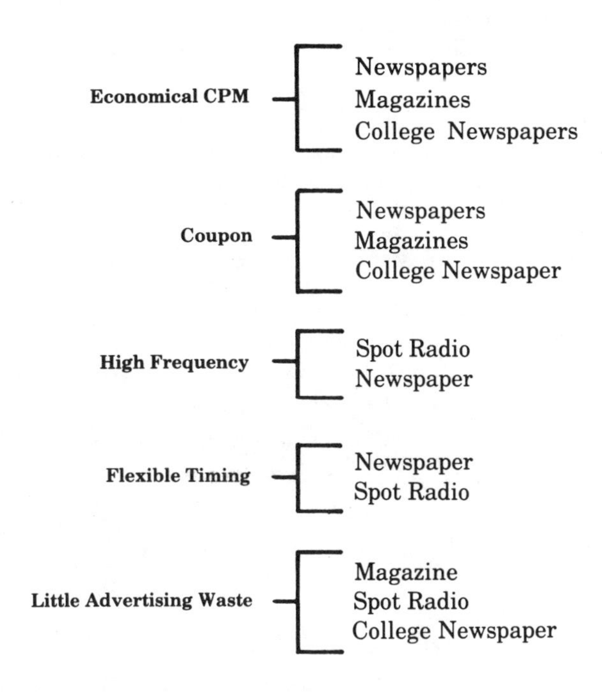

COST EFFICIENCIES OF VEHICLES

Newspapers will have an average cost per thousand (CPM) of $3.42.

Magazines will have an average CPM of $4.67. This number was reached by taking the CPM of the magazines used by Skytrain and finding an average.

The CPM of college newspapers will be $5.26. An estimated CPM for spot radio is $0.59 (based on 30-second commercial between 7-11, Monday through Friday).

The CPM of the primary target will show how efficient each medium will be. The CPM of the primary target group relates to the anticipated sales levels of the chosen newspapers.

The average newspaper CPM for the primary target group is approximately $22.54.

The average magazines CPM for the primary target market of the chosen magazines is $12.50.

The CPM of the primary target group of college newspapers is $9.07.

CONTINUITY

During the marketing period, continuity will be of major importance. The propensity to consume will be highest during the spring, summer, and fall months. It is important to have continuity during these months with some periods having more concentrations than others within these months. The very highest concentrations should occur just before the very highest propensity to consumer periods. (This will be during summer months and before holidays in the spring and fall months.)

Newspaper advertising will begin in April because this is just prior to the time when foreign travel consumption begins.

Magazine advertising will begin in March because of the longer life of magazines. Also, magazines start earlier so a little more frequency of magazines can be achieved. Magazine advertisments will run in December to reach the holiday foreign vacationers. College newspaper advertising begins in February and March to reach students before the spring break holiday.

Spot radio will begin in May because spot radio is being used as a reminder. It will be necessary to have these radio commercials on during the time of foreign air travel peaks.

TABLE 2

Flow Chart

	Jan.	Feb.	Mar.	Apr.	May	Jun.	Jul.	Aug.	Sept.	Oct.	Nov.	Dec.
Newspaper				X	X	X	X	X	X			X
Magazine			X	X	X	X	X	X	X			
College Newspaper		X	X		X							
Spot Radio							X	X	X			

SELECTION OF MEDIA VEHICLES

Newspapers will be selected on the basis of: (1) the cities they are located in (they must be in the top twenty-six counties). The newspaper must have the largest circulation of any paper in the city; (2) The CPM of each of the newspapers; and (3) the propensity to consume of each specific market. Table 4 combines these criteria into a vehicle rating factor (VRF). The cities comprising the twenty-six cities are then ranked by the VRF. The thirteen cities with the highest VRF will then receive more advertising than the thirteen cities with the lowest VRF. The selected newspapers are listed in parentheses under the city name.

College newspapers will be selected on enrollment. The larger colleges have a higher percentage of students from the twenty-six largest cities than the average college does.

Radio stations will be selected in the two largest cities (which are located in the two largest counties). Radio stations must be "Top Hits" radio stations.

Magazines will be selected on the basis of reach of the primary target group. *Playboy* reaches 31.4 percent of the primary target group. *T.V. Guide* reaches 28.3 percent. *Penthouse* reaches 20.6 percent.

ADVERTISING UNITS

Newspapers: In all newspapers (college included) a 500-line advertisement will be used. This will be large enough to receive attention. It also will be large enough for effective use of the coupon. This size will not be over the limits the budget allows.

Magazines: Full page 4 color ads will be used in *Penthouse, Playboy,* and *T.V. Guide*. The impact of this size and quality of advertisement will be needed to make it stand out in these vehicles. Most of the advertisements in these publications are of this size. If the advertisement were smaller or black and white, 2-color or 3-color, it would get lost in the crowd. The impact of the advertisements are important in this medium because frequency is not possible to attain. Attention must be gained by impact.

Spot Radio: Advertisements will be 30 seconds long. This is used as reminder advertising so it will be distributed in New York and Los Angeles.

DISTRIBUTION

Newspapers and spot radio advertisements will be distributed regionally to reach the specific target area. Magazines will be distributed nationally, because regional distributions would not efficiently reach the target markets.

Spot radio will be distributed solely in New York and Los Angeles as it will be used as reminder advertising.

Newspaper and spot radio advertisements will be distributed through the week. The newspaper advertisements for group 1 newspapers will come out in the Wednesday and Friday editions. Radio advertisements will run during weekdays 7:30-11:00 p.m. The latter part of the week (wednesday, Thursday, and Friday) will receive the spot radio advertisements.

BUDGET ALLOCATIONS

Newspapers will receive approximately 50 percent of the advertising budget. They are the primary medium. They will also have a large total audience impression.

Magazines will receive approximately 40 percent of the budget. It is a more expensive medium. They do reach the target group effectively.

Spot radio receives 5 percent of the budget. Effective penetration in New York and Los Angeles can be achieved with this percentage of the budget.

College newspapers receive the remainder of the budget — 5 percent. This economical medium will reach target audience at a low CPM.

MEDIA BUYS

Newspapers: The group 1 newspapers (according to Table 4) will have the frequency of two 500 line advertisements per week during the heavy marketing periods. These periods run April through September. This will be thirteen newspapers running forty-eight advertisements a year each.

The group 2 newspapers will have the frequency of one 500-line advertisement per week during the heavy marketing periods running April through September. This will be thirteen newspapers running twenty-four advertisements each a year.

TABLE 4

	Circulation[1]	% of[1] Coverage in City	Line[1] Rate	CPM[2]	Propensity of City for Foreign Travel	VRF[3]	Approx. Approx. No. of T.G. Reached	CPM for T.G.
1. Los Angeles, Ca. (Times)	1,020,208	24.3	4.00	1.96	155	79.1	101,331	19.74
2. Boston, Mass. (Globe)	506,114	26.5	3.21	3.17	180	56.8	67,575	23.75
3. Sacramento-Stockton, Ca. (Bee)	186,300	23.9	1.05	2.82	151	53.5	15,774	33.28
4. Philadelphia, Pa. (Bulletin)	516,872	27.8	2.40	2.32	117	50.4	89,238	13.45
5. Portland, Ore. (Oregonian)	241,264	45.1	1.45	3.00	147	49.0	34,276	21.15
6. Hartford-New Haven, Conn. (Courant)	211,016	32.1	1.15	2.72	118	43.4	38.520	14.93
7. Denver, Col. (Post)	262,952	33.6	1.36	2.59	110	42.5	34,272	19.84
8. New York, N.Y. (News)	1,824,836	26.2	10.10	2.77	115	41.5	?	?
9. San Francisco, Ca. (Chronicle Examiner)	488,782	36.1	3.75	3.84	158	41.1	68,590	27.34
10. Seattle-Tacoma, Wa. (Times)	245,614	26.4	2.23	4.54	156	34.4	32,208	34.62
11. Washington D.C. (Post)	561,640	36.0	3.94	3.51	118	33.6	72,360	27.22
12. Houston, Tx. (Chronicle)	322,762	31.6	2.00	2.85	73	25.6	54.036	18.51
13. Milwaukee, Wisc. (Journal)	334,167	67.0	1.60	2.39	61	25.5	69.680	11.48
14. Cleveland, Ohio (Plain Dealer)	379,615	26.5	1.96	2.58	61	23.6	33,390	29.35
15. Dallas-Ft. Worth, Tx. (Times Herald)	250,505	26.9	1.55	3.09	71	23.0	44.923	17.25
16. Chicago, Ill. (Tribune)	762,810	23.3	4.46	2.92	65	22.3	106,947	20.85
17. Detroit, Mich. (News)	633,708	38.2	3.52	2.78	57	20.5	120,712	14.58
18. Cincinnati, Ohio (Post)	187,000	31.5	1.12	2.99	59	19.7	29,610	18.91
19. St. Louis, Mo. (Globe Democrat)	271,755	26.1	1.64	3.02	53	17.5	42.543	19.27
20. Baltimore, Md. (Sun)	174,013	42.5	2.40	6.90	114	16.5	53,975	22.23
21. Indianapolis, Ind. (Star News)	214,979	45.3	1.56	3.63	56	15.4	36,693	21.26
22. Atlanta, Ga. (Constitution Journal)	216,532	42.7	1.65	3.81	55	14.4	52,094	15.84
23. Tampa-St. Petersburg, Fl. (Tribune Times)	187,947	26.2	1.31	3.49	46	13.2	2.270	29.41
24. Pittsburgh, Pa. (Press Post Gazette)	190,812	38.8	2.13	5.58	67	12.0	60,916	17.48
25. Miami, Fl. (Herald News)	447,057	45.6	4.19	4.26	45	10.56	41,496	50.49
26. Minneapolis-St. Paul, Minn. (Star Tribune)	227,378	41.8	2.49	5.48	55	10.0	58,520	21.27

1. Source: Aug. 12, 1978 SRDS-Newspapers
2. Based upon a 500-line ad
3. Vehicle Rating Factor $= \frac{\text{Propensity for Foreign Travel}}{\text{CPM}}$

Group I	964,800
Group II	+ 355,200
	1,320,000
18.5 percent production costs:	244,200
Total cost of newspaper:	1,564,200

College Newspapers: (See Table 5) College advertisements will run twice a week during marketing periods. These periods are the last two weeks in February, the first two weeks in March and all of May. This will be a total of sixteen advertisements in college newspapers.

Line rate for top 100 college	27.92
Lines	× 500
Cost per advertisement	$ 13,960
Time advertisement runs	16
Space cost	223,360
(Production) 18.5 percent of space cost	41,321.60
Total cost of college newspapers	$264,681.60

Magazines: *Playboy, Penthouse* and *T.V. Guide* will carry Skytrain advertisements. These will run once a month for eight months during Skytrain's heavy marketing periods. Advertisements will run March through September and in December to reach foreign travelers who travel over the Christmas holidays.

	Full Page 4-color	8 Times
Playboy	36,955	295,640
Penthouse	31.085	248,680
T.V. Guide	61,000	488,000
	129,045	1,032,320

Space cost for magazines	$1,032,320.00
(Production) 18.5 percent of space cost	190,979.20
Total spent on magazine	$1,223,299.20

Spot Radios: Radio spots will be purchased in Los Angeles and New York.

Time cost for spot radio	91,848.83
(Production) 6.5 percent of time cost	5,970.17
Total spot radio cost	$ 97,819

Totals:

Newspaper	1,564,200.00	49.7%
College Newspaper	264,681.60	8.4%
Magazine	1,223,299.20	38.8%
Spot Radio	97,819.00	3.1%
Total	3,149,999.80	100%

TABLE 5
Budget by Month and Media

	Newspaper	College Newspaper	Magazine	Spot Radio	Total (Month)
January					
February		$ 55,840			$ 55,840
March		55,840	$ 129,040		184,880
April	$ 220,000		129,040		349,040
May	220,000	111,680	129,040		460,720
June	220,000		129,040		349,040
July	220,000		129,040	$30,617	379,657
August	220,000		129,040	30,616	379,656
September	220,000		129,040	30,616	379,656
October					
November					
December			129,040		129,040
Total (media)	$1,320,000	$223,360	$1,032,320	$91,849	$2,667,529

TABLE 6
Schedule

	Newspaper	College Newspaper	Magazine	Spot Radio
January				
February		○		
March		○	*	
April	+ + + +		*	
May	+ + + +	○○	*	
June	+ + + +		*	
July	+ + + +		*	-
August	+ + + +		*	-
September	+ + + +		*	-
October				
November				
December				

○ = four 500-line advertisements in each of the top 100 college newspapers.
* = three full page 4-color advertisements (*Playboy, Penthouse, T.V. Guide)*
+ = thirty-nine 500-line advertisements, twenty-six in Group I newspapers and thirteen in Group II.
- = 48 Gross Rating Points of spot radio in Los Angeles and New York (24 each); the advertisements must run between 7 and 11 p.m., Monday through Friday.

CONTINGENCY PLAN

1. If sales goals are not being met, advertising should be scheduled closer together to get a very large impact in a short amount of time. This should be

done at the times when demand for foreign air travel is at its peak. College newspaper allotment of the budget should go to newspapers because at the time of intense advertising colleges will not be in session. Newspapers can reach the highest number of people. The advertising that was to run in December, should be rescheduled for the heavy travel months. Magazine advertisements should run in the heavy months also (May, June, July, and August). Other magazines that reach the target market will have to be selected to handle the extra advertising.

2. If demand for flights exceeds the supply of flights, advertising should be spread out over more of the year. The peak travel times would be oversaturated with demand at this time. All advertising in June and July should be rescheduled for the fringe times of March and September. The same units of advertising would be used, they would be spread out over a longer period of time.
3. If demand is heavy at all times a decision about extending the service should be made by the controllers of Skytrain.
4. If competition begins to advertise head-on, continue to use the planned media schedule. The differences of Skytrain must be emphasized. The competition would like to see Skytrain to back-off. Skytrain must fight for its share of the market.
5. If disasters of any type affect foreign air travel, pull all possible advertising that is to run. Newspapers, college newspapers, and spot radio will be relatively easy to put a hold on. The magazine advertisements will run as scheduled because it would be very difficult to know in time to take them out. The advertising should be rescheduled as soon as conditions return to close to normal.

ENDNOTES

1. *Sales and Marketing Management;* January 1978.
2. *Ibid.*
3. Barban, Cristol & Kopec; *Essentials of Media Planning,* p. 15.
4. *Ibid.*, p. 14.
5. *Ibid.*, p. 74.
6. *Advertising Age,* June 20, 1977.
7. *Advertising Age,* Nov. 21, 1977.
8. *Advertising Age,* June 20, 1978.
9. *Advertising Age,* November 21, 1977.
10. *Sales and Marketing Management,* January 1978.

SOURCES

Sales and Marketing Management; January 1978.
Essentials of Media Planning; Barban, Cristol & Kopec
Advertising Age, November 6, 1977.
Advertising Age, June 20, 1977.
Advertising Age, November 21, 1977.
American Research Bureau (ARBitron) Spot Radio.
BBDO
LNA Multi-Media Report.
Standard Director of Advertisers, 1978.
Standard Rate and Data Service for Spot Radio.
Standard Rate and Data Service for Newspapers.
Standard Rate and Data Service for Consumer Publications.
Advertising Media Sourcebook and Workbook; Barban, Jugenheimer, Young.
Target Group Index (Foreign Travel).
Target Group Index (Males).
Cass National Rate Book and College Newspaper Directory.

Index

Advertising Age, 47
Advertising environment, 85
Advertising mix, 5-6
Advertising objectives, 15-16
Advertising weights, 61
American Research Bureau (ARBitron), 48-49, 110-111, 160
Area of Dominant Influence (ADI), 49, 154
Audience, 51-54, 75-79
Audience considerations, 21-22, 105-126, 139-141
Audience quality, 75-76
Audit Bureau of Circulations, 52, 107-108

Bleed, 164
Brand Development Index (BDI), 64-68, 178
Broadcast Advertisers Reports, 41
Broadcast cost estimates, 99-102
Budget allocation, 152-153
Business Week, 47
Buying Power Index, 34

Category Development Index (CDI), 66-68, 178-179
Checking, 7
Circulation, 51-54, 106
Circulation, 53
City and County Data Book, 34
City Zone, 108
Closing date, 166
Column-inch, 162
Competition, 40-42, 70, 83-84, 147, 149-150
Consumer profile, 6, 20-21, 45-54, 151
Content, 60-61, 137-139
Contingency plan, 23, 153-154
Continuity, 7, 17
Control of message, 84-87
Cost, 60
Cost considerations, 127-134
Cost per rating point, 24, 98-102
Cost per thousand, 24, 88, 102-104, 127-134, 143-144, 166-167, 183-184
Coverage, 106-107
Creative considerations, 82-83
Cumulative rating, 107, 119, 180-181

Daypart, 169
Demographic characteristics, 47-48
Demographic matching approach, 20
Demonstration, 83
Discounts, 162-173
Designated Market Area (DMA), 49-50, 154

Editor and Publisher Market Guide, 34
Estimating, 93-103, 160-161
Executive summary, 148-149

Financial considerations, 88-89
Fixed rate, 169, 172
Flight, 22-23
Frequency, 17, 80, 107, 114, 119, 123-126, 185

Geographic selection, 59-71, 81-82
Grid rates, 170-172
Gross rating points, 21-22, 120-123, 159, 167, 173, 182-183

Hiatus, 22-23

Impact, 17, 78, 83
Intermedia, comparisons, 133-134
Irritation, 80

Leading National Advertisers, Inc. (LNA), 41-42
Length of message, 81
Line (agate line), 162-163
Location, 85-86
Logistics, 7, 27-29, 61

Magazine concept, 86
Magazine cost estimates, 103-104
Market-by-market efforts, 61-63
Market profile, 6, 33-44, 151
Marketing and Media Decisions, 47-48
Marketing interface, 11-12
Marketing mix, 5-6
Marketing objectives, 15
Marketing orientation, 13
Mechanical considerations, 87-88
Media characteristics, 75-91
Media clutter, 141-143
Media cost references, 94-99
Media effects, 28, 137, 141-143
Media efficiency, 88
Media evaluation, 26, 89-91
Media, importance of, 3-5
Media information sources, 32-56, 94-99
Media mix, 17
Media objectives, 16-19
Media performance, 61
Media planning unit, 12
Media process, 8, 11-29
Media quality, 137-144
Media Records, 41
Media report, 147-155, 203-217
Media selection, 24-27, 151-152
Metropolitan area, 33, 38, 108, 114
Milline rate, 128-129, 181
Monitoring, 161-162
Mortality rate, 81
Multiple spotting, 81

National Association of Broadcasters (NAB), 142
Negotiation, 161
New product introductions, 70
Newspaper cost estimates, 98-99, 102-103
Nielsen, A. C. Company, 40, 48-50, 111, 120-122, 160

Objectives, 14-19, 150
Orbit, 86, 170
Outdoor cost estimates, 99

Perishability, 81
"Piggyback," 81
Preemptible rate, 169, 172
Price considerations, 88-89
Product protection, 81
Product turnover, 70-71
Product user approach, 21-21
Profile of U.S. Consumer Market Segments, 46
Promotion mix, 5-6
Public policy, 86

Quintiles, 54

Radio All Dimension Audience Research (RADAR), 111
Rating, 21-22, 106, 120, 179
Reach, 17, 107, 114, 119, 123-125
Readers per copy, 182
Regionality, 43-44
Regulation, 86-87
Repetition, 79-80
Retail Trading Zone, 108
Rotation, 170
Run of press, 163-164
Run of station, 170, 172

Sales and Marketing Management, 34
Sales data, 64-67
Scatter package, 86, 168
Schedule, 22-23, 63, 153
Selectivity, 77
Selling Areas-Marketing, Inc. (SAMI), 38, 40
Share of audience, 106, 179-180
Showings, 173
Standard Rate and Data Service, 34-35, 88-89, 97-98, 154, 162, 164, 168
Starch, Daniel & Staff, 46
Statistical Abstract of the United States, 46
Strategies, 6, 19-27
Survey of Buying Power, 34

Tactics, 6, 27-29, 159-173
Target group, 6, 20-21, 45-54, 151
Target Group Index, 35-38, 48, 51, 53-56, 109-110, 154
Target market, 6, 33-44, 151
Timing, 22-23, 68-71, 79-81
Trendex, 42

Unduplicated audience, 106-107, 117-118, 132-133, 184-185
Units, 6, 152

Vehicles, 6, 152

Wave pattern, 22-23